UIDE D0247184

# TRAINING CONTRACT SUCCESS

*"The aim of the guide is to help you secure your job as a trainee solicitor. It is written by solicitors who have successfully been through the Training Contract recruitment process, for people who are about to go through the process. It is all about passing on our knowledge and experiences, as many aspiring solicitors would stand a better chance of getting a Training Contract if they were aware of what law firms expect of them. Whilst you have the ingredients to determine your ambition,* Ultimate Guide to Training Contract Success *has the recipe to assist you to gain entry into the legal profession."*

**Ultimate Law Guide**

**Published by Ultimate Guides**
**Copyright © Training Contract Success Limited 2008**
**C.Robinson, K.Owusu-Bempah**
**All rights reserved**
**The Authors have asserted their moral rights.**
**All Design and Graphic works by creative designer Nadim Antonio DeGouveia-Akhtar**

# Contents page

**Introduction**

The Legal Landscape      **9**

**Chapter 1**

Getting Started      **15**

**Chapter 2**

Life as a lawyer – An overview of the legal profession    **23**

    i.   **Solicitor v Barrister – which is for you?**

    ii.   **What work do Solicitors/Barristers undertake?**

    iii.   **The route to becoming a solicitor or barrister**

    iv.   **How to become a solicitor**

    v.   **The life of a trainee solicitor**

**Chapter 3**

What makes a successful lawyer?      **46**

    ➢ *All-round portfolio of skills*

**Chapter 4**      **51**

    i.   Which way do I go?

    ii.   Get on the right road: Which firm to choose

    ➢ *Factors that affect the choice of where to apply*

**Chapter 5**

Demystifying legal practice areas      **58**

**Chapter 6**                                                        **66**

What are law firms looking for?

**Chapter 7**

Marketing yourself effectively                                       **75**

    I.  How can I make myself stand out?

   II.  Self-Assessment: What is my Unique Selling Point (USP)? belief and confidence

> *SWOT analysis*

> *What firms are looking for*

> *Know yourself inside out*

> *Spin yourself into a firm*

**Chapter 8**

Networking for success and self-promotion                           **85**

> *Making the most of career fairs*

**Chapter 9**

Getting to grips with "**Commercial Awareness**".                   **96**

> *Commercial awareness case study*

> *Commerciality test*

> *The City and law as a business*

**Chapter 10**

Improving your CV and covering letter –

*Top CV tips that work*                                              **117**

> **Examples of covering letters**

> **CV examples**

## Chapter 11

The application form                        **134**

> ➢ *Examples of application forms*
> ➢ *Applications record*

## Chapter 12

i.    Succeeding at the interview            **160**

> ➢ *Background research and practical tips*
> ➢ *Different types of interview*
> ➢ *What the firm wants*

ii.    Know yourself inside out

> ➢ *Interview techniques*
> ➢ *The BIG DAY*

## Chapter 13

How to answer those tough training contract     **183**
Interview questions

> ➢ *The most common training contract interview questions*
> ➢ *How to structure your suggested answers*
> ➢ *Useful questions to ask at your interview*

## Chapter 14

Assessment days/centres                 **199**

> ➢ *Group exercises*
> ➢ *The case study*
> ➢ *Psychometric tests*
> ➢ *Writing letters*
> ➢ *Presentation tips*

**Chapter 15**                                                  **213**

How do you decide between two offers of a training contract?

> ➤ *What are the factors that make a good Training Contract?*
> ➤ *Which firm is "right" for me?*
> ➤ *Negotiating an offer*

**Chapter 16**

Finishing the LPC without a training contract      **217**

> ➤ *Other opportunities in the legal market*
> ➤ *Never lose faith – Perseverance is the key*
> ➤ *Post graduate study – LLM*

**Chapter 17**

Meet our friends                                 **227**

> ➤ *Our friends provide top tips and practical advice on how they secured training contracts at their firms'.*

**Chapter 18**

Ultimate Law Guide's 10 step strategy for training      **247**
Contract success

**Chapter 19**

Useful websites and contact numbers      **249**

**Chapter 20**

Diversity and the law      **255**

**Conclusion**      **259**

**Acknowledgements**      **261**

Appendix 1      **262**

Appendix 2      **269**

## Why I founded Ultimate Law Guide

When I was going through the training contract application process, there lacked a singular, all—encompassing, useful source of reference to turn to, for practical advice and guidance during the early stages of my career when it was so vital to think ahead, roadmap and navigate the journey to becoming a solicitor.

Successful career planning involves careful and thorough consideration of where you want to be and how you are going to get there. *Why is this important to students aspiring to become solicitors?* Simply because, securing your training contract and thus becoming a member of this important profession is no mean feat, it is an extremely challenging yet worthwhile career path.

Everyone requires mentoring at some point during their careers. However, many of my peers from similar underprivileged backgrounds to myself did not actually receive such support or encouragement when they were starting out, and preparing to launch their legal careers. I remember seeing many of them slip through the net and left behind in the search to secure training contracts at law firms. The main reasons behind this were due to not having the right support network of expert advice and guidance to help them plan their legal careers properly. As a result, they were not sufficiently informed or adequately prepared for what it takes to get into the legal profession.

Many of these students lacked an awareness of the various routes into the legal profession, and did not fully appreciate what qualities law firms expect of a budding solicitor. Consequently, these talented students missed the recruitment milk-round when larger law firms recruit their lawyers two years in advance of the training contract commencement date. A number of my peers encountered these stumbling blocks and unfortunately, believed there was no alternative but to abandon their dreams of a legal career, which was not only a huge disappointment, but a waste of potential, resources, money and time.

I am really determined to address this issue, and this is why I founded **Ultimate Law Guide.**

Part of the philosophy behind my service is to give something back to the next generation, by *guiding tomorrow's leading lawyers today* via this career guide, the website **www.ultimatelawguide.com**, career skills workshops and mentoring / coaching programmes that we run at law schools and universities throughout the country. Ultimate Law Guide provides practical solutions to many of the common pitfalls involved in trying to forge a legal career, through sharing my own first-hand experiences and knowledge of successfully going through the demanding training contract selection process, and my time spent training, then qualifying at a leading City law firm, and practising as a commercial solicitor at a global blue-chip company.

Ultimate Law Guide sends the elevator back down to bridge the gap between education and employment. My team and I help students to unlock their potential and tap into their talent, raise their aspirations and inspire the confidence to succeed during their studies and the career management process. There is a huge diverse pool of talented young people from all backgrounds, and it is important that they are all provided with the best possible chance to gain access to the legal profession. This career guide offers a helping hand to make this happen.

Ultimate Guide to Training Contract Success provides a real and significant difference to improving your prospects of achieving that much coveted first job in law. The top tips and anecdotes will help to develop your commercial awareness; raise the standard of your applications; and polish your interviewing technique. It will also help you to attain that all-important work experience in order to gain an invaluable insight into what legal practice is all about. Work experience is the key to building up your CV and becoming more marketable and attractive to prospective employers. Work experience will provide you with a platform to acquire know-how, build professional networks, hone your skills and develop the self-confidence and character required to give you the edge and achieve Training Contract Success, and go on to have a rewarding legal career.

**Craig Robinson**

## Note to all Readers

This guide is written with every effort to assist you to secure a trainee position with a firm and with the best intention of covering all aspects of the training contract recruitment process. It has been put together by members of the Ultimate Guide Team, who are lawyers that have successfully been through the recruitment process recently. Although we certainly believe that the tips in this guide will help you to increase your chances of securing a training contract when combined with your own focused planning and determined approach. Please note that this guide is a combination of our experiences and serves to highlight the methods and techniques that have worked for many of us in the past and under no circumstances can we guarantee that you will secure a training contract as a result of reading this guide.

We would also mention that in no way is anything which is written in this guide associated with any law firm, company or organisation other than Training Contract Success Limited. Where we have included our own opinions and opinions of individuals (particularly in Chapter 17), these views are in no way whatsoever linked to or connected with the organisations that these individuals work for or have previously worked for.

**Ultimate Law Guide Team**

Introduction

## The Legal Landscape

Securing a training contract can be one of the greatest challenges for an aspiring solicitor, because qualification as a solicitor depends on whether you are offered a training contract by a law firm. A training contract is the two-year period of practical based training awarded by a law firm to an aspiring solicitor.

### Why is entry into the legal profession so challenging?

The fierce competition for securing a training contract is common knowledge among students. Law firms receive thousands of applications for a small number of places so they can afford to be selective. Because of this, the training contract recruitment process is extremely challenging for many applicants.

There is a huge disparity between the number of applicants searching for training contracts and the number of training contracts actually available in the legal recruitment market. According to the latest report by the Universities and Colleges Admissions Service (UCAS), published in February 2008, 84,860 applicants chose to read law, confirming that law is the most popular degree course to study at university. UCAS further revealed there were 22,260 applicants accepted on to law courses in universities around the country.

There are 6,376 students studying the CPE/PgDL each year, and in the academic year of 2008/9, there were 10,601 full-time places on the LPC with an extra 2,948 part-time places. The Solicitors Regulation Authority (SRA) confirmed that there were **6,303** training contracts registered from 1 August 2007 to 31 July 2008. It is thus easy to see why it is increasingly difficult to secure entry into the legal profession, simply due to the numbers, with lots more places available on law courses than there are training contracts.

The challenge of securing a training contract is further compounded by those students who have already completed law courses in the previous years, and are still searching for that elusive training contract. In addition, there are student barristers who are changing direction to become solicitors, legally trained professionals working in alternative careers hoping to return to the law, plus mature students and legal executives aiming to further their careers by qualifying as solicitors. The gulf between available training contracts and the increasing number of aspiring solicitors clearly shows that the recruitment market for trainee solicitors is hugely oversubscribed.

## The current graduate recruitment market

After years of a buoying graduate recruitment market, according to the Association of Graduate Recruiters (AGR), this year is set to become one of the toughest years in which to graduate. According to research recently published by High Fliers, the UK's top graduate employers have slashed their recruitment targets by 17 per cent for 2009. The hardest hit sector is in investment banking and finance where entry-level vacancies have been cut by 44 and 47 per cent respectively.

One knock on effect of the difficulties in the current economic climate is seeing more graduates who previously wanted a career at the investment banks now targeting a career in law, viewing a legal career as an alternative challenging, interesting and rewarding career option. Some graduates tend to regard law as a safer bet in the current economic climate compared to other sectors because, law firms have kept their recruitment targets static in spite of the cutbacks in the wider graduate recruitment sector. The College of Law and BPP confirmed this trend by reporting the number of non-law graduates applying for the Graduate Diploma in Law (GDL) course to convert to a career in law has soared by 20 per cent this year.

The great surge in graduates who would previously have opted for investment banking are clearly now turning to a career in law, which clearly means competition for training contracts is set to intensify even further. This academic year there will be even tougher competition, and graduates will have to complete more applications for possibly even fewer jobs. Students /

graduates will have to work even harder to get noticed, stand out from the crowd and improve their prospects of securing a training contract.

We recognize that you are not immune from the effects of the economic downturn. But you do have <u>Ultimate Guide to Training Contract Success</u> to turn to for everything you need to know, and to walk you through every aspect of the training contract recruitment process. It is written from the perspective of people who have recently and successfully been through the selection process. Our guide is a reference book which can be dipped into at every stage of your career planning and will provide you with top tips and practical advice about how to go about securing your training contract. We answer all your questions on how to write top-level application forms, what skills and experiences law firms look for in prospective trainees, interview techniques and advice on what attributes make a successful solicitor.

Whichever type of firm you are heading to on your training contract journey, this guide will help you to focus your preparation and overcome the common stumbling blocks, whether you are managing the anxiety of a nightmare application form, the big interview day or struggling to maintain your self-belief and confidence.

We have written this guide principally to reflect our own experiences of the recruitment process and ultimately to help you progress in your future legal career. We will share with you our own personal 'winning ways' and make your journey to securing a training contract, an easier road to travel. We guide you through each stage of the selection process, highlighting areas of difficulty and covering some of the most frequently asked questions; from what is commercial awareness to how you can differentiate yourself from other applicants.

Members of our team trained as solicitors at top City law firms and have been through the gruelling training contract recruitment process. Through first-hand experience and the accounts of our friends and colleagues, we were able to formulate various effective techniques and collate a vast amount of useful information and best practices. We received many training contract offers between us and would like to pass on to you the secrets of our success.

Training Contract Success is about thinking and planning ahead, being organised, having a clear focussed strategy, persevering and being determined. We believe that sharing our ideas, practical advice and sound guidance will help hone your skills and equip you with key tips, techniques and relevant information that will help you to differentiate your approach and avoid those common pitfalls. In fact, all the critical things necessary to land a training contract offer!

Our strategies are most effective when implemented over a period of time. Please do not wait until the day before the deadline. For some students achieving a training contract offer is a huge task, and the process should not be underestimated. With firms receiving 2,500 applications for fewer than 100 training contracts at the largest firms you must be realistic and appreciate what it takes to land that much coveted first job in law.

This guide should not be viewed as an overnight recipe for training contract success. If you combine the content of this guide with a focused work ethic, we are sure you will gain positive results. The process for any job may be a rollercoaster ride – in the sense that you build up to your first interview, get the nauseous feeling in the pit of your stomach on the day of the interview and the rush of adrenalin while you're in the 'hot seat,' and you either come out at the end of the ride with the supreme feeling of success or the anti-climax of disappointment. You will need to be prepared for the ride.

This guide will equip you with useful knowledge to assist you in your journey but you will still need to apply yourself and become a student of the recruitment process. This means learning as much as you can about the process and looking beyond the basics of simply completing an application form and attending an interview. Instead, you will learn what the role of a solicitor actually involves, including the highs and the lows, and figure out why you are suited to this type of career. Once you have found your source of motivation for a legal career, making applications and attending interviews becomes much more rewarding.

Knowing why you really want a career in law creates the desire to apply yourself in a determined and disciplined way. It is important to have the picture of yourself as a lawyer at the back of your mind, and it is this vision that you are working towards. Talk to the people around you who can advise and help you, why go through the process blindly? Listen actively, and absorb the advice given to you and apply this to formulate your own unique approach. Do enough research to be able to plan your career and obtain work experience in areas of law that you find interesting. This will help you to make an informed choice about where to begin your career.

You are no doubt waiting for the door to open to an exciting, challenging, rewarding and lucrative career as a lawyer. There is no reason why you should not succeed once you have worked out the best type of firm for you. There is a wealth of resources available to guide you in the right direction – starting here!

Here is a quick synopsis of what you will learn from this guide:

- Understanding the legal scene and the route to becoming a solicitor.
- The most elusive of recruitment criteria – getting to the bottom of what commercial awareness in business and law is really all about.
- The best way to differentiate your application and stand out from the crowd; including advice on drafting your CV and preparing covering letters and application forms.
- General advice to prospective trainee solicitors commencing their law degrees, Common Professional Examination/PgDL and Legal Practice Course.
- Considering options available to fund these courses.
- How to promote yourself effectively through marketing techniques, networking and expanding your list of contacts - and spinning yourself into the law firm of your dreams.
- Why so many applicants fall at the first hurdle and how to ensure that your application doesn't end up being rejected.
- Gaining a competitive edge by matching your skills with firms' requirements and standing out from the crowd.

- How to get your application noticed.
- Top tips and strategies to overcome the hurdles of interviewing.
- Things that prospective employers look for.
- Meet our friends – a section written by trainee friends providing top tips and practical advice on how they secured their training contracts!
- The importance of vacation placements and maximising the value of work experience.
- Choosing between two training contract offers. What factors make a good training contract?
- What to do if you finish your studies without securing a training contract.
- Unconventional routes for aspiring lawyers to enter the legal profession.

Only a handful of lucky candidates will end up receiving an offer from every single firm they apply to. However, lots of students receive rejection letters for the hundreds and thousands of graduate jobs in the market, simply because they haven't found the correct approach, but don't lose heart. Do not let yourself become one of those students left frustrated and disillusioned by the whole recruitment process.

We understand the anxieties that all graduates face, especially those wanting to get into such an extremely competitive marketplace. Some will struggle to cope with financial pressure or a succession of rejection letters, and give up. For others the biggest worry will be which glamorous destination to spend the summer break or having the hassle of sending the firm's application in before the deadline. In either case, don't allow yourself to be the student who loses focus for whatever reason. With our success strategies you can overcome the challenges and gain a competitive edge over others competing for the same places by developing the right portfolio of skills and work experience, and achieve training contract success!

*"You must believe in your ability to get the law job you are searching for."*

**Ultimate Law Guide Team**

Chapter One

## Getting Started

For those who are able to secure a training contract, a career as a solicitor offers tremendous opportunities. A career in the legal profession is intellectually stimulating, demanding and highly rewarding, with newly-qualified lawyers at the biggest firms being paid in excess of £60,000 per annum. The legal profession is well-respected and a lawyer's job is well paid. In addition, the work of a lawyer is very interesting, varied and can offer opportunities such as working in-house at a large multi-national company or overseas.

Law firms seek to recruit the best and brightest talent available in order to remain ahead in this fiercely competitive marketplace. Traditionally, lots of City law firms tended to recruit from established "red brick" universities, and those who didn't attend those institutions found it harder to make their way through the process. Over the last few years, reports in the legal press and indeed many firms in their recruitment literature suggest that lots of law firms actively seek to widen the pool of talent from which they draw new recruits. It is now common to see the number of different universities firms have recruited from in their graduate literature. The message is clear; as long as you can meet your chosen firm's selection criteria, you will not be precluded on the basis that you did not attend a traditional "red brick" university.

## A-Levels

Although some firms are specific about their entry requirements, we have looked at many websites where law firms talk about the requirement for good or strong A-levels. From our personal experience, what is deemed to be good or strong will largely depend on the type of firm where you will be applying to. If your dream is to work in one of the top City firms, you must keep in mind the fact that you are competing against some of the brightest graduates in the country. It goes without saying then, that for these types of firms only the highest academic results will be good enough.

If your aim is to work for a high street practice the academic requirements may not be as stringent and we have seen examples where people have been able to sell themselves on experience alone.

## Degree results

Law firms look for evidence of $1^{st}$ class or 2:1 grades throughout your university years. This is because the job of a lawyer is intellectually rigorous, and demands a capability of clear and lucid thought, and the ability to process and assimilate large amounts of information, and find solutions to complex problems. You must be able to show that you have the intellectual ability to make it in the legal profession, and the best indicator of this, is measured by your academic record.

The minimum entrance requirement for securing a training contract at most leading firms will typically be a 2:1 degree or higher, with some firms also specifying three strong grades at A-level to further refine the selection criteria of their recruitment process. The divide between a 2.1 degree and a 2.2 is clearly very important when it comes to applications for training contracts, because the larger law firms' receive thousands of applications for a much smaller number of training contract places.

More and more graduate recruitment teams at law firms are using online application forms, where the class of your degree is used as a numerical criterion on which to select applicants, and without a 2.1 or higher it's more than likely that your application will be declined before it has even gone before the eyes of a graduate recruiter.

The importance having a stellar academic track record cannot be stressed enough – so undergraduates study hard! If you are still at university and look like you're heading towards getting a 2.2, carefully look at ways to improve your study methods to increase your chances of fairing better in your exams.

## I only have a 2.2 in my degree - can I still secure a training contract and become a lawyer?

Having a 2.2 degree classification will not necessarily preclude you from having a career in law, but it certainly makes it even more difficult than it already is to achieve a training contract. Our experience from people we have spoken to who left university with 2.2 degrees is that you will have to work extremely hard to secure your training contract.

Here are a few tips which may help if you find yourself in such a position:

✓ **What can you offer a law firm regardless of your degree?** It will be difficult for a graduate recruiter to see past your degree classification, unless you can display some other outstanding qualities, such as language skills, commercial awareness, and excellent work experience, which may set you apart from other good candidates, who will invariably have a 2:1 in their degree. The challenge is working out how outstanding you have to be and in what way.

✓ **Gaining relevant work experience** can assist you to overcome a blip in your academics. Analyse what you have to offer and where you want to work (focus on what law firms interest you, and what those firms look for in their candidates), you can then decide how much work you need to do in order to get where you want to be.

✓ **Gaining work experience develops your skills and enhances your CV.** The harsh reality is that with a 2.2 degree you will be looked upon less favourably by most law firms, and one of the best options are to build up your experience, for example, gaining paralegal experience before immediately applying for a training contract, or by gaining commercial experience at a leading blue-chip company for a couple of years (as other career sectors are more flexible than law). This will boost your chances of securing a training contract.

*Case study:* Our friend got a 2:2 in their degree, and initially found it very difficult to get that all-important first job in law. She gained work experience at a City law firm as a paralegal and worked extremely hard, which impressed the partners she *worked for, to the extent that they offered her a training contract interview. When the partners asked her to explain why she only achieved a 2.2, she explained it was largely a result of too much socialising at university, but she had now learnt from these experiences and was much more focussed, motivated and determined to succeed in her professional career. Our friend was subjected to a far more gruelling interview than the standard applicant but had proved her capability on the job doing trainee type work.*

*At the interview she was able to demonstrate her commitment to a legal career, honesty, a maturity of thought and a strong willingness to learn. Our friend was subsequently offered a training contract with the firm.*

It is therefore worth remembering that experience can provide a useful way in. It can prove to a prospective employer that you're committed, dedicated and passionate about becoming a lawyer. It also prepares you for the world of work by developing your professionalism.

✓ **Further work experience can help you develop useful contacts.** Legal and commercial work experience demonstrates you are capable of working in a challenging, dynamic environment – and more importantly – that you can do the job of a lawyer. You will still have to work hard to get your applications noticed, (which is where effective networking and self-promotion comes in, *see chapter 8 for help*). Although, it is worth remembering that law firms will be more likely to consider employing you once they see a gleaming CV filled with excellent experience as it provides evidence that you are capable of proving you have what it takes to succeed in a legal career.

✓ **Carefully research and tailor your applications** to the firms you apply to. This will help you get your approach right, and you will stand a better chance of getting through the application stage. Focus on putting your energy into each specific application to a firm where you realistically stand a chance of an interview. Many of the larger corporate-commercial firms advertise specific requirements on their website. Use this information to ascertain whether there is a realistic prospect of you getting interviewed by this particular firm.

✓ **Contact the law firms directly to see if they are prepared to offer interviews to candidates with a 2:2**. Before making training contract applications consult the online sources and legal magazines (*see chapter 19 for further details*), as these sources usually inform you of the minimum academic requirements. Some firms may consider your training contract application as a whole, so if you do not meet a specific requirement, it may still be worth applying. However, make sure you contact the graduate recruitment department and inform them of your position and ask whether they would still consider you. You may find that they ask you to apply anyway as you have something on your CV which makes up for your academic results. There is nothing wrong with contacting a firm to ask how stringently their requirements (as advertised) are adhered to.

✓ **You may have to lower your expectations, and be more open-minded about where you would like to commence your legal career.** Consider working for a smaller firm that may be more willing to offer you the opportunity of becoming a solicitor. Once you are qualified, you can always move on. However, a note of caution is that, where you do your training contract will have a considerable bearing on where you can go once you qualify, and therefore impacts upon your overall career prospects.

✓ **If you have genuine mitigating circumstances do not be afraid to mention them**, as firms are always prepared to listen. Explain your situation to the graduate recruitment officer, and provide a detailed explanation (with supporting evidence) why your degree results do not serve as an accurate representation of your actual ability and intelligence. Draw on examples of when you have demonstrated the skills required for the job. Explain why you want to be a lawyer, and why their firm in particular is right for you, and the reasons why you are extremely determined to work for them. If you make a good impression you may be fortunate enough to be awarded with an interview.

However, be careful when mentioning mitigating circumstances which may have affected your grades. We have seen graduate sites which report that law firms are increasingly rejecting students whose mitigating circumstances consist of being involved in too many extra-curricula activities while at university. The logic behind this appears to be that firms expect the trainees they employ to be well-rounded individuals who are organised, able to prioritise and multi-task effectively without losing focus on the task at hand.

✓ **Good references.** If you have a top academic reference to support your degree, and reinforce your intellectual ability and all-round portfolio of skills, it can help to improve your prospects of law firms looking past your academic "blip" and go towards helping you secure that elusive training contract.

✓ **Carefully consider further study. Undertaking a LLM masters or postgraduate degree** may help you to draw a line under your undergraduate degree and increase your knowledge of a practice area that interests you. There is no guarantee that an LLM qualification will actually improve your employability. However, if you are interested in a particular area of law, for example, human rights and public international law, it may serve as a useful building block to increase your knowledge, and help to make you more marketable if you then apply to a law firm or organization which specialises in this field. *(Review chapter 16 for further information).*

So, if you do have a 2:2 degree, don't abandon your dream of becoming a lawyer. Although, you must take a realistic look at the type of law firm you want to work at, and consider whether you are likely to meet their entrance requirements? Are you ready, willing, and able to commit the time and energy to overcome the hurdles that having a 2.2 is likely to bring?

## Must I have a law degree?

In the same way that you do not need specific A-levels to embark on a law degree, you will not be required by any law firm to have done an undergraduate degree in law in order to secure a training contract. In other words, non-law degree students are at no major disadvantage in the trainee recruitment market. The fact is, a substantial number of trainees have a degree in a subject other than law and, if you read the trainee recruitment literature, you will see that many firms actually welcome the mixture of skills this brings. If you are a non-law student it may be the case that your motivation to become a solicitor will be tested at interview and the firm may be interested to hear why you chose your degree discipline. However, the only real disadvantage for you is the extra year spent at law school completing the CPE or PgDL, which we describe in more detail in the following chapter. Although, for some students, spending an extra year as a student before facing the real world is viewed as a real added bonus.

## Consider why you are joining the profession

Our advice to all students is to consider what motivates you and where your interests lie. Working in the law will be more rewarding if you are interested enough in the work you are doing. When making career decisions remember the most important aspect of working for a law firm is enjoying the work you do:

✓ Do you have a real and genuine interest in the law?
✓ Do you believe you will find the role as a solicitor enjoyable and challenging? If so, why? Always think of reasons! If you are only pursuing this career path for the money or you're blinded by the stories of prestige and glamour then think again, as this attitude is unlikely to sustain you through the testing interviews, and the challenging tasks a legal career brings.
✓ Consider whether you would be prepared to invest your own money to put yourself through your law studies, if you had to.
✓ Have you researched extensively, read widely and targeted law firms carefully?
✓ Remember, you must think ahead, plan carefully, be organised and have a career strategy in place!

## The Legal Landscape: Points to Ponder

The competition for training contracts is incredibly fierce. Prospective trainees must think ahead and be well prepared for a legal career. Law firms seek to recruit the best talent because clients expect the best service. Points to remember for training contract success:

- A legal career is challenging, demanding, interesting, and financially rewarding.

- Your competition – how can you get ahead?

- The academic criteria against which law firms judge prospective trainees.

- Consider the financial cost of your legal training.

Chapter two

## An Overview of the Legal Profession

### *What do Solicitors do?*

Solicitors give advice and assistance on legal and commercial matters. They are instructed directly by clients and are typically the first point of contact for clients. Clients can range from individual members of the public, businesses, companies, government organisations and charities.

The work of a solicitor varies a great deal depending on the area of law in which they practice. Most solicitors provide different types of legal advice. Solicitors tend to advise their clients over the telephone, by e-mail, by a face-to-face meeting, and representing them in court. Solicitors can also be advocates (appear in court) by gaining higher rights of audience.

Solicitors have much more direct contact with their clients than Barristers have. Solicitors research points of law, negotiate, prepare / draft contracts and other legal documents. Most solicitors work in private practice, being based in offices. Other solicitors work in central and local government, or in-house in a commercial or industrial organisation.

Solicitors are governed by a professional body called the Law Society.

### *What do Barristers do?*

Barristers also offer advice on the law. The key difference is that barristers specialise in advocacy – which is, submitting the legal arguments of your case in court. Many would-be barristers are attracted to the prospect of having a job that involves standing up, speaking in public and arguing cases in a formal setting. Many aspiring barristers are also interested in the traditions and formalities of working in the English court system.

Barristers receive their instructions from a solicitor. When not appearing and advocating in court, Barristers work in office buildings known as sets of chambers, where they prepare their cases in anticipation of matters being litigated. The legal arguments are known as their submissions and skeleton arguments. Barristers also provide legal opinions for solicitors when asked to consider a particular question of law.

Barristers automatically have higher rights of audience in the higher courts. They are often required to wear wigs and gowns in court.

Barristers are regulated by a professional body known as the Bar Council.

## Solicitor –v– Barrister – which is for you?

If you have reached a crossroads in your career journey, where you are unsure whether you would like to be a barrister or solicitor, we would urge you to get some work experience at a law firm (known as vacation placement), and chambers (known as mini-pupilage). This will help you to find out for yourself what sort of working life is "right" for you, and what sort of branch of the legal profession you will enjoy the most. Gaining experience will help you to become better informed when making those all-important career-decisions.

Below is a list that may help you decision making process:

- Solicitors are involved commercial transactions from its commencement to completion. Barristers will not necessarily get the same exposure to a deal, as they only tend to get involved on an ad-hoc basis through providing a legal opinion on a point of law.

- Solicitors tend to work in larger teams with a good support networks of legal secretaries and paralegal. Barristers often work more independently, with some support from a pupil barrister.

- A key distinction between a solicitor and barrister is the way they are remunerated financially. A solicitor is employed by their law firm and paid monthly just like any other employee of a company. The role of a solicitor therefore generally provides more financial certainty, (particularly at the junior level) as they are employed by a law firm on an annual salary and benefits package. Some barristers are employed by law firms, but they are mostly self-employed, where the onus is on the barrister to bring in their own cases and clients. The income of barristers is derived from the fees they charge whilst appearing at court and preparing the cases for the client.

▪ Some students are attracted to the Bar for flexibility it offers, as they are able to take time out if they wish, and do not have to work for someone else.

Please see the following diagram on the route to becoming a Solicitor or Barrister, or for more information, refer to the Law Society's guide to becoming a Solicitor, which can be accessed                                                             at **www.lawsociety.org.uk/becomingasolicitor.law**

## The route to becoming a Solicitor or Barrister

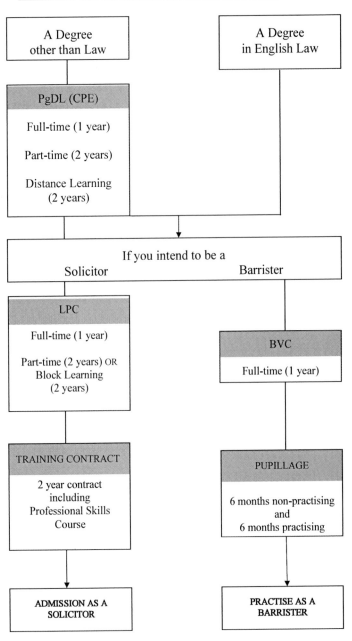

| A Degree other than Law | A Degree in English Law |

**PgDL (CPE)**

Full-time (1 year)

Part-time (2 years)

Distance Learning (2 years)

**If you intend to be a**

Solicitor          Barrister

**LPC**

Full-time (1 year)

Part-time (2 years) OR Block Learning (2 years)

**BVC**

Full-time (1 year)

**TRAINING CONTRACT**

2 year contract including Professional Skills Course

**PUPILLAGE**

6 months non-practising and 6 months practising

**ADMISSION AS A SOLICITOR**

**PRACTISE AS A BARRISTER**

**How to become a Solicitor**

Aspiring solicitors should be realistic about what studying and practising law involves. Do not be misled by fantasy tales or 'fat cat' stories and myths of mega-rich lawyers. The truth is, only a select few see such glamour and normally after many years of hard work! Make sure you really want to become a solicitor for the right reasons and ensure you really know about the advantages and disadvantages.

The majority of law students become solicitors by completing a three-year law degree, a one-year Legal Practice Course (LPC) and a two-year training contract as shown in the diagram opposite. Those who study a non-law degree must complete a law conversion course before undertaking the LPC. These courses are known as the Common Professional Examination (CPE) or the Post-graduate Diploma in Law (PgDL). Both the LPC and law conversion course last full time for the one-year course and can also be taken as a part-time two year course. Both the CPE and PgDL courses are very similar in content and nature. The law conversion course covers the seven foundations of legal knowledge: Criminal law, Equity and Trusts, Property and Public law, Obligations: Contract and Tort, and European law.

Most large commercial law firms recruit their trainees two years in advance, the aim being to spot the brightest talent in the legal market while they are still at university. This is one of the main reasons why prospective trainees must be forward-thinking and aim to apply early during the second year of your degree course or year 3 if you are a non-law student. In any case you will want to apply well before the firms' application deadline.

The firms that recruit trainees two years in advance normally fund the successful applicant's law school fees and also provide maintenance payments to help with living expenses. Given the huge costs for those studying for a legal career, landing a training contract with one of the larger commercial firms brings the added benefit of sponsorship during your studies, another reason why training contract places at these firms are so highly sought after. Many regional and provincial firms may recruit one year in advance, and high street and smaller sole practices tend to recruit trainees as and when there is a business need to recruit and/or a vacancy arises.

## 1. First year law and non-law undergraduates

✓    For law undergraduates make sure you get excellent marks in the foundation subjects required by the Law Society. These are contract, tort, criminal, public law, land (property), European Community law, equity and trusts.

✓    It is important that you apply for internships and work experience to get a feel for what life as a solicitor is really like. Additionally, you will be able to demonstrate an interest and commitment to the legal profession.

✓    When selecting electives on your degree course, choose options which complement your career objectives. For example, if you intend to apply to city firms, it makes sense to pursue corporate/commercial options. Remember, the strength of your academic results is what counts. Ensure you work hard to achieve and maintain good grades.

✓    Choose electives in areas which you are most interested in. If you enjoy these subjects you are more likely to achieve a 1st or high 2:1 and gain a broader knowledge. Consult students in the year above to ascertain the quality of teaching for a particular elective and how challenging students have found it. That said, bear in mind when reading for any degree that no subject is easy and there is no substitute for hard work.

✓    There is a popular myth in some places that your first year grades are irrelevant because they do not count towards your overall degree result. Do not buy into this! Law firms will ask you for all your grades and most law firms wish to see evidence of consistent 1st or high 2.1 grades across all three years.

✓    Build up your CV with lots of extra-curricula activities, for example, travel, involvement in university committee, sport, music and developing a proficiency in a foreign language.

## 2. Second Year

✓ Ensure you obtain vacation placements and internships at law firms. It is a good idea to apply to a variety of firms to gain experience in a wide range of practice areas that appeal to you.

✓ Set up a calendar of events and deadlines for your applications.

✓ Once you begin to build up your profile, it is time to prepare your CV. Your search for a training contract should really kick off in the autumn.

✓ Begin researching the different types of law firms in order to assess which type of firm will best suit you.

✓ Produce a record of all your completed applications and responses received and any follow-up action that may be required e.g. chasing firms for responses or obtaining feedback on your application if you have been rejected.

✓ If you receive rejection letters, it is important not to lose your hope and motivation. Discuss your feedback with friends and your careers advisors to gain constructive advice, encouragement and positive support.

✓ Be organised and prepare a timetable of all the action points we have advised you on.

## 3. Final Year

✓ The key word is FINALS! It is crucial that your main aim is to work towards achieving top grades across all your subjects.

✓ By this stage you may already have a training contract offer. If not prepare yourself for the task of making training contract applications and balancing the hectic schedule of study.

✓ It is now time to apply for a place on the LPC. Those students who are offered a training contract may well be sponsored by their firms, but many others will have to fund themselves.

✓ If you are accepted onto the LPC then the Law Society will automatically ask if you would like to join as a student member. The Law Society also recommends that your university send copies of your exam results to them, so they can check your grades.

✓ Obtain a certificate for the completion of the academic stage of legal training.

## Final Year non-law students

✓ Final year non-law undergraduates who have made the decision to become solicitors must apply for places on the CPE or PgDL. The course fees are currently between £4,000-£7,000, depending on the course provider and the location.

✓ Some firms will fund the CPE/PgDL fees if they offer you a training contract.

✓ At this point you should update your CV and begin sending off those vacation placement and training contract applications later in the year.

✓ Your Law degree or CPE/PgDL certificate shows you have satisfied the Legal Knowledge requirement of the Law Society. To qualify as a solicitor, you must use your law certificate within seven years from 1st October of the year in which you obtained your law certificate.

Deciding to pursue a career in law is a huge financial burden. CPE/PgDL course fees and living expenses are very expensive, so you really need to carefully consider your funding options. As previously mentioned, you may receive sponsorship for cost of the CPE/PgDL if you have a training contract.

Many students pay for the CPE/PgDL themselves through existing savings or with parental help. Other sources of funding available include loan packages such as Career Development Loans and Professional Development Loans which are available through High Street banks. When considering your funding options you would be wise to check your repayment obligations and consider taking out repayment insurance in case you do not find a job in time to meet your commitment to repaying the debt.

The Law Society offers bursary schemes to a small number of exceptional students each year, who are experiencing considerable financial hardship. Bursaries are awarded for CPE, PgDL and LPC students only. Application forms are available from the Education Department of the Law Society. Various charities also offer scholarships or financial assistance. You can find out about these by contacting the Law Society.

During the autumn term of the CPE/PgDL, you will have to apply for a place on next year's LPC. If you have not managed to secure a training contract you should apply as early as possible. Continue the process of sending out strong applications and note that many students do actually start the CPE and LPC without having secured a training contract.

## Mature students

Some mature students often have concerns about how their application will be viewed by prospective employers. We always suggest to mature students to focus on the skills and experiences they have gained during their previous career, which, if marketed effectively on their application forms will provide a competitive advantage over other younger applicants.

**CASE STUDY:** *The challenge for mature students is researching and finding out which individual firms are really "right" for them. As a mature student I was concerned about how law firms would perceive me, but I decided my age and the fact that I have two children, would not be a barrier for me to enter the legal profession. I knew that I had to build up my CV in preparation for submitting polished top-level training contract applications.*

*I thoroughly researched the practice areas and law firms that interested me, and I considered Why I wanted to join a particular firm? Where I wanted to apply?, What the firms look for in their candidates, closing application deadlines etc. I built up my CV with law-related volunteer work, undertook a range of extra-curricular activities – which complimented my enthusiasm for the area of law I was interested in. I contacted 5-10 of my preferred firms, and enquired about open days and vacation placements to learn more about the sector I wished to enter. I asked to shadow a solicitor for a week or so. Some of these firms were quite amenable for me to come in and complete a number of work placements, which helped me to gain a greater insight into my desired practice area and enhanced my CV at the same time. I believe my work experience was invaluable and it was my launchpad to being awarded a training contract.* **Olivia Bailey**

We advise mature students when completing their application forms to concentrate on highlighting the relevant skills and experience which you have developed throughout your earlier career, and most importantly: **Consider how this will benefit the law firm you are applying to from a business perspective? Will there be a business need to hire you?** For example, if you wish to become a corporate finance lawyer, and your previous career was in project finance, banking, or hedge funds, you are highly likely to have built-up useful contacts from this sector, developed skills and experiences which would make you an asset to any law firm. It is therefore important in your employability stakes to be able to sell your ability and knowledge to be a good lawyer, to show a propensity for being able to bring in business and to manage others.

Your previous profession should demonstrate your ability to balance and manage competing responsibilities. We trained with colleagues in their 30's and 40's, who informed us that they had to carefully consider the decision to change from their previous careers. We found those colleagues were extremely focused on embarking on a legal career. They informed us that the partners at the firm had been impressed by their ability to maintain jobs, as well as juggling assignments and meeting training contract deadlines, during their LPC.

Re-training as a solicitor brings added challenges to mature students, such as changing the course of your, and perhaps your family's life direction, coupled with the cost of legal training makes the decision for mature students to become solicitors a huge one. We know of mature students who have re-mortgaged and even sold their houses to fund their journey to becoming a solicitor. However, we would add that by deciding to pursue a career in law at this point in your career you are demonstrating a great deal of commitment to becoming a lawyer.

Many law firms appreciate having older trainee solicitors at the firm for their mature, calm and serious approach to working on legal work. One mature applicant noted that, at their interview they were able to have an extremely engaging conversation with the partner at the law firm. Much of the interview had been based on what they had done with their lives up to that point, because many law firms place a great deal of value in having life experience. A large number of mature applicants are awarded training contracts by law firms, because of these very reasons.

It is important to remember that, the function of a trainee solicitor is to learn how to be a good solicitor, but at most firms the role also involves additional responsibilities of being a fee-earner and generating profit for the firm. The older trainees are likely to be more commercially aware, better organised, and also be more adept at managing their time effectively and talking to clients.

**Our Top Tip: Carefully consider a firm that will embrace your life experience, and the skills you've gained from a previous career. Select a firm that offers a good legal career together with a flexible work/life balance. Perhaps even contact the firms you are interested in directly over the telephone for an informal chat. Our chapter on networking will also be of use to you in your pursuit of Training Contract Success. All the best!**

### Student Membership of the Law Society

During your CPE/PgDL year, you are required to enrol as a student member of the Law Society in order to commence the LPC. The Law Society will then send you an application form to complete and return. The cost of student membership is currently £80. In addition, a reference must be completed by your tutor on the form before you return it to the Law Society. The Law Society will then send you a letter confirming your student enrolment. Being a member of the Law Society enables you to gain access to assistance and a wealth of information and guidance.

## Vacation Schemes

For dedicated and determined law students, summer holidays are synonymous with legal work placements, known as vacation schemes. Vacation schemes are the best way for students to; gain an insight into how a law firm works, get to know a firm, develop a feel for the firm's office environment and how a particular law firm operates. Any type of legal work placement will help to give you an insider's view of the work solicitors undertake, which is all-important in helping you make sufficiently informed decisions about which type of firm you want to work for in the future.

Most City law firms have vacation schemes during the Christmas, Easter and summer weeks. These schemes usually last 2-4 weeks and students are paid around £250 per week. Check the deadlines on the websites of law firms, and apply well in advance of the specified deadline. Legal work experience is very important. It will equip you with practical experience within a legal environment and will demonstrate your interest in working (especially if unpaid) for a law firm, and a long-term commitment to spend your future career as a solicitor. They are marketed as a two-way process meaning that by the end of it, the firm will have assessed your ability and you should have an idea of whether the firm is right for you.

If a summer placement is your aim, apply around December as deadlines are usually in February. Most firms tend to adopt a first-come-first-served approach and will call you for interview as and when they receive your application, so be organised and apply before the rush which culminates around the impending deadline date. You should be aware that some law firms are in such demand that they fill up their places allocated for interviews before the deadline.

Check whether the law firm only considers second-year undergraduates or third-year non-law undergraduates for vacation schemes. Some firms have a strict policy on this and you should find out before you spend hours applying. Firms usually accept vacation scheme applications until late January/early February.

Gaining legal work experience gives you an opportunity to build a rapport with the firm, and you may impress them if you show great enthusiasm and a willingness to work hard. If you do, you should be well on your way to getting a training contract interview. Vacation schemes are the "try before you buy process," and form a large part of the selection process and will enhance your chances of obtaining a training contract at the firm if they make a good impression with the firm.

Law firms are attracted to students who have a number of vacation schemes on their CV because it shows that those applicants have reached the decision to become a lawyer with their eyes wide open, and are therefore more likely to have a long-term commitment to a legal career. It also shows those candidates are in great demand from many other law firms as well and that the applicant has built-up their commercial acumen with useful legal experience.

## Post-vacation placements

After your vacation placement, if you are still keen to join that particular firm, you might want to follow up and write a thank-you letter or e-mail to your supervisor, explaining the reasons why you enjoyed your placement and indicating whether or not you will be applying for a training contract with the firm. Firms have a structured procedure for applying for training contracts following work experience and although this gesture alone will not get you a job it can never hurt to write and thank somebody for having provided you with a fantastic opportunity.

If you have gained some work experience at a law firm, and you are now planning to make an application to a firm, you may want to consider the following non-exhaustive list based on your experience of the firm:

✓ the nature of the training programme
✓ the overall friendliness of the firm
✓ what really interests you and what will give you job satisfaction
✓ the quality of individuals in the firm
✓ the firm's main areas of expertise
✓ the firm's overall reputation in the legal world
✓ the financial help offered by the firm for LPC/CPE
✓ the trainee retention rate

✓  client base
✓  the size of the firm
✓  the facilities at the firm
✓  trainee salaries / assistants' salaries
✓  how many partners trained at the firm
✓  foreign travel and language grants
✓  opportunities for further training and development

Personally, we wouldn't advise students to spend every summer holiday completing placements. Combine your work experience with other interesting activities to demonstrate you are a balanced and well-rounded individual. Graduate recruitment departments are attracted by those who follow interesting pursuits such as travelling, and having creative pursuits will spark an interest in your application and generate good conversation at your interview.

*My vacation placements were a great opportunity to shine. You will usually be at a firm for 2-3 weeks and work in one or two departments assisting partners and qualified lawyers in transactional matters. Firms will also run case studies and teamwork exercises as well as organising various social events. At the end of the period both parties may be keen to continue the relationship and the opportunity of an offer being made and accepted in September could be increased.*

*During one of my vacation placement, I sat for two weeks, with a solicitor who set me most of my tasks. This included legal research, delivering legal documents, attending client meetings, contacting other jurisdictions for information on cross-border transactions, preparing for presentations to recruiters, proof-reading contracts and photocopying. I found out at an early stage that any budding future lawyer must be prepared to work long hours. Always be sharp and alert, think on your feet and be ready to impress. Vacation placements look good on your CV and give you an invaluable pool of information to draw from at interviews. Use vacation scheme interviews as early practice for training contract interviews.*

**Craig Robinson**

Our advice to anyone wanting to join the legal profession is that gaining legal work experience is of utmost importance to helping you decide whether the job of a lawyer is for you, and to test if this is something that you can see yourself doing for the rest of your life.

## What if I am unable to get a Vacation Scheme?

Vacation schemes are notoriously very difficult to secure because there are fewer places available on these schemes than there are actual training contracts. This is compounded by the fact that some of the brightest applicants accept several vacation placements during a single summer. Law firms understand how difficult it is to land a vacation scheme, which is why they value all sorts of legal and commercial work experience, whether in a bank, estate agents or accountancy firm because it will help to boost your commercial acumen, which is very important to law firms (see chapter 9 for commercial awareness).

Some law firms also offer alternative opportunities in the form of Open Days and Skills Workshop sessions to build up your experience and understanding of the realities of working for a law firm. These alternative options are worth applying for, if you are unable to secure a vacation placement.

Consider making new contacts whenever the opportunity arises, make friends with the trainees you meet, speak to the associates you shadow and keep in touch (see chapter 8 for further advice on networking).

## 4. The Legal Practice Course (LPC)

The vocational stage of training to be a solicitor is a one-year, full-time (or two-year, part-time) course designed to bridge your undergraduate degree and your training contract. The course is designed to provide students with sufficient knowledge and skills to ensure that you are well-equipped to undertake all the tasks under your training contract (under supervision) and to be able to cope effectively as a trainee solicitor. Generally, the LPC focuses on practical skills, such as interviewing and advising clients, writing and drafting, communication skills (advocacy), practical legal research, practical group discussions, with emphasis on group work in tutorials and workshops. The

LPC is renowned for its continuous assessment and examinations throughout the year.

The content of the course is broken down into five core areas – business, property and litigation (both civil and criminal), pervasive subjects, skills assessments, i.e. interviewing clients and advocacy, plus electives. The compulsory subjects on the course are regarded as core areas of legal practice. The LPC is designed to bridge the procedural elements with the substantive law. Other core areas known as "pervasive subjects" are professional conduct, client care, Financial Services Act, Solicitors accounts, EU law, probate and administration of estates, principles of estate planning, trusts and taxation. The LPC is aimed at developing a more commercial focus to meet the growing needs of law firms.

The LPC also permits a certain amount of specialisation through a range of optional subjects. LPC students with training contracts should always liaise with their training principals prior to selecting their optional subjects.

The LPC is a demanding course, in the sense that you are constantly assessed throughout the year and a great deal of preparatory reading is required for lectures and workshops, which means excellent organisation, prioritisation and time management skills are required to cope effectively with the challenges of the course.

**Our Top Tip: Students preparing to embark on this course must be sure they understand the nature of the course and the volume of work involved. Work hard towards the prestige of having your name published in The Times newspaper once you pass the LPC!**

## Financing the cost of your legal studies

Lots of LPC students will be sponsored by law firms and others will have parental help, but for some, the cost of funding the LPC can be a huge financial burden. LPC fees range from £5,000 to £10,000 depending on which area of the country you choose to study in. As with the CPE and PgDL there are scholarships and bursaries available. You might also think about taking a break from your studies to gain experience and save money to fund your legal training yourself. This may be a sensible option for lots of students, and would demonstrate your commercial acumen regarding the financial planning and funding of your legal career. For those of you who find yourselves in that position, the financial cost of becoming a solicitor may make you question your commitment to pursuing a training contract. Speaking realistically, law students who fund themselves will incur an average debt of around £25,000-30,000.

## LPC without funding

Students should also bear in mind that living expenses during the vocational stage of training can drive debts up by another £5,000-7,000. In addition to being careful and prudent with your finances at the outset of your degree, our practical advice to students who have not managed to obtain the necessary funding for the CPE or LPC is two-fold; firstly, assess your desire to enter the profession. If you are certain a career in law is for you, you should not be put off by financial worries. Your determination to achieve your goal should be enough to see you through. After all, your legal training is an investment for your future. Indeed, we have many examples of friends who started the LPC without training contracts who by the end of that year had managed to secure jobs. It is also the case that some firms will pay some or part of your LPC fees retrospectively.

Secondly, consider the option of doing the CPE or LPC part-time. Although it takes two years instead of one, you can learn as you earn. Some individuals are, in fact, commencing their training contracts with smaller firms as they study the LPC, highlighting the flexibility of some firms.

## 5. The Training Contract

The training contract is the final hurdle to qualifying as a solicitor. Every firm will have a different approach to their training contract, and the level of responsibility and type of work you will be given is dependent on the size of the firm and the areas in which they specialise. The Law Society sets out strict guidelines for firms ensuring that future solicitors maintain a good standard. This includes undertaking the Professional Skills Course (PSC) as part of the training scheme for solicitors - you cannot qualify as a solicitor without passing the PSC. This is a modular course which aims to ensure that you have reached the appropriate level of skills and knowledge during the Legal Practice Course and the training contract.

The Training Regulations, 1994, require trainees to spend at least four months each in three areas of law, with at least one of these seats incorporating non-contentious/contentious work. Most training contracts are divided into four seats where trainees spend time in different departments, usually at 6-month intervals. It is designed to provide a breadth of experience in a minimum of three and usually four practice areas of law and, the seats mould the trainee's aspirations and clarify their interests. Under close supervision by a partner or senior associate, a trainee will undertake practical work in research, drafting, attending meetings and client conferences, and provide support for a period of over six months. It gives the firm an opportunity to get to know the individual – and for the trainee to prove their worth to the people who will decide their qualification prospects at the end of the two-year training period.

It is probably helpful to think of the training contract as an apprenticeship. These two years provide an opportunity for a law firm to build upon what the trainee has already learnt by combining it with practical work experience under the supervision of a solicitor with at least five years, post qualification experience.

What you learn during your training contracts will depend on your firm and your supervisor. If you join a large commercial firm, you are likely to spend six months in four departments giving you different exposure. However, at a niche practice the main concentration may be on a single area of work, your options may be limited and trainees must ensure that the firm will provide them with training in the minimum of three practice areas as required by the Law Society.

The Law Society's Legal and Education department have a standard form Training Contract that all law firms will have to adhere to and are prohibited from excluding any express terms in the standard form. However, firms can incorporate additional clauses as long as they do not conflict with the Law Society's standard form. If there is any conflict the Law Society's terms will take precedence. An example of this standard form Training Contract is in Appendix 1, which details the obligations of the training establishment and the trainee during the training contract. You may want to read this document to understand all of the important requirements that the Law Society sets out. Your firm should ensure that once your training contract is signed by both parties, it is registered with the Law Society within 28 days. Once this is done, you will receive a letter from the Law Society confirming the date your training contract commences and the date that it will end.

## Salary

The Law Society sets an annual minimum wage for trainee solicitors. In 2008, the minimum salary levels for trainees working in Central London, is £18,420 per annum. For trainees working outside London, in England and Wales the new minimum salary is £16,500 per annum.

It is worth noting that the majority of the top 100 law firms pay well in excess of the Law Society minimum. Law firms are not obliged to retain you after you complete your training. However, the trainees who manage to convince their colleagues and supervisors that they are a reliable and safe pair of hands, are likely to have impressed the firm sufficiently enough to be retained and offered a job on qualification.

## The Life of a Trainee Solicitor by Justin Deveraux

*During my interview for a training contract, I said I was looking forward to exciting work coupled with interesting and challenging clients. As a trainee I am now concerned about surviving - keeping my head above water while making a good impression and living up to everyone's expectations. I'm now 6 months into the job and I still have a million questions. Most importantly, where do I turn to for help with unfamiliar tasks? From my experience, I knew the best people to gain information from were the trainees and newly- qualified lawyers. As a new trainee, I knew that firms perceive trainees as an investment for the future, the life-blood of the firm. I began quickly learning that trainees are expected to ask questions but to also think carefully, laterally and independently before-hand.*

### My First Seat

*Colleagues described my first seat as a baptism of fire! The transition from your legal studies to becoming a full-time trainee is a testing moment for all aspiring solicitors. After years of attending lectures the reality of life as a lawyer was about to be experienced first-hand. My first mission was to embark on my banking seat in a senior assistant's office and hope things worked out.*

*During my first day of training, I was advised to have an open mind because practising the law is very different from studying it. Friends at smaller firms admit that they were given a caseload from the outset and expected to make an immediate impact. Larger firms have the luxury of being able to offer a full suite of induction courses at the start of each seat, accompanied by lectures from partners and the internal training team.*

*At that early stage, I had no idea what I wanted to specialise in, but fortunately a partner provided me with some much needed guidance, something along the lines of:*

**"Whichever practice area you decide to specialise in, it is imperative that you have a good grounding and knowledge of the major areas – not least because most transactions today will have implications across several fields. With the intensification of globalisation, modern lawyers need an international outlook to business as**

**companies expect to transact business regardless of borders, and want a seamless service from their legal practitioners in various jurisdictions."**

*Further pearls of wisdom arrived from a senior associate who remarked:* "Work hard and do what's asked of you and the next two years will be fine." *It was reassuring to hear these words and to be on the receiving end of hints and tips from seasoned lawyers. I felt privileged to be gaining such excellent advice.*

**Highlight of my first seat**

*Whilst acting for a global bank on a huge leveraged finance deal, I worked on various finance documentation on a transaction with a capital value of just under £1billion. I collected all the conditions precedent (CPs), conditions which the borrower has to satisfy before the bank will be willing to lend the money. My role as trainee was to ensure that each document had been accounted for.*

*As a result of the mad rush at closing, I had managed to mislay a vital document. I assured my supervisor that everything was under control. However, without this one document, we could not give confirmation that the CPs had been satisfied, the funds could not be transferred to the borrower. I knew for sure the original document was somewhere on or near my desk, it had to be!*

*Confidence, poise and self-conviction were key in knowing how to cope and re-assure my supervisor that "all was well" - i.e. looking in control on the outside while beginning to fret on the inside! I managed to locate the document; I had mistakenly put it in a pile of documents I had given to my secretary. I quickly learned how to survive my first seat. I learnt how to handle a potentially deal-breaking matter without losing the trust of my supervisor.*

*Organisational skills are one of (if not) the most important attributes a trainee can have - being able to prioritise and manage time. Those are some of the things that a trainee will receive praise for. I recently assisted a senior lawyer on another deal and needed to prioritise a huge workload and getting these basics correct gave the lawyer the comfort that I was completely on top of my work. As I prepare to move on to my next seat, phone conversations with my predecessor indicate that I'm in for another shocker; the reality is that I may have to spend the first Monday of my second seat working through the night. Not a problem... if I survived my first seat, I can survive anything!*

**Our Top Tip: Start thinking about paying attention to detail on your CV and application forms and answering questions succinctly. Once you start your training contract, your supervisors will expect you to accurately implement every single instruction. Avoid making elementary mistakes by getting the basics right! Focus on your spelling and grammar, and the readability of your documents and always use spell check to verify the accuracy of your work.**

### Qualification as a Solicitor

Once you have finished your training contract, the Law Society will send you an application for entry onto the Law Society's roll of solicitors. You can then apply for a practising certificate and, if you wish, join the Law Society as a full member. Many newly-qualified solicitors prefer to stay at the firm where they trained, where they are familiar with both the staff and the firm's unique way of working. It is unlikely that a firm will have invested the time and resources in training you if it was not considering you for a place at the end of it. That said, it is possible that the firm's staffing requirements have developed in a way that was not anticipated, (e.g. through a merger or a downturn in a particular area of work) and there are no longer places available for newly-qualified lawyers.

### Associate / Assistant solicitor

Once qualified and employed by a firm, you will be an associate/assistant solicitor, normally working under the supervision of a partner or senior solicitor. Consequently, you will work on a fixed salary and may be lucky enough to receive performance-related bonuses.

The working life of a solicitor varies considerably according to the type of firm you work for, the partners supervising you, the areas of work in which you are practising, and your own abilities. Generally, you will be expected to work hard and take responsibility with minimal supervision. The next step up for a solicitor is to become a senior assistant/associate, then a partner.

## Partnership

The ultimate career ambition for most solicitors in private practice (i.e. working for law firms) is to become a partner. Law firms are partnerships; they are owned and managed by the partners. (Salaried partners have a similar status to equity partners but do not have a share in the firm's profits). The length of time it takes to become a partner will depend on both the individual and your firm. Generally, a solicitor can expect to wait up to eight or more years post qualification for partnership at a large commercial firm and perhaps only four years at a smaller, less commercially-orientated firm. Again, much will depend on your own abilities and probably a bit of luck!

---

**OVERVIEW OF THE LEGAL PROFESSION: Points to Ponder:**

Students may not always realise all of the options which are available to them. Once you reach the crossroads where you are required to make the important decision of which pathway to take, in order to make the best choices you need to be well informed. Points to consider are:

- What options do you have?

- What do solicitors and barristers do?

- How do I even become a solicitor or barrister?

- What are vacation schemes, the CPE and the LPC?

- What is expected of you as a trainee?

---

Chapter Three

## What makes a successful lawyer?

There are many characteristics required to become a top lawyer. From our experience the key qualities that help make a successful lawyer are:

### All-round portfolio of skills

A successful lawyer will possess a portfolio of skills and abilities, including a mix of excellent technical attributes - the ability to think laterally, drive and determination to get the job done. You will be expected to know the law, and have the ability to listen carefully to clients in order to implement their instructions and assist them in making difficult commercial decisions.

### First-class communication skills (written and oral)

A solicitor must have superb communication skills and be able to speak confidently and credibly to a client by providing advice in a clear and coherent manner. Effective communication helps to build a rapport and trust with a client. Great lawyers also use their communication skills to negotiate favourable terms for their clients.

*Great lawyers are technically excellent, assertive and respond quickly to the needs of their clients, so that clients believe you are always accessible. Excellent legal advice involves providing legal and commercial solution to for the client, consistently keeping the client updated and well-informed. I have observed that clients appreciate pragmatic forward thinking by their legal business advisors. Successful lawyers invariably speak the same language as their client, possessing the innate skill of being able to; interpret matters from the client's perspective, unravel complex legal jargon and, communicate advice in a viable way.*

**Craig Robinson**

## Careful attention to detail and finely tuned drafting skills

Having a thorough and meticulous approach is an important attribute for a solicitor; drafting extensive legal documents accurately is an essential part of the work most solicitors undertake. An efficient solicitor will pay tremendous attention to detail and leave no stone unturned in ensuring the accuracy of their documents. They will have the ability to remain focused, by paying attention to the key issues at all times.

## Commercial acumen

Successful lawyers invariably have great commercial awareness. In the legal arena the role of a solicitor has evolved from being a sound technician of the law to having all-round business skills, a legal advisor will often be called on to provide a commercial steer to the advice they provide. Today a lawyer must have an in-depth knowledge of the mechanics of their client's business, and its clients expect their lawyers to have a full understanding of their strategic goals and marketplace, with legal advice being applied in the commercial context in which a client operates.

A good grounding and knowledge of the major areas of law is also of the utmost importance because some transactions will have implications across several fields. With the continuing presence of globalisation, commercial lawyers need a global outlook to business, as companies expect to transact business regardless of borders, and want a seamless service from their legal practitioners in various jurisdictions.

## Effective at managing their clients' expectations

Those lawyers who are able to effectively manage the expectations of their clients will invariably establish a good reputation. This can only be achieved by providing the quality of work they expect. Client care is part and parcel of a lawyer's job. Good lawyers are client-centred and focused on adding significant value to the delivery of their service to clients.

Client Relationship Management is a key element to this and involves looking to the long term by building a strong positive rapport with clients, by cultivating and developing relationships with new clients and effectively maintaining and managing long-lasting relationships with existing clients. Lawyers who can demonstrate an understanding of the commercial environment in which a client operates and find workable practical commercial solutions to meet the challenges faced by clients will exceed the expectations of the client.

## Time management and organisation skills

A successful lawyer will be able to manage their time extremely efficiently, and have effective organisation and prioritisation skills of the highest order to ensure they are able to keep on top of their tasks and meet deadlines. As a solicitor, you will learn that your time is your most valuable commodity. You will charge your clients for the "billable" time you spend advising them.

## Effective team player

Teamwork is critical to success in business. Lawyers must be able to work collaboratively and effectively in a team to achieve set goals, as well as being equally adept at working independently and autonomously. There can be periods when you work very hard and for long hours on a transaction. Nobody is going to respond well to a team member who sulks about having to work past midnight or pulls a long face when given a task to do in the evening. You won't be the only one so it's unlikely you'll get much sympathy. You will be much more of an asset to the team if you smile and get on with it. You must be committed to helping your colleagues meet deadlines around a transaction, and enjoy the buzz of working on a deal.

## Passion for your area of practice

A legal career can provide you with a high degree of job satisfaction as it will constantly test your aptitude. The opportunity to be a part of a respected profession, the learning involved with keeping pace with constantly evolving legislation and precedents, provides the potential for a dynamic career. As a trainee you will make your way through four or more seats and at the end of your training you will select an area of law which you feel suits you best. If you have a keen interest in your chosen area of law, this is likely to provide you with energy and enthusiasm for the work you undertake, which will help to make you career progression much smoother.

## Highly self-motivated

Good lawyers will be highly self-motivated and possess a proactive, can-do positive attitude. They will be able to think laterally around problems and they will in most cases be fired up with enthusiasm for the work they do. Reputable solicitors tend to possess a strong work ethic and are prepared to go the extra mile for their clients.

## Calm under pressure

As professionals, lawyers must be calm, poised and unflappable under pressure and be able to keep emotions from influencing their decisions. Ultimately, clients want their lawyers to have the presence of mind to think clearly and quickly on their feet (especially during meetings) and be able to adapt to deal with the most difficult problems.

## Polished interpersonal skills

The best all-round lawyers tend to be personable, and are able to demonstrate exceptional people skills when cultivating useful business contacts, which may develop into an increase in work for the firm.

**Our Top Tips: If you feel that you do not possess these qualities at present, don't despair! Remember that law firms are looking for potential. The key qualities at this stage are whether you have the confidence, discipline, ambition and personality to succeed. Are you hungry enough to make it in this highly competitive legal market? What makes you tick? Does your desire to succeed as a lawyer come from a motivation to make money or a passion for a particular area or to exceed client expectations and ultimately help people?**

**When we started applying for training contracts, most of us knew that success would not arrive overnight! But we worked tremendously hard and remained determined, and had a good work ethic, persistence, self-discipline, with dedication and a strong desire to achieve, we managed to reach our goal! Now so can you!**

## What makes a successful lawyer: Points to Ponder

In order to project the qualities you need to be successful at interview, you need to start moulding yourself in to the image of a successful lawyer. The transition starts now. Remember:

- The requisite portfolio of skills for lawyers.

- Which characteristics make the difference and why?

- How you can adopt these characteristics to become successful in your search for a training contract.

## Chapter Four

## <u>Which way do I go?</u>

In your pursuit of a career in law, it is absolutely vital you know what you want and exactly where you are heading. To get ahead, you must choose the right road to the right firm!

In order to decide which type of firm is right for you, your starting point must be to research the firms you are interested in and prepare a shortlist of the law firms to which you will apply. Assessing a potential firm is fundamental, as you will be spending at least two years of your life there as a trainee. Do your research! Look at the practice areas and any recent examples of the firm's work which most appeal to you. Whilst it is not easy to make such decisions two years in advance of commencing your practical training, you should try to make as informed a choice as possible, because the place you work in has to be right for you.

In our discussions with training contract applicants we have found that many aspiring solicitors choose firms that will not suit them simply because they fail to carry out enough research and are not aware of all the opportunities. A great first step for students applying for training contracts is to find out everything you possibly can about the work the firms undertake.

One student we spoke to had written to a lawyer regarding an article she had written which he found to be of particular interest. This may sound slightly too keen to some readers but through a series of meetings that student was able to find out more about the area of law he wanted to practise. The message here is to reach beyond your comfort zone!

**Our Top Tip: You are realising that the law is a profession for which you need to plan ahead. Generally employers recruit during the penultimate year of the law degree, which means it's never too soon for students to plot their path from school to university to a solicitor's office. It does pay to be organised.**

Use the work experience you have gained during your studies to assist you in getting on the right road. For example, assess your vacation scheme placements and ask yourself how much you enjoyed the experience. Combine this with extensive research and read as much as you can and as widely as possible from law websites, legal magazines which all include features about various practice areas and differing types of firms. If you look on the website of any firm, you can see the areas of law they practise in. Also, go along to your university careers centre, graduate open days, career fairs, and consult lawyers that you gained experience from during your vacation placements or any solicitors or barristers you may have come into contact with. They will always have a wealth of knowledge and experience you can use to help you in your search for a training contract.

All law firms have a selection criterion for choosing their applicants. In the same way, you must also formulate your own criteria for the firms you chose to apply to. The more you expose yourself to the different types of law firms and the culture of the firms, the easier it will become to select the ones which most closely match your criteria.

**Our Top Tip: Keep files on firms that you are really interested in joining, for example, press cuttings and internet archives. Consulting websites such as RollonFriday.com, Legal Week, lawcareers.net, Chambers and Partners student directory, Lex, Target law and Lawyer2B, will greatly assist you in building up a database of current issues and news regarding your chosen firms, while helping you ask and answer questions appropriately at interview.**

## Selecting your law firm

Before you begin looking at any specific jobs it is helpful to understand the nature of the environment in which you will one day be working.

Many students have told us how difficult they find it to distinguish between some law firms. Here is an overview of the different types of law firms. Each will offer different types of work and the culture may be different.

**Big city firms** are the largest employers of trainee solicitors. These firms fund the CPE/PgDL and LPC for their future trainees through sponsorship, and provide the added benefit of giving students maintenance expenses to support them through their studies. It is hardly surprising that competition for places at these firms is extremely fierce. The salaries are excellent and they are combined with very challenging work that may often involve working long hours.

**Magic circle,** A group of five law firms: Allen & Overy, Clifford Chance, Freshfields, Linklaters and Slaughter & May make up the Magic circle. These firms fall under the category of big city firms but are distinguished by being the largest, in terms of the value of their transactions, the size of the firms and the number of trainees they recruit. They are the apex of city law firms, consistently at the top of the legal rankings table. These firms are corporate institutions and their work is based around finance, banking work and mainstream corporate work.

**International:** These comprise of nearly all the magic circle firms and they handle all aspects of cross-border business and financial law. With multiple offices throughout the world's major financial centres, there are likely to be good opportunities to travel, which is why students who are able to speak foreign languages fluently gain an edge. You will work for multinational clients in multi-jurisdictional legal and commercial sectors, on matters of high-value complex transactions, commercial awareness being integral to the work you do. Almost all of these firms are based in the City of London and have offices in the major cities around the world, providing a great opportunity to work on the biggest deals at the cutting edge of corporate and finance law with opportunities to travel overseas on transactions and secondment to the client's international offices.

**US firms:** The last two decades have seen an influx of US firms to London. They challenge and compete with other major international city firms for corporate and commercial work. Some of these firms also specialise in hi-tech areas such as telecommunications and IT. Although corporate activity remains their mainstay, they regard themselves as very much global law firms rather than US firms with City offices. They recruit only a handful of elite students and offer the highest trainee salaries in the City.

**Major national**: Such firms offer a wide range of high-quality commercial work for both public and private companies. These firms tend to have very good support facilities, large numbers of lawyers and high levels of remuneration. Although UK-based many of these firms will have strong associations with firms in other countries.

**Medium-sized**: These firms generally work for some major Public Limited Companies and some larger regional companies as well as private clients. A mid-sized city practice will provide a full range of commercial and corporate services but may not have the cross-border expertise of some of the larger City firms.

**Regional:** These firms offer broad-based legal services throughout the country from a number of big regional commercial centres, such as Birmingham and Manchester. They are often the product of mergers between strong regional practices. Work tends to be of a domestic nature using expertise across the country wherever appropriate. Regional firms operate from either a single office or several offices in a particular geographic region. Their clients are mostly the public and private companies in the region.

**Niche and specialist:** These are small firms which offer high-quality work in a specialised field. Often they are innovative and provide a high level of personal service. Some niche practices are experts in one particular area of law such as media law. Students must be aware that these firms often have only one or two trainee vacancies per year. Working in a specialised practice area, you must be determined to spend a career in that field as opportunities for change may be limited. Mature students with industry experience generally have a competitive advantage over younger students for these jobs. At interview, you need to be particularly convincing on why this area is for you.

**High street:** High street firms generally give their trainees hands-on work with a tendency towards a mixture of family law, criminal, private client, wills and probate, tax, divorce, personal injury and Conveyancing. However, some are known to specialise. Your working hours and salary will generally be less than your City counterparts and your work/life balance will certainly be healthier with early responsibility. The high street lawyers we have spoken to feel they work in a personally rewarding environment. Training is perhaps less structured than the training you'll receive at other firms. These firms may pay slightly less than the large City firms, but staff often report better working hours and flexibility in their training. Trainees that are part of a small intake often report an incremental increase in their level of responsibility in tandem with their development, with a great deal of client contact

**In-House:** Training within large companies is quite rare for many aspiring solicitors and only a handful of training contract opportunities are available at some of the big brand name companies specialising in telecommunications, utilities or media. The advantage of training in-house is the specific on-the-job training and closer involvement in the business decision-making process, which invariably demands excellent commercial awareness in order to understand the key issues of the business and the wider industry. Prospective trainees with ambitions to work in-house should carefully research which companies offer training contracts and perhaps contact companies directly to see if they would consider hiring a trainee solicitor. In addition, contact the Commerce and Industry group at the Law Society for further information. (*See chapter 17 which profiles Maria Christou, who is training in-house at Motorola*).

**Government:** There are also training contracts available in the legal services departments of local government. Each borough council's legal department offers at least two training contracts annually. The Government Legal Service also offers training contracts in different government departments, such as the Department for Trade and Industry. It may also be worth considering applying to public bodies and organisations such as the Crown Prosecution Service (*see chapter 19 for contact details*).

**Factors which may affect the type of firm you choose.**

**Geographic area** - The question here is where do you see your long-term future and which area of law do you want to practise in? Regional firms in particular will be concerned about trainees having some connection to the area. With the stiff competition for jobs, many firms are aware that some trainees are flexible about where they train because they are determined to qualify. However, some of these firms fear that, once qualified, the solicitor will move on to another firm in a different part of the country. Proving to the firm your strong local connections and commitment to investing and spending your career in the region is a pre-requisite.

- Consider the difference in the type of work you may experience in different regions
- Think about whether the opportunity of a secondment to a client or a seat in an overseas office appeals to you and;
- Think about where the firm is located.

**Size** - Do you see yourself working in a large organisation as one of around 100 trainees? The biggest law firms are not necessarily going to be the right choice for you; not all prospective trainees will be suited to working for the big firms. While it is true that the training programme at these firms tends to be first class, well-structured and organised, training at smaller firms also has some great advantages e.g. some smaller firms are able to offer trainees greater responsibility from an early stage.

**Reputation/Culture/Ethos of a firm** - According to the recruitment brochures, each firm has its own definable culture. You must assess the type of culture which appeals to you. The only way you can truly find this out is by visiting the firms on vacation placements and open days to observe the dynamics yourself. If you attend open days or vacation schemes, pay close attention trust your first impression and natural gut instinct to aid your decision. Think about whether you could see yourself being happy at the firm. Look at how formal or relaxed they are and whether any busy lawyers are willing to take the time out of their demanding schedule to talk to you.

**Type of work** - You must ensure you carry out sufficient research so that the firms you apply to offer the type of work that you would like to do. However, if you already know which practice area you want to work in, research whether the firms are recommended and highly regarded in that practice area.

## The Training element

- ✓ How is the training structured?
- ✓ What are the benefits and opportunities on offer to trainees?
- ✓ What is the turnover of staff?
- ✓ How many trainees are kept on at qualification?

## How to find the information

✓ Look at the firm's website, brochures and directories, (Chambers and Partners directory, Legal 500, LawCareers.net are all excellent sources). Make sure you know enough to show a specific interest in the firm's areas of practice, history and any involvement in cases or transactions reported in the legal press.

✓ Have a genuine interest in the practice areas of the firm; it is unprofessional to waste your time and the firm's time if it transpires that you want to be a human rights lawyer when you are interviewing at a corporate firm.

✓ Training contracts are available at a diverse range of places and not just at law firms. Many websites list recent vacancies.

✓ Contact the firm's marketing department for up-to-date literature.

✓ Use your network of contacts to get a behind-the-scenes view.

---

### Get on the right road to choosing a firm: Points to Ponder

Targeting the right type of firm for you is essential. You can save hours of time in filling out application forms if you target the right type of firm from the outset. The best way to ensure whether a firm is worth applying to is by thorough research. In addition, your training contract will run for a period of two years and it is important you assess whether the practice areas undertaken by the firms you have targeted match the type of work you want to do. Remember:

• There are different types of law firms – which type of firm is right for you?
• The criteria you should be thinking about when deciding which firm suits you.
• How and where to find out information about law firms.

Chapter Five

## Demystifying Legal Practice Areas

During your research into legal practice, you may have studied or discovered an area of law which appeals to you the most. Some students, especially if they haven't studied law, will not be familiar with the specialist areas of law. We have set out below a brief explanation of the main practice areas.

## Banking and finance

This area ranges from simple bi-lateral lending between a bank and a company to the cut and thrust of a huge syndicated loan. Banking and finance entails the legal side of constructing, structuring and implementing commercial loan agreements. For example, Jumbo syndicates provide loans to help finance large-scale corporate acquisitions, such as Vodafone's £13bn merger with Airtouch, a telecoms company. Keeping abreast of global corporate transactions will develop your commercial awareness. You should try to familiarise yourself with banking terminology, e.g. underwriting, security, and leveraging. Specialist banking and finance work will include real estate finance and tax-based structured financing, and both of which are fairly self-explanatory.

## Construction

Construction work is in essence split into contentious and non-contentious work. On the contentious side of things you will inevitably find yourself in court when things go wrong, for example, over the delay in completion of a major building project or when a building turns out to be defective or collapses! The non-contentious side will involve negotiating and drafting contracts for building projects between the various parties (contractor, surveyors, etc.) and perhaps amending one of a multitude of standard form contracts widely used in the industry.

## Corporate

Corporate finance involves firms acting for public companies which have shares listed on the London Stock Exchange and AIM. The area covers Initial Public Offerings (IPOs), the process by which a firm floats its shares on the Stock Exchange, for example Google's flotation in New York during August 2004, mergers and acquisitions (M&A) and restructurings and raising finance.

The need to be commercially aware is clearly seen in this area of law. Lawyers will work closely with bankers, accountants and companies. They will need a good understanding of the client's business, the sector within which it operates and a thorough understanding of the roles of the other professional advisers.

In these types of deals lawyers will structure the deal alongside other professionals; where they negotiate, prepare and finalise documentation, provide advice on the transaction, and carry out "due diligence". This term refers to an investigatory process by which lawyers will investigate the affairs of a company which may be the subject of a takeover or a merger, such as any contracts the company has entered into, whether there is any outstanding litigation and any legal or financial commitments which could affect the commercial position of a company after the completion of the transaction. The work may have an international aspect to it or competition issues may arise. Other key areas that may be involved are banking, employment and IP.

## Criminal

Criminal law at a solicitor's practice will involve work related to prosecuting or defending those accused of committing offences, from minor road traffic offences to more serious ones. Most of these firms are based on the high street and will also offer expertise in areas including child abuse and sexual offences, drug-related offences, fraud, mentally ill offenders, and serious violent offences. However many larger corporate firms will advise on white-collar crime.

The international aspect of criminal law will encompass European Human Rights, terrorism, murder, serious fraud, organized crime, international drugs trafficking, money laundering and war crimes.

## Employment

Law firms will work closely with employers and employees in this practice area. This is an extremely important practice area; it deals with any company's most valuable asset – its people. The work will range from lifestyle concerns (parental rights, career breaks), to restructuring companies, including redundancy. Employment will also cover areas such as workplace discrimination and employment litigation. In many firms a large part of the employment department will be concerned with providing ancillary support on employment aspects of large corporate deals, for example, mergers and acquisitions.

Many firms have built reputations for acting for employees or alternatively employers in employment disputes. In both cases lawyers will need to be sensitive to the expectations of the parties, and the commercial nature of the employer's business as well as the litigation concerns of the employee.

The field is noted for its frequently changing law and best practice guidelines, such as the recent legislation on Age Discrimination and the impact this will have on employment methods of many companies.

Lawyers will always need to be well-versed on the latest cases and judgements; in addition, an integral part of a lawyer's role may also be to assist in helping other members of the firm get to grips with such changes.

## EU and competition

Lawyers will generally advise on different types of regulatory work. This will include advising on compliance planning, cartel offences, and regulatory investigations. The larger city firms will handle large scale and high-profile antitrust litigation cases. International firms will deal with the increasing anti-trust legislation in countries across the world. The nature of the work requires an in-depth understanding of how various sectors and industries operate.

The legislation involved in this area seeks to curtail the abuse of a dominant position by a company, or anti-competitive restrictions on trade in the European Community.

## Family law

The major areas of family law are separation agreements, divorce, financial settlements and court orders following divorce, disputes involving children and contact/residency orders, cohabitation, pre-nuptial and pre-registration agreements and civil partnerships. This area of the law is constantly in the media. Recent examples include the high profile divorce of both Paul McCartney and Roman Ambramovich.

Family law is a very demanding practice area, and requires practitioners to have the ability to empathise with their client in difficult circumstances, as well as being sensitive and understanding to their client's needs. Equally important is the need for family lawyers to have sound judgment, formidable negotiation skills and great attention to detail when settling family disputes. With constant developments in case law and legislation it is integral that family lawyers keep up with the changes in the law.

## Intellectual property

Intellectual property is the general name for a set of intangible rights relating to ownership of original works. Ownership of these rights grants a monopoly over the use of the creation, and are usually a trade mark, copyright, patents or design rights. Businesses are increasingly recognising the need to protect designs, packaging, inventions and trade names.

The work in this area will generally fall into two categories: Hard IP - which is scientifically based, such as patent work, which involves the protection of inventions and processes. And soft IP - which involves the protection of copyright (essential to authors and musicians), trademarks (essential for companies to indicate to the public where goods originated from), design rights (manufacturers) and passing off. Other associated rights may arise when providing advice, such as confidentiality and those relating to information technology and the Internet.

Non-contentious IP work - This will generally involve a client wanting to buy or assign intellectual property rights for commercial purposes, or, on a corporate transaction, checking the title to IP rights which have been claimed.

Contentious work - The basis for this type of work is that a person's rights have been infringed, e.g. a manufacturer selling a product under a trademark may bring an action against someone else selling a product under the same mark. The firm will naturally advise on what can be done to stop the infringement and perhaps seek settlement, as litigation can be extremely complicated and expensive.

## IT/ Technology/ Telecoms

The incredible growth of the internet, the convergence of IT, digital technology, new media and telecommunications industries, has led to rapid developments in technology in industries around the globe. This is an exciting area of practice for many lawyers as it is constantly in a state of rapid development. The work involved for lawyers is wide-ranging and varied. Clients may be developing or using leading edge systems or innovative inventions/projects.

A great deal of the legal work in the IT industry covers advising, negotiating and drafting commercial contracts, software development agreements, web hosting agreements, computer licences, maintenance and outsourcing agreements to litigation involving the ownership of software and Intellectual Property.

Intellectual Property is very important to this area of the law and a good understanding of this subject, competition law and contract law is fundamental to advising clients effectively on the creation, protection, exploitation, and enforcement of the rights involved in advancements in technology. Some of these inventions are so valuable that they become a litigious battleground in industries whose businesses are threatened by new advanced digital technology or are in danger of being destroyed by technological developments or the loss of the Intellectual Property Rights itself. For example, see the Blackberry dispute between the US companies RIM and NTP.

## Litigation

Litigators act for clients involved in disputes. Litigation is a process by which one party brings a claim against another party having recourse to the courts in order to resolve the dispute. Commercial litigation is extremely broad, and once qualified lawyers will tend to specialise in areas ranging from patent litigation to insurance or professional negligence. There are other methods of resolving disputes, which will form part of the litigator's armoury of skills. Sometimes contracts between two parties are drafted to include a reference to binding arbitration in the face of any disputes. These are normally confidential. Alternative Dispute Resolution (ADR) is another method which is quicker and more cost-effective. It involves negotiation by a mediator. If no agreement can be reached the party will still have the right to litigate.

The work will involve case analysis and preparation, research, instructing counsel, attending meetings and case management conferences with others involved in the case (such as witnesses and experts) and attending court.

## Personal injury

A lawyer's role is to advise and provide assistance to the people injured in accidents – at work, at home, on the road, or elsewhere. In many cases, someone else is at fault and responsible for the injuries, and the people are entitled to compensation for their injuries and loss of earnings. Personal Injury law involves; advising the client on their legal entitlement and helping them to negotiate their compensation and/or instituting legal proceedings. Those interested in this area of the law will require a good understanding of the Civil Procedural Rules, the law of tort and negligence.

## Private client

In commercial firms the term "private client" refers to individuals as opposed to corporate organisations. The individuals are largely non-UK based, high-worth individuals. Law firms will advise banks and trusts on aspects of trust law. Through a trust an individual can hold assets, for example, holding funds in an offshore jurisdiction while at the same time making tax savings. The work can involve thinking up and implementing appropriate tax advice for clients.

## Project finance

This covers the long-term financing of infrastructure, power and energy projects where the debt and equity which are used to finance the project are repaid from cash flows generated by the project once it is up and running. Project finance is of a very commercial nature and could involve building things such as roads, wind farms, dams and power stations. Project finance is a broad mix ranging from work more akin to corporate transactions to pure finance related work.

## Tax

Tax legislation is known for being very complex. There are various forms of taxation; corporation, personal (including income tax), property tax (including Stamp duty) on the sale of property, inheritance tax, international tax and VAT. Clients will require personal and/or commercial tax advice and planning. Tax lawyers invariably have a great understanding of technical points of the law, meticulous attention to financial details and corporate law and will of course enjoy reading the annual budget.

## Property

The bread and butter for this type of commercial lawyer will obviously be the buying and selling of commercial property. A large company may want to purchase the freehold interest of a property in the middle of a city in order to redevelop it. On such deals lawyers will normally split into teams. For example, some will negotiate the purchase contract while another group may investigate the freehold title and others the planning permission. The same team may advise on how the purchase is to be financed.

Aside from buying and selling, firms are involved in complex finance transactions relating to property, in addition to various urban regeneration schemes such as the numerous projects undertaken following the bombing of the city centre in Manchester in the lead up to the 2002 Commonwealth games.

## Media and entertainment

Media and Entertainment lawyers practice a vast range of commercial law. Much of the work will be contractual. It may cover aspects of Intellectual Property including trademarks, data protection or sponsorship. You will also advise on employment law issues, property transactions and even crime. This area of law has an extremely wide ambit. If you are working in-house for one of the sporting bodies you are likely to be dealing with much regulatory and governance work. From this you can see that as a media lawyer you will need to be grounded and keep a firm interest in all areas on which you envisage your client may need advice. For this sector you will need especially good interpersonal skills. The clients you are dealing with may not be corporate clients and they may expect their lawyer to be at their disposal.

---

### Demystifying legal practice areas: Points to Ponder

After reading this chapter, ensure you understand the type of law which is practised at the firms you are thinking about applying to. Be able to explain briefly the type of work each area involves.

Below are the questions you could very easily be asked at an interview. Ensure you look impressive on application forms and at an interview by getting to grips with the different types of law, it might also give you an idea of the type of lawyer you want to be.

- What does banking law involve?

- Have you ever wondered what corporate lawyers actually do?

- What's so private about private client work?

- Which areas of law are you most interested in and why?

---

Chapter Six

## What are law firms looking for?

When talking to the graduate recruitment managers of leading law firms about what they look for in desirable candidates, there are qualities and aptitudes that come up time and time again. Law firms spend a phenomenal amount of time and money in their search for talent, and in developing their trainees to become talented lawyers and future partners of the firm. This is why they have spent a great deal of time considering what attributes make the "brightest talent", and invariably seek to recruit only the very best and most able people.

This chapter provides a detailed breakdown of the type of skills that firms look for when selecting their candidates. While there are a portfolio of different qualities and characteristics required to be a successful lawyer, it is worth noting that law firms do not expect the finished article, but graduate recruitment managers often tell me that they are looking for "projected ability" and real potential.

It would be naive to assume that every firm is looking for precisely the same attributes, but below are some fundamental qualities which tend to underpin what most firms look for in their trainees. As we have mentioned previously, the legal recruitment market is an extremely competitive market place, which is why you must ensure that by the time you reach your interview for a training contract, you possess an all-round portfolio of skills – a briefcase of outstanding qualities and abilities, and are able to demonstrate that you possess the skills and personal qualities that firms look for in candidates. You can do this by promoting yourself effectively on both your application forms and at the interview stage.

**\*A stellar academic record:** Law firms seek to recruit students who have achieved excellent academic grades consistently throughout their education. The work of a lawyer is intellectually rigorous and demanding, and recruiters will base your ability to cope with such demands, on the marks you have achieved at school and university. This is because law firms view your academic grades as one of the key indicators of intellect and a benchmark of your capability, which is why the reputable commercial law firms request the very best qualifications.

You must be able to show that you have the intelligence to make it in the legal profession. The minimum entrance requirement for securing a training contract at the leading commercial firms are typically a 2:1 degree, often accompanied by a further request of three A grades at A-level to further refine the academic criteria of their recruitment process. That's not to say that it is impossible to get a training contract with a 2:2, just that you either (i) have to be able to show that are capable of better, but due to mitigating factors (eg, illness or bereavement) you were unable to achieve your full potential, or (ii) have to do further research to find those firms for whom the 2:1 isn't a pre-requisite for employment.

However, law firms have become aware that strong academics alone will not make a successful lawyer, and also look for other skills. For example, achievement in sport, commercial experience, interesting hobbies, and language skills can provide you with a strong competitive edge in the legal recruitment market.

**Our Top Tip: Balance your academic studies with activities from other areas of your life, thus creating an exciting array of achievements that illustrate you have lots to offer. This will almost certainly impress recruiters.**

*__Teamwork:__* At law firms you will need to be a good team player  because the way the profession works is more and more about using teamwork and consensus to reach the best possible outcome for all parties, whether it be in transactions, mediations or arbitrations. Negotiations are based around working with teams which often not only includes working with your colleagues in your department, but those from other groups to form multi-disciplinary teams, which also has input by the client, and other professionals. The ability to work collaboratively and effectively with others is of fundamental importance to working at a law firm.

When you become a trainee there will be occasions where you will not know the answer to a problem. You will often save the client and yourself time by sourcing assistance from your colleagues, as they may have worked on similar transactions or previously researched a particular issue that you are working on. This will be much easier if you get on well with colleagues enough to ask for their views on a particular matter. There is no point in trying to reinvent the wheel, and lawyers will generally work closely to pool together their experiences and resources.

One of the most important skills you'll need to be a successful solicitor is the ability to be a useful member of a team. When applying, ensure that you highlight your examples that show you are a good team player and leader whilst you were at university, and during your past work experiences.

*Interpersonal skills* – There is little point in being the brightest person in the class if you can't talk with people. Any lawyer must be able to communicate effectively with their client. Your ability to empathise and interact with others in such a way as to engender confidence, form lasting relationships, and clearly explain complex situations in a clear manner is integral to the role of a solicitor.

In addition, having good "people skills" will help you to interact with a wide variety of characters at your firm, and fit into the culture of the firm. On a daily basis, you will need to tap into the know-how of different people in order to get-on. For example, the librarians and secretaries play such a pivotal role in the daily function of a law firm. If you build up a good rapport with your secretary, your work may get put to the top of the pile, and your quick turnaround of your work will impress your supervisor.

The most successful lawyers tend to be personable, and able to work effectively with people by building, developing and maintaining relationships with clients and colleagues alike. As you progress through your career your firm will expect you to build up a list of contacts and eventually win new business. Marketing opportunities are very important and you need to be able to show clients that as well as being a fantastic lawyer, you are good value in a social context.

*Communication* – Being able to communicate clearly and effectively on paper or face-to-face/over the phone underpins the role of a solicitor. This is because the role of a solicitor largely involves being able to advise, and negotiate effectively with their client and the other side to ensure a deal runs smoothly. The use of clear and succinct language will be valued by both your clients and colleagues. Client care is fundamental and possessing excellent communication skills will help you to communicate ideas and advice to your clients.

Your communication skills are tested throughout the training contract application stage. At the application stage – you will impress potential employers by clearly explaining your skills and experiences in a concise way by using headings and numbered bullet points. At interview, law firms will be impressed with candidates who provide answers that are structured, succinct and tailored to the questions. Too many candidates either talk excessively when they could have explained concisely the point they are trying to get across, or do not go into sufficient depth when describing their skills and experiences.

One of the things that many interviewers will assess is whether they would feel comfortable putting you in front of a client. It is one thing to have first class academic grades but applicants may still fail to land a training contract if they cannot demonstrate the ability to communicate well at the interview.

*__Commercial acumen__ - Based on talking to recruiters up and down the country this is the single most desirable attribute in a future trainee, and is becoming more and more important. So that trainees emerge not only as a good lawyer but a sound business advisor to clients too.

This phrase drives fear into the hearts of many students as it is the least understood. But, simply put__, it is developing an understanding of the business environment in which law firms operate. You appreciate the role of a commercial lawyer, and the commercial context in which they provide the legal advice.__

The best way to demonstrate that you have what it takes to cut it as a commercial lawyer is to start thinking commercially, and from a client's perspective as early as possible. As a commercial lawyer you need to understand your clients' businesses in order to give them the best legal advice. Recruiters will look for candidates who have a keen interest in, and understanding of, the business world.

A commercial client will not care about the technical meaning of legal terminology, but she will care about the impact that it may have on the transaction at hand. For City firms especially, legal advice always takes on a business element and every student needs to be commercially aware, so that they will be able to contextualise their advice to the client.

The hit UK BBC series *The Apprentice* is a good example of what is meant by commercial acumen. **Sir Alan Sugar** informed us that he was *"looking for someone with an eye for profit, a mind for new ideas, a flexibility of approach and a buzz of energy that means they will be hungry to help me build my successful business."* When law firms are recruiting prospective trainees, a candidate will only get ticks in these boxes if they are able to sell all of these qualities to the firm and more.

**Our Top Tip: It is not enough to show firms you have commercial awareness by knowing who their clients and direct competitors are. Law firms want more! You must not only keep abreast of recent deals but also show an appreciation of how lawyers can be proactive and anticipate the legal and commercial points that arise in transactions. This is the only way to show firms that you have the potential to think commercially.**

* **Dedication to the profession** – With intense competition for places, it is vital students demonstrate a long-term commitment to a career in law, which can be shown through work experience. It is important that you acquire some work experience which shows you are interested in pursuing a legal career. Law firms see little difference between law graduates and non-law students. The key to showing your commitment is by expressing your long-term goals at the interview.

*ial**Attention to detail** – When lawyers draft contracts, a single word in the wrong place can change the emphasis of a clause and possibly the outcome for your client. As a lawyer you are expected to have a thorough, accurate and meticulous approach. Committing any glaring grammatical or punctuation mistakes on your application form is the easiest way of showing sloppiness - mistakes like this will send your application straight to the rejection pile.

\***Honesty and integrity** – Clients expect lawyers to work to a high moral standard and ethical code. They will only instruct solicitors they can trust. Solicitors' professional conduct rules are strict guidelines ensuring lawyers always act in their clients' best interests. Furthermore, client confidentiality and professionalism are paramount to safeguarding the reputation of the legal profession.

\* **Pro-activity -** Firms like applicants who display initiative and a get up and go. They are also impressed by candidates who value their skills and strengths. This can be demonstrated by the way in which you apply to the firm – for example, asking the graduate recruitment manager at a careers event for a weeks unpaid work experience, on the condition that once you impress the firm – they will offer you a job. Further, you may be able to point to examples of your proactive nature in past experiences, and extra-curricular activities.

\* **Ambition -** Many aspiring solicitors are extremely ambitious and driven. In such a competitive business, you should have a clear and realistic plan of where you imagine your career heading in the next 5-10 years, and whether it is your ambition to be a partner at a law firm, or to move in-house.

\***Image is vital** – Show yourself in the best possible light by projecting a professional and businesslike appearance. Your attitude is equally important, and being motivated and enthusiastic is important. Before a firm commits to employing you, they will want to be sure that their clients will see you in a positive way. First impressions always count for so much. Even when filling out application forms, think about the image you are conveying.

\* **Enthusiasm and Energy** – Demonstrate a real interest for the firm you are applying to and the type of work they do. This passion will enable you to talk about the firm and the reasons for your application in a vibrant and memorable way. You will naturally come across as highly-motivated and this type of enthusiasm can be infectious.

\* **Individuality -** Always be yourself and do not try to be someone that you think firms are looking for. Firms don't want order-following clones on the career treadmill! They want to see a variety of individual personalities with a sense of humour, sparky characters with have an ability to think outside and around the box. At interviews, always give answers that are personal to you, rather than the answer you think they want to hear.

* **Sense of humour** - Allow your personality to shine through at interview. Firms want individuals who are not afraid to be themselves and who are not overly self-conscious. Throughout your legal career you will have to socialise constantly. During the course of your training contract, you may end up working into the night on large transactions. At 3am any associate will appreciate working with someone whose personality helps to boost the morale of the team.

***Extra-curricular activities** – Your interests and hobbies can be an incredible selling point. This is your opportunity to showcase your personality. How else will you show that you have developed into a well-rounded individual? Law firms aim to recruit a variety of individuals, and the way you spend your free-time adds flavour to your credentials.

There is an art to talking about your extra-curricular activities *(see Chapter 11 on application forms).* As well as engaging the person reading your application form with your answers, show how you manage your time, your leadership qualities and that you are an interesting and fun person to work with. Use whatever you say to reinforce to the recruiter that you have all the qualities they are looking for.

***Legal/commercial work experience** can be the decisive factor at interviews. Lots of savvy candidates will use this kind of experience to highlight the transferable skills they have learnt. This experience will provide you with an opportunity to illustrate your commercial awareness, and recruiters will always find this a point of interest. If you have good experience a large portion of your interview may be taken up discussing what work you have previously undertaken.

Eye-catching experience can make a significant difference to being selected for interview. If you do not yet have any work experience it is necessary that you do your best to find some. If you are interested in a particular area, there is no better way of expressing your interest than having gained solid experience in this area of the law. Gaining an insight into the realities of working life also shows you appreciate how academia translates into the day-to-day practicalities of working as a lawyer. Believe us when we say that the two require completely different sets of skills.

Any vacation placements will be an advantage, and if marketed effectively could give you an edge that differentiates you from other applicants with similar academic grades.

- ✓ Remember that excellent work experience is nearly as valuable as every legal qualification.
- ✓ For those of you, who have not yet managed to get work experience, sign up with a placement agency. These agencies specialise in obtaining work experience for students.
- ✓ Employers prefer to recruit graduates with some commercial experience whether voluntary or paid.
- ✓ Contact local advice centres to gain some pro bono work experience.
- ✓ Contact charities and local papers for volunteering opportunities.

**Our Top Tip: Devising a skills table is a particularly useful technique to highlight your skills against the firm's criteria in preparing your application forms and interviews.**

**List a number of skills (such as legal experience, problem solving, commercial awareness etc) and then think of examples of how you have used/developed these skills. Try to find two examples from each of your education, work experience and extra-curricular activities. Aim to use as many different examples as you can in order to reflect your varied experience and well-rounded personality. The aim is to show that you have a wide range of experiences. By doing this you will be able to answer most of the skills-based questions on an application form, as well as those that interviewers throw at you. Below is an example of a skills table with examples of different experiences:**

| CRITERIA (SKILLS) | Experiences / Background demonstrating skills in action |
|---|---|
| Commercial Awareness | ✓ Young Enterprise Scheme<br>✓ Legal and commercial work experience at City firms. |
| Teamwork | ✓ University Law<br>✓ Committee organisation of annual Ball.<br>✓ Gap year reconstruction project in Cambodia. |
| Interpersonal skills | ✓ Holiday job |
| Communication skills | ✓ Teaching English in Japan<br>✓ Volunteer work and pro bono experience. |
| Attention to detail | ✓ Editor of university newsletter<br>✓ |

## Do you know what the law firms want from you? Points to ponder:

- To perform well at interviews and assessment centres you must really know what qualities firms look for in candidates.

- What are the main qualities that law firms are looking for in prospective trainees?

- Devise a skills table: Consider your own experience, how can you demonstrate to firms' that you possess the key qualities which could well ensure your success during your training contract?

- Can you demonstrate to firms' you have the ability to think commercially?

Chapter Seven

## Marketing yourself effectively

### How can I make myself stand out?

The way you come across is just as important as what you say. In a competitive marketplace, the need to market your skills effectively and stand out from other talented students has never been more important.

Your career success will depend on more than impressive legal knowledge, you must aim to demonstrate that you have an interesting personality and the interpersonal skills needed to grab the attention of the recruiter in such a way that they will find it difficult to forget you. As we have previously mentioned, law firms look for potential, and they will want people who not only have the requisite skills and attributes to succeed at their firm but people who also possess something unique. You will need to highlight that you have the total package of skills the firm is looking for.

**Languages** are a clear advantage when applying to international law firms. Languages are viewed as very useful, especially if a student has gained experience abroad. Studying a language that is uncommon will attract the attention of firms especially if they happen to have an office in that language area, or if a firm has plans to expand and open other offices abroad, people with the relevant language skills could be crucial in this process. In addition, clients or colleagues often require documents to be translated. Sell your linguistic ability; make sure the firm knows exactly how proficient you are in the language.

**Personality** – The interview is partly a personality test. At your interview the firm will be trying to assess whether you will fit in. As a lawyer you will need to make the client confident in your ability. The firm will want to see you at your most charming, witty and thoughtful. Demonstrate this by showing that you are someone who is also good with people, friendly and confident. You can even get your personality across on the application form by showing your range of interests and achievements.

**Travel** – This can be a hot interview topic if you undertake exciting "off-the-wall" activities on your travels, or especially if combined with work experience. As the saying goes, there is nothing like travel to broaden the mind. There are a whole host of things you can get involved in when you travel abroad, carry out voluntary work, teach English, do charity work, learn a language; activities such as these look impressive on the application form and are great talking points at interview. International vacation placements in Europe or around the world are also highly regarded as they combine travel and work experience.

**Extra-curricular activities, hobbies and interests** – Never underestimate the importance of these types of activities. As you will see later in the book, there is an art to talking about extra-curricular activities. There are lots of things that you can get involved with at university and elsewhere. For example, charity and community involvement, human rights campaigning, other volunteer work, school and university positions of responsibility, music and sports, debating, public speaking, leadership and team-working abilities are valued highly, as are writing articles for a journal or legal publication.

Having unusual hobbies or extra-curricular interests will make you stand out from the crowd and demonstrate you are a balanced and well rounded person. Tell the firm all about your deep sea diving expertise. How many other people will have this on their CV? Interviewers will be interested in talking about your work experience at the International Criminal Court or what it was like to play for the youth academy elite of the England Rugby team. Being a trained magician in a circus or spending weekends tank driving will naturally make the reader spark an interest in your application as you are likely to stand out from the crowd!

**Awards and achievements** – The importance of highlighting these skills is obvious but you have to sell your awards and achievements in a way that sounds impressive. Tell the recruiter if you were 1 out of 300 students awarded the Contract Law prize or if you were placed 2nd out of 2000 international competitors at the Chemistry World Cup and be prepared to answer in depth any questions about those achievements.

## CASE STUDY

*I decided to take a gap year and set up and manage my own bar on the island of Madeira. I saved money and borrowed money from friends and family in order to fund this venture. I gained excellent experience running the business for two years and dealing with a variety of people. I met some lawyers and managed to network effectively which led to me spending a further six months in Lisbon working for a law firm, while my assistant ran the bar. My goal is to work in corporate law. My entrepreneurial spirit and track-record provided a unique selling point, which has attracted the attention of many firms I have applied to.*

**James Diaz, law student**

## Self-Assessment: What is your Unique Selling Point? (USP)

When companies make products or deliver services they focus on their major strengths that make them different from any other products in the market. To achieve a Unique Selling Points (USPs) is to stand out in the minds of the consumer. Law firms are looking for people who shine in the ever popular legal recruitment field.

The aim of your USP is to differentiate yourself. You have to assume that most graduates entering law firms have attained sound academic qualifications. The way you stand out from the crowd is by how you describe and discuss your personal experiences.

Highlighting your USP's can sound like blowing your own trumpet but modesty will leave you waiting a very long time for a training contract offer. In today's legal recruitment market, applicants cannot afford to rely solely on their academic track record. Law firms want more, an all rounder - **the total package,** but don't forget that even the most fantastic products need to be marketed correctly.

Analyse your qualities and ask questions such as: How would people describe me? What am I really like? Consider your main skills and abilities. What do you really want from your career? What makes you suitable for the job? Identify your best skills and promote these in a positive way.

One of the best ways of analysing yourself and evaluating your personal traits is through a SWOT analysis. Look at your positive and negative points and collate information, as if you are selling yourself as a product.

**SWOT your way to success**

SWOT stands for 'Strengths, Weaknesses, Opportunities and Threats'. This procedure is commonly used by companies to analyse and assess their current position and future prospects. You may also use it to gauge your skills and abilities. In interviews you can avoid giving stock answers by preparing an analysis of your skills and qualities in the form of a SWOT analysis:

**SWOT ANALYSIS**

**1. Identify Strengths and Weaknesses (internal)**
**2. Identify Opportunities and Threats (external)**
**3. Prepare a Working Document.**

List the positive and negative aspects of your personality under the SWOT headings. This is a valuable piece of self-analysis. Many people know what they are good at but what about the opposite? Consider your weaknesses, you may be asked to detail these at interview. Honesty is the key to painting an accurate picture of yourself and assessing where your future lies. Get a close colleague to check it to see if they agree.

**Example:**

- ✓ **Strengths -** Highly motivated/ enthusiastic/high energy levels/ tremendous work ethic. List specific achievements.
- ✓ **Weaknesses** – Inconsistent grades? Are you working hard enough? Solutions – What are the reasons for this? Are you prioritising your work/social life balance correctly? Organising and prioritising is the key to time management and preventing the accumulation of stress when impending deadlines are drawing closer. Are you shy? Embark on a public speaking course, practice giving presentations.
- ✓ **Opportunities** – Are you able to build contacts in the legal field during work experience. Use your contacts for advice and guidance and opportunities such as further

work experience. Further study – will doing an LLM, non-legal masters or the New York Bar to enhance your CV?
- ✓ **Threats** – Consider the competition from non-law students, international students and mature candidates. Think about what you can do to put yourself at a competitive advantage.

By identifying these key features of your personal strengths and weaknesses and by beginning to work on them, the process will give you the focus to steer your career in a positive direction and enable you to work on your weak points. Also remember that even your strengths can be improved upon. This process may also help you decide which firm is best for you.

## Self-belief and Confidence

*Many people succeed when others do not believe in them, but rarely do people succeed when they do not believe in themselves.* **Craig Robinson**

Self-belief is a prerequisite for training contract success. It is as simple as that! How can you expect prospective employers to show faith and invest money in training you, if you do not exude the right level of self-assurance? Self-belief comes from within. Your inner voice is often your harshest critic but for the vast majority of law students your academic and extra-curricular achievements are proof that you can become successful in achieving your career goals. Do not listen to anyone who tells you that you can't make it, this will only work against you - create your own destiny. Be structured and logical and plan your approach, it is infinitely better to have some kind of strategy.

Learning how to think positively and successfully is the first step, positive visualisation equates to positive realisation. Self-belief is the first stepping stone to building your confidence. This is critical for any type of success in law and business. You need to be certain that you have what it takes to succeed: there is no room for self-doubt. It is common knowledge that the majority of people who are taken on as trainees at law firms are confident in themselves and their ability to deliver to the highest standard. There is no way you can compete if you think of yourself as any less.

**Our Top Tip: You have to believe it to achieve it! With the right strategy in place, success is achievable.**

*Look at your greatest achievement and be confident that it was YOU that made it happen! A can-do attitude is vitally important as you can do anything you put your mind to. There are thousands of people from all backgrounds practising law and working around the country in top firms and global companies, there is no reason why this can't be you!*

**Graham Cutts, Lovells**

We know of capable students who had excellent CVs and should have walked into training contracts but were rejected after interview due to a lack of self-belief. This lack of self-assurance is easily detected. One way of building up your confidence is by making friends with positive people who have the characteristics you admire. These are the people who can make a genuine difference to your approach. Observe the source of their confidence, observe the way they interact with others and implement what you see. Speak to your friends and ask them how you come across. Find yourself a mentor, someone who is in a position you aspire to, listen to the advice they give and mirror their positive qualities. Join social clubs where you can build up your confidence by interacting with others. Get away from negative people who constantly remind you how difficult it is to make it in the legal profession, for whatever reason.

We cannot re-iterate enough that nobody can give you confidence in yourself except you! Before interview start visualising yourself as a lawyer and you won't feel overwhelmed in the presence of your interviewers. Believe in the skills that you are bringing to a prospective employer. You need to have enough belief to market yourself impressively.

*I was a very capable law student with top marks but suffered from being very nervous. I paid a huge price for this lack of self-belief, since my more confident colleagues landed the top jobs from firms that had rejected me. My feedback was always the same: I needed to be less shy, self-conscious and come out of my shell.*

**Michelle Turner**, law graduate

Self-belief does not replace the practical skills necessary to do the job of a lawyer. However, there is little point in trying to achieve goals if you do not believe you can make it. Do not let fear stop you from getting that job in law that you desire! **Fear is simply False Evidence Appearing Real!** Don't let this kind of anxiety keep you from becoming what you aim to be – a successful lawyer.

Successful people tend to have a starry vision of the future - which they maintain in order to achieve their goals - qualify, and become top lawyers. They have the self-discipline, confidence, persistence, self-belief and are rejection-proof! If you truly aspire to work in a certain field, you have to go that extra mile and be inventive, disciplined, diligent and highly self-motivated.

Self-belief will maintain your motivation; it will keep you going when you are feeling overwhelmed by the process. This is not just motivational rhetoric; lots of students have felt dejected at some point. Do not be that student who is ready to give up because of the pressure involved in the recruitment process. You must be committed and dedicated enough to work consistently until the opportunity for success arrives.

*What we think determines what we believe; what we believe influences what we choose; what we choose determines what we are, and what we are attracts what we have.*
**Charles Khiran**, life coach on personal effectiveness

So far in this chapter you have learnt that achieving a training contract really does involve believing in yourself, focused planning and devising career goals. To achieve your goals in life you must be committed to dedicating much of your time towards reaching your goals. Students must evaluate themselves. Try creating a step-by-step career strategy. We carefully implemented a plan of what we wanted to achieve by the end of the year. It is important to write your goals down to measure your progress and evaluate the effectiveness of your actions as you make progress.

## What are the primary benefits of goal-setting?

*My chosen goals enable me to remain persistently motivated, dedicated, determined and focused about what I am working towards. Securing a training contract for me was a really hard slog – but the reward was worth it. I kept my goal of becoming a qualified lawyer at the forefront of my mind at all times and never lost sight of what I was trying to achieve. Goal-setting is useful but do not be overburdened by your goals! Once you achieve your goals, don't stop! A successful person continues reinventing their goals.*
**Craig Robinson**

Do not try to force your goals. If you do not reach your ambition of securing a training contract by a target date, do not give up. With the right attitude and application – it can happen. Perseverance is the key. Remain committed, question whether your strategies have been appropriate and evaluate whether you need a new strategy.

**Our Top Tip: Goals must be specific, relevant, measurable, attainable, realistic, motivating, challenging, time-scaled, positive, clear and written down. Share your goals with supportive people who can encourage you and offer you constructive criticism.**

## SPINNING IT TO WIN IT

We have asked you to picture yourselves as lawyers and you may be reading this wondering why you need to pretend that you've achieved something before you actually have. Unlike the television show "Faking it", we are not asking you to pretend you have made it already without achieving the necessary qualifications and experience. All we are saying is that you should visualise how you can be successful. Let us explain how this might work in practice.

Government officials have their very own PR machines also known as "Spin Doctors" who have the mandate of ensuring their client is presented in the right way and projects a positive image. Why can't would-be solicitors use a similar technique? This simply involves putting a little gloss on your achievements, experiences and attributes in order to make them shine and resonate, thereby marketing ones-self in the best possible way.

You may have only sold two cars at a profit in your holiday job as a car salesman, <u>but do not sell yourself short</u>. Promote what you did to make it sound impressive on your application form or in your interview, as long as what you say is underpinned by honesty and supported by concrete examples. Remember, what you are doing is trying to make your experiences as attractive as possible. You will see exactly how to sell yourself in this way in our section on application forms (*see chapter 11*).

*My position as a data input administrative for an investment bank increased my commercial acumen and understanding of the City, and the business of investment banking. Once I developed more skill and experience, I began performing the role of a business and research analyst. I noted this on my application form for a training contract, and was invited to an interview. At the interview, I conveyed the image of having started out as quite low in the company and working my way up through the ranks of the organisation. The law firm were so impressed by my initiative, ambition and work-ethic I received my training contract offer the following day.*

**Jenny Jackson, a trainee solicitor**

At the interview put a similar positive slant on the things you say, to help ensure you leave a lasting good impression. Make sure every point is telling. Do not be afraid to highlight your achievements in the best possible light!

**Top Tip: Picture yourself as a successful commercial lawyer working on multi-million and multi-jurisdictional transaction with a high-profile client. You must believe, see and think like an excellent solicitor on the day of your interview. By picturing yourself in this way, you will be developing the mentality of a successful solicitor and increase your confidence levels. However, be careful and bear in mind that you must maintain the correct balance so as not to display misplaced confidence.**

## Marketing yourself effectively: Points to Ponder

The mentality of a training contract winner: The way you come across is just as important as what you say. In such a competitive marketplace, the need to market your-self effectively in order to stand out from the crowd of other talented aspiring solicitors has never been so important.

This chapter demonstrates the strategies in which you can differentiate yourself from other applicants by finding your Unique Selling Point.

We also show you how to evaluate yourself with a SWOT Analysis and self-assessment techniques, including:

- How to think like a lawyer.

- How to boost your confidence levels and self-belief in order to perform well at interview and continue to apply for training contracts if you begin to doubt yourself, because you must believe it to achieve it!

- Set yourself achievable goals because success is an achievable target.

- How to market yourself effectively and spin yourself into a firm.

Chapter Eight

## Networking for success and self-promotion

The famous adage: *"It's not what you know, it's who you know"*, has never lost its relevance in the world of business. It was true in the past and it remains true today.

**Robert S. Gardella,** the author of The Harvard Business School guide to finding your next job places a great deal of importance on networking to hone your skills and improve your chances of achieving a great job and successful career

Networking can be an important step to a career in law and certainly a stepping-stone to progression during your career. The hard truth is that many people are presented with opportunities through people they already know, whether friends, relatives, colleagues, classmates, or acquaintances, which is vital given some jobs are never even advertised. You may be able to network successfully to uncover hidden job opportunities. Often, finding opportunities in this way can give you an advantage over other candidates because you will have been referred by somebody, and in business, people often place some emphasis on these types of referral. However, one thing is for certain, even if you make useful contacts you will still need to show that you possess the relevant skills in order to secure the job you are applying for.

*Gardella* asserts that the best way of undertaking a job search is by tapping into personal networks, by *"Planning your work and then working your plan."* The author's optimum piece of advice is to build a database of contacts, which includes their names, referrals, e-mail correspondence, how and when you made contact. Furthermore, you might devise a network tree diagram and go beyond existing contacts and share the details of contacts with colleagues, expanding your database both vertically and horizontally. To summarise these concepts:

**Vertical Networking** means developing contacts with people in positions of authority. These could be graduate recruitment managers, assistant solicitors and partners.

**Horizontal networking** involves networking at your level. This may include your colleagues who have already secured training contracts or any trainees you know. It is very important to keep in touch with former colleagues, as they may let you know if plum opportunities come up to help you in your career progression.

## What is effective networking?

The secret of networking is really just about getting on well with people. One of the best resources available to a job seeker is people whom they know. Networking is about the building of relationships, asking for information or help and looking at ways in which you can help others. Tapping into your existing network can start with focusing on your own family, friends and acquaintances for immediate contacts then casting your net further afield. This is a vital first step to effective networking, as you should remember that you are a part of other people's networks.

You will be at a huge advantage if you can find people who can tell you all about their experiences as practising solicitors and their experiences of the training contract recruitment process. When you are looking for a training contract, you should inform people around you about your search. You never know whom they might put you in touch with. Always keep a record of your contacts.

> *I knew people in the City and asked them directly for career advice. I met up with these individuals and showed a keen interest in the work they undertook. My contacts helped me a great deal, by providing mentoring support, reviewing my CV and application forms and pointing out how I could improve, which made all the difference as I became more informed about the opportunities that were available.* **Alex Ansah, US law firm**

## First steps to successful networking

Basic networking can lead you to many useful contacts. When you start networking, you'll be surprised by the way that the people you meet are connected. Despite how unconnected you think your family and friends are; there is a theory that a chain of people connects us with some influential people who might be able to assist us in one way or another. Look at the social networking sites *Facebook*, *LinkedIn*, or *Bebo*, and you'll be surprised at how many times somebody you know pops up on another person's page.

Networking is about getting to know people who can open your world up to new opportunities, and if you make a good impression among the contacts you meet, don't be surprised to find yourself talked about in very positive terms. When liaising with potential contacts, be polite, respectful and clear about the help you are seeking. You should find that most people will be flattered that you thought of asking them for guidance to steer you in the right direction.

To network successfully, you should keep a comprehensive, up-to-date database of people whom you have met, and remember which contacts can assist you and who you can help in return. The more people you know, and the wider you make your networking pool, the greater your chances of being recommended for a new opportunity.

## One-to-One networking: How do I make contact with people?

You have a much better chance of effective communication and negotiation when meeting people face-to-face or, by writing to thank them for taking the time out of their busy schedule to give you advice. For example, if you spoke to a contact at a careers fair, you might e-mail or write to thank them for advice they had given you. In networking, polite and sincere gestures can go a long way and help you to build your network of useful contacts.

## Developing effective networking strategies

**Following up -** Developing follow-up strategies is one of the key elements to successful networking. Always tell your new contact that you will get in touch with them at a future date. When an aspiring lawyer makes a follow-up call, this is known as a "warm call" because you have already met your contact, and a rapport may have already been established at the initial meeting. Providing that meeting went well, your contact will be more likely to go out of their way to help you in the future, where they might not, if you were simply "cold calling" them out of the blue.

**Elevator pitch** is a concept borrowed from our U.S. neighbours. Many recruitment specialists suggest having a 90-second *elevator pitch*, practised for situations when you might meet people. Having something to discuss and gauging the interest of contacts underpins networking, because networking only proves effective when there is give and take. Put yourself in your prospective contact's shoes: if someone makes a good impression on you and has an interesting conversation, then you are much more likely to remember them.

**Effective self-marketing:** Self-promotion is an integral part of successful networking. You will need to talk yourself up in a measured way, so that your contact is aware of your credentials. It's a means of getting ahead and standing out. This will be invaluable in the recruitment process if your contact mentions that you are an interesting, witty and accomplished individual.

**Our Top Tip: The key to productive and successful networking involves seeking out the opportunities you are searching for, coupled with looking at ways you can add value to somebody else's quest for opportunities. Remain in touch with existing contacts, keep on the look-out for new additions to your contacts list and introduce them to your other contacts to strengthen ties.**

**Developing your contacts: What do you stand to gain from networking over the long-term?**

Networking can be a long and time-consuming process and you may need to invest a large amount of your time and energy getting to know people and building up a rapport with them. Your success in the legal profession can be influenced by the quality of the relationships you build and develop during your career. However, networking is not an overnight key to success, in many cases it is a long-term strategy. The best connections are built up by expanding your network of contacts over a whole career.

You will find networking easy if you learn to show a genuine interest in people. Effective networking is not about using people, but genuinely asking for help and providing help in return when appropriate. When you get to the interview stage you might mention a relevant person you have met on your career journey. This might be someone who works for the organisation whom you found impressive and approachable. This type of mention if done tactfully does two things: it shows the firm that you have gone the extra mile in your research, and it shows on a balance of probabilities that having established a good rapport with your contact, you would be the kind of person who would fit in well at the firm.

## Developing your networking strategy: Casting your net

As we have mentioned before, the wider your network of contacts, the more opportunities are likely to come your way and potentially assist your career. In order to network successfully in the legal profession, you will need to have a clearer focus. Without a clear focused aim, networking is just ineffective socialising. If you know what you need, you are better equipped to direct your focus on the right kind of research.

For example, you know that a leading lawyer at the law firm you want to work for is going to be at a particular event. Undertake a little research on that person beforehand, consult their career biography details on their firm website, check chambers and partners, they may be recommended as a leading lawyer in the Legal 500. At the event, if you have the chance to speak with your potential contact, remember, you are likely to impress them with your knowledge about their career and the particular transactions and cases they have worked on. In this way, you are much more likely to make the kind of impression that will ensure they remember who you are.

## What is the importance of networking for lawyers?

Law firms operate as businesses, and people do business with people that they like. You may have heard somewhere that business is about people and not paper. The ability to detect opportunities in the business environment and attract clients is critical to sustaining any business. As your career progresses, you will see how lawyers rely on their network of contacts to bring in business from clients who are likely to be long-term contacts. The message is to keep in contact with and maintain professional relationships in order to be at the forefront of your contact's mind when the right opportunity arises. Building strong businesses in the legal profession relies on lawyers developing excellent networking skills.

**Our Top Tip: To become a top lawyer you need to know how a top lawyer acts and thinks, so get in touch with a lawyer who works in your chosen field and gain some useful advice to guide you in the right direction. People are usually flattered when you ask them to be a mentor. Mentoring is all about building up a relationship and learning from someone. This can be achieved by making contact with a person and setting up a meeting to ask specific questions about the firm they work at. Ask them questions and learn from their approach to how they have become successful in their legal career. Have your CV ready in case they ask to see it. Show a genuine interest in their career background and remember to ask for their contact details and business cards. People are often impressed by this kind of initiative and enthusiasm.**

## Where can prospective trainee solicitors network?

You can network anywhere - at Christmas parties, law talks, seminars, careers fairs/events, university alumni meetings, and during work experience placements and vacation schemes. You can meet contacts absolutely anywhere, so never miss an opportunity to strike up a conversation with people.

To get the best value out of networking you need to undertake research before the event, otherwise you will be walking into a room of 100 people with no idea of who anybody is. You will either spend hours indiscriminately working the room, or use your time speaking to someone unable to help you. As a future lawyer your time is your most valuable commodity, so don't waste it. Aim to identify who you want to speak to beforehand, then Google the names of these individuals, so you know what is going on in their practices, and you will increase the likelihood of making a favourable impression with these potential contacts.

## Alumni

Some universities offer access to alumni networks. Most universities now have online alumni in some form. Contact your university for further details of alumni networks and events to attend.

## Social and business events

Many students are filled with dread when faced with the idea of networking, traipsing around a room filled with complete strangers. Networking is not something that should be feared, or looked down upon as overly sales-like. You should embrace it as a challenge and see that it can be the perfect way to market your skills.

## Career fairs

Careers fairs are an opportunity to meet recruiters and get ahead. Law fairs are a valuable source of information about opportunities in the legal profession, both for those who are studying law and for non-law students who are considering a career in law. The fairs will give you an opportunity to talk informally to a range of legal professionals, from graduate recruitment to trainees and qualified solicitors.

*"You really can't get too much information when it comes to making such an important decision as where to train as a solicitor. Career fairs can help you to meet trainees and graduate recruitment from the firm to develop a more informed view and sense of where you might see yourself spending your legal career".*                                        ***Justin Deveraux***

Students should not just go around the stalls collecting free sweets and pencils. Career Fairs represent the start of the recruitment process and are an opportunity to make a positive impression on a graduate recruitment team who may one day be interviewing you for a training contract.

Is your university holding a career fair? It is important you attend, try to extract as much information as possible and aim to make a good impression on the firms. The law fair calendar starts in October and continues until February. Held at universities nationwide, many of the fairs are open to all students. However, others restrict entrance to students of the host university, so check before you go. With over 30 law fairs held at institutions around the country, you can be selective about which law fairs you attend. Find out from the relevant careers service which firms/organisations will be taking part. By doing this sort of preparation, you'll choose the fairs that match your criteria and will be beneficial to you.

## How to get yourself into a conversation

At networking events, it is difficult to interrupt a group's discussion; but by introducing yourself (using professional etiquette), and then simply listening and asking questions at the right time, you can ease your way into a conversation. Some students will stick to key contacts like glue – avoid this approach! Mingle as much as possible and bear in mind that throwing your CV or your contact details at these people should also be avoided. When you do meet people, refrain from asking for a job straight away! Keep your ears peeled, listen actively and attentively, and express a keen interest in their firm and the work they do. When you make contact, thank them for taking the time to talk to you.

Do not be distracted by the champagne and smiling faces at these events: always be on the look-out for networking opportunities. In the world of business, it is the people who make an institution successful, and your ability to fit in is crucial to your success. When meeting existing and prospective contacts, always aim to remember names and faces and make a concerted effort to get to know people. Set yourself a goal before you get to the event. For example, you could aim to meet approximately five contacts. Only offer to exchange your details at the end of a conversation, once you have had time to make a positive impression.

*Careers fairs are a crucial chance to speak to graduate recruitment or trainees who are acutely aware of the process you face and know about the type of experience you are likely to have at the firm, therefore talk to them directly and ask probing questions and gain a real feel for what they perceive the culture at the firm to be.*

**K.O.B, trained at a magic circle firm**

## Maximising your time at events to further your career

Here are a few tips to help you:

1. Get a copy of a map of the careers fair, so you can plan your route to finding the law firms that you are interested in.
2. Dress smartly and comfortably and make an effort to impress graduate recruiters.
3. Career fairs are marketing and networking opportunities! Do not think firms will hire you there and then but approach each stall as though you are striving to make a favourable first impression. These fairs are, first and foremost PR for law firms. If you make a positive impact on the representatives of these firms, they are more likely to make a note of your name.
4. Every careers fair is different. Do your research and ensure you attend events that are conducive to your career goals. Fairs will either be information-giving events or recruitment events where exhibitors are looking to fill vacancies. Check your careers service first.
5. Many law firms are asked the same bog standard questions: set yourself apart; avoid asking the same old thing. Prepare a few pertinent questions beforehand, with the aim of actually wanting to learn something.
6. Consider the size and practice areas of firms attending the careers fair and analyse which firms appeal to you.
7. Do not approach potential employers with a casual attitude, as if you are not really sure why you are attending or the idea of a career in law is just a passing whim. Questions like: "Why should I consider working for you?" don't go down well with professionals who have given up valuable time for your benefit. Approach the law fairs with a professional attitude.
8. Students should try to attend careers fairs at quieter times and thus be able to get more out of these events. If you go along at a quiet time (i.e. at the beginning or the end) you will not have as many students competing for the attention of representatives but will have a better chance of ensuring your name sticks out in the mind of recruiters.
9. Ask for the business cards of the representatives of law firms that interest you. This will assist you in your applications and interviews.

10. Arrive prepared so that you know which firms you want to speak to and you utilise your time effectively. Make sure you know what each firm does.

11. Fairs are informational settings that create a platform to network. We do not advise giving out your CV. It may not go down well. Instead make initial contact and get the low-down on tailoring your application to get into that firm.

**Our Top Tip: Make the most of law fairs to help you decide if a legal career is the right career choice for you, or alternatively to identify which area of law will suit you best. Fairs really are great opportunities to meet professionals and address the issues that concern you. The experience can only inform your choice of firms later on and will make you feel more confident at the interview stage.**

**Another Top tip: Do not pester your contacts; appreciate and understand that professional people have extensive workloads and busy schedules. Be careful not to forget people when contacts have ceased to be useful; they may be of help to others. If you ask for advice and people refuse you, do not take it personally. Remember that not everyone you meet will be in a position to help you. Don't be afraid of rejections, being proactive in your networking gets you closer to your goal of landing that dream job. Always remember to thank any contacts who have helped you along the way and keep them updated regarding your career decisions and developments.**

## Networking for success and self-promotion:

Networking effectively can put you in a better position when it comes to making applications and attending interviews. The principle behind networking is taking the initiative to meet people who can assist you in your career planning. In this chapter we explain the most successful ways you can use networking as a way to make contacts in the profession.

- Understand how successful networking works in practice.

- Discover how to network in a room full of strangers.

- Learn how to build a rapport and follow-up with your new contacts.

- Understand the importance of getting out there and attending law firm recruitment and marketing events, to meet the people at these law firms, so you can begin to find out whether you can see yourself working for a particular law firm.

Chapter Nine

## Get to Grips with commercial awareness

Law firms want people who have an all-round portfolio of skills and – above all – who are commercially aware. Commercial awareness is frequently highlighted as the key characteristic sought by law firms when they are recruiting trainee solicitors. Law firms often inform us that a lack of commercial awareness is the reason for rejecting bright students.

The concept of commercial awareness often strikes fear into the hearts of students, because many students are unsure about what commercial awareness is, and whether they have any, which is clearly hindering the chances of otherwise good prospective trainee solicitors securing a training contract. So, what on earth does it mean? And how does someone display their commercial awareness?

### What is Commercial Awareness?

Broadly speaking, the essence of commercial awareness consists of: An understanding, and interest in the business of a law firm, the clients, the environment in which they operate in, and understanding the role of a commercial lawyer.

1. **Your client**
   - Being able to communicate effectively with clients.
   - Developing an understanding of your client, their business as a whole, and the wider environment in which it operates, so that you can contextualise your legal advice.
   - Having n awareness of the key issues (current and future) facing a client's industry and knowledge of their competitors, so that you develop the ability to see the complete picture.
   - An ability to see things from the client's perspective when providing legal advice. So, you understand their priorities, and appreciate the legal needs of a law firm's clients, the business needs and industry in which those clients are operating in.

## 2. **Law is a business**

- Understanding that law firms are themselves commercial entities in business. The key driving force behind the practice and business of law is profitability, and making money is achieved by meeting the needs of its clients, and building the reputation of the firm in order to develop the business through retaining existing clients and attracting new clients.

- *"Do you have an interest in, and understanding of how law firms become successful?"*

- The law is a business, lawyers charge for their time (a lawyer's most valuable commodity), and aim to provide a service which encourages the client to retain the services of the firm in the future. As a trainee solicitor you will also charge for your time and as a result become involved in billing the client for the work you undertake, and you may become involved in networking, and assisting in the preparation of pitches/marketing your law firm's legal services to prospective clients.

- The largest law firms specialise in corporate and commercial work, and they aim to recruit lawyers who possess the skills and character that will be suited to working in a corporate environment.

- You must understand how a law firm's business is run (internal), the importance of providing an efficient and cost-effective legal service,

- the market conditions and wider environment in which law firms operate (external),

- understanding the legislative, political, economic and social framework in which law operates,

- keeping abreast and up to date on current business issues and recent commercial transactions.

### 3. **Understanding the role of a commercial lawyer**

Law firms want their lawyers to understand what their clients do, how they do it, why they do it, so that you are fully informed when advising them on the best course of action of a particular transaction.

## Why is Commercial Awareness so important?

Law firms consider commercial awareness to be an essential competency in their future trainees. Graduate recruitment will only offer positions to candidates who are commercially astute or, at least demonstrate the potential to possess commercial awareness in their application for a training contract. Being commercially aware will therefore give you an edge in the employability stakes for securing a training contract.

Commercial awareness is an important criterion for law firms in their recruitment of their lawyers, because top City law firms' recruit their trainee solicitors two years in advance, and this decision is based on a projection of your ability and your understanding of the role of a commercial solicitor.

The cost to a law firm in training and developing each trainee during a training contract is in the region of £250,000. It is therefore vital that firms are confident that their money is being invested wisely. In addition, many law firms' aim to hold on to this "investment" beyond the training contract period, and regard their trainees as the future life-blood and partners of the firm, which is why firms expect candidates to show a real commitment to spending their future career at the firm. It is important that you can justify why a firm should plough hundreds of thousands of pounds in training you?

As an applicant, firms will want to know that you have the potential to be commercially aware, and whether you have shown signs of being business savvy through your experiences. So, that you have the capability to emerge as a good lawyer and sound business advisor to your clients.

## Are you commercially aware?

As a student or graduate you will not be expected to be an expert on the mechanics of the business world, but law firms are looking for basic knowledge and a real enthusiasm for business matters, and more importantly, the ability and willingness to think commercially.

Law firms want trainee solicitors who not only know about strict legal principles, but want students who can relate to clients, and appreciate the commercial context in which they apply their advice to clients.

## The role of a commercial lawyer

Law firms work hard to win clients and prestige in an increasingly competitive market for legal services. It is a pre-requisite for a commercial lawyer to be commercially aware, because you need to understand your clients' businesses in order to give them the best legal advice.

*Essentially solicitors' who are commercially aware:*
- Have an awareness of the legal and business challenges for the firm in the legal market.
- Consider how their law firm can progress, and bill higher profits than their competitors.
- Appreciate the changing needs of their clients and are able to cultivate and develop long-term relationships with their clients.
- Know their firm's mission, values, vision, strategy, & business plan.

When working with clients, successful commercial lawyers are able to view situations from a commercial or business perspective, as well as a legal perspective. Solicitors are required to be technically excellent, and it is a given that you know the law. But you will also have to be able to explain complex legal issues in the context of your clients business. This often involves taking a step back and carefully analysing a set of circumstances from different angles, and asking "who are the key stakeholders in this matter? What are the risks and concerns involved in this situation?, what questions would they ask?". Stakeholders include customers/clients, employees, directors, shareholders and professional advisors (eg, lawyers, accountants).

Commercial lawyers deal with more than just the law, they anticipate what the issues are for a client's business at an organizational, local, regional, and a global level. They are able to keep abreast of issues which have a bearing on the work their clients undertake. The legal profession has to consistently adapt and respond to changes and developments in the economy, which may affect a client's business operations. In the modern legal arena the role of a solicitor has evolved from being a sound technician of the law, to an all-round business advisor. A commercial lawyer must be able to assist clients to achieve their business aims, by delivering a pragmatic, solutions-orientated commercial steer to their clients to help them resolve matters which help to safeguard and enhance the financial viability of a client's business. It is therefore important to understand the need for businesses to be cost effective and the importance of client relations.

### ➢ *What do clients want from their solicitor?*

Clients seek solicitors that speak the same language as them, and understand their business needs. Clients are impressed by lawyers who are able to understand what they are seeking to achieve, and deliver a seamless service of legal advice that meets their objectives and adds-value to their business.

Some clients are hands on and prefer to be involved in the process of finding a solution. Knowing your client and having the interpersonal skills and charisma to develop a long-lasting relationship with your client is vital. Clients want to be kept updated and informed at all times by their legal advisor. Clients want to be kept up to date by their solicitor, so a solicitors responsiveness, accessibility, availability and communication skills are thus paramount to the delivery of a first-class service.

As lawyers ourselves, we know the significance of being commercially aware, the impact commercial awareness has on the quality of legal advice and, the overall success of one's professional career if they have business acumen. In addition, recruiters will look for candidates who have a keen interest in the legal sector, and their particular firm above any other.

**Our Top Tip: Avoid commerciality at your peril! Legal advice often takes on a business element, and no student can afford NOT to be commercially aware. If you do not develop your commercial awareness, you will only let yourself down and highlight a serious weakness in your application.**

## Becoming commercially aware

You cannot gain commercial awareness overnight. In order to become commercially aware for the purposes of your training contract interview and for your future career, you will need to dedicate time to reading about the world of business and finance if this type of work interests you.

> *Let's analyse the building of commercial awareness another way*

Imagine if somebody were to question you on a television show you had only watched a handful of times. You may be able to talk about what you have seen but perhaps not convincingly and comprehensively. You are sure to miss out detail in terms of characters, plot development, or even clues as to how the story will unravel. This analogy reflects the building of commercial awareness. In order to talk confidently and have substantiated opinions, you should aim to follow the business press on a daily basis in the weeks preceding your interview. You can then build up a progressive picture of the major stories.

Interviewers will not expect you to have detailed knowledge of everything in the FT. However, they may expect you to focus on the key events and topics of interest, which will put you in an excellent position to think practically and logically when answering the question at your interview. By reading about key topics on a daily basis, you will slowly begin to build up a clearer picture of the issues, almost like discovering how a plot is unfolding in a TV series. You will see who the key players are, the major issues, and in most cases you will be able to deduce the implications of the certain events.

Financial journalists will invariably give their opinions on the issues of the day. Start thinking about whether you agree or disagree, and the commercial advantages and disadvantages of how various deals are being handled. This is the best way to develop your understanding and develop your own views. Naturally, there will be aspects you find particularly interesting, all of which you can discuss at interview.

*For example*, currently occupying the pages of the business broadsheets is the great fall of Lehman Brothers as a consequence of the current difficult global economic climate. Also, Lloyds TSB are proposing a deal to takeover Halifax Bank of Scotland (HBOS), which may change the face of banking in the UK. In effect, the buy-out was a rescue, as HBOS shares had been driven down amid concerns over its future.

The buyout will create a super-bank with nearly a third of the British mortgage market. In normal market conditions this deal would have caused competition law implications for the UK mortgage market, as the combination of Lloyds and HBOS (both UK banks) in the mortgage market would be potentially anti-competitive as there would now be less choice for customers. However, Chancellor Alistair Darling confirmed the government would waive competition rules to ensure the deal went through.

The deal also sparks fears of thousands of job losses at HBOS, due to the possible closure of duplicate Lloyds TSB and HBOS branches and head office departments being merged, which also brings up employment law issues, if staff are going to be made redundant.

NB. It is always worth considering what the key commercial issues will be, and what the legal implications are likely to be.


## Raising Commercial Awareness

So far, you will have learnt that commercial awareness is an outlook; a way of thinking that must be developed over a period of time. The bottom line is - if you wish to pursue a career as a commercial lawyer, you must become commercially aware. You can only do this by dedicating time to getting to grips with the world of business and finance. The following tips will point you in the right direction:

## Follow the business news daily

Candidates often make the big mistake of thinking that reading the Financial Times the day before or, on the morning of the interview will provide enough knowledge to bluff their way through the pressing issues currently in the global economy. This really is the wrong approach! Any seasoned interviewer and lawyer will be able to expose your limited knowledge, which will create a negative impression.

Reading the Companies and Markets section of the FT may seem a daunting prospect, but it is actually made easier by having a focus. If you find stories you are interested in, why not follow up by using the internet to locate other stories which cover different views? Look at the rest of the industry; are there other interesting and relevant things happening? What is your opinion on how things will develop?

There is a plethora of general information available. Take the time to keep abreast of the legal and business press, such as, the business pages of the major broadsheet newspapers will provide a useful background to the big issues in the commercial arena. The Times, the FT, and the Economist are very good at breaking down the key components of the major matters. Watch/listen to business related programmes in the media (TV and Radio). For example, Working lunch, the Apprentice, Dragon's den, world business review, and the Money programme will provide a useful insight into the major issues currently facing businesses.

**Keep up-to-date with news in the legal market:** Monitor the legal press, the Lawyer 2B, Legal week student, The Lawyer, Legal Business, The Gazzette are also useful publications that will help you find out which firms are working on the high-profile deals.

Read the graduate recruitment brochures of the law firms that interest you. Peruse the websites of law firms and their clients. Review their recent news and press releases section, which will provide a useful insight into the current matters the law firm are involved in. Read articles which cover issues the law firms that you intend applying to, keep a file on the information you have collated, in case you are invited to attend an interview at any of those firms. Look on *RollonFriday's* "inside information" section on law firms, which should cover most of the background you will need. Be pro-active and look out for the clients of a law firm, recent deals the firm have acted on, and what is happening in their client's marketplace?

**Research:** Use the search navigation space on websites, such as, lawcareers.net, The Lawyer, and Legal Week to keep up to speed on developments in various legal sectors. Ensure you are aware of the major current issues affecting the legal market, such as, recent transactions and forthcoming legislation. Consider the commercial implications for law firms and their clients business. Subscribe to our commercial awareness forum through our website www.ultimatelawguide, to gain free access to articles from the legal and business environment. Read articles from publications such as, The Economist, and Practical Law Company ("PLC").

**Commercial/legal experience:** Your past work experience may have enhanced your commercial awareness. Attaining experience at a law firm will provide a useful insight into working life in a dynamic office environment. If you are unable to get legal work experience, do your utmost to gain some commercial experience.

You will need to show that you have undertaken roles in the past which have exposed you to business matters. It is important that you are able to discuss your experience, and evidence the transferable skills you developed, such as teamwork, analytical skills, communication skills and working with customers in a pressurised environment.

The type of work from which you can draw commercial experience might surprise you. Some of you will be saying to yourselves that you have only had work as a sales assistant. Try to convey your experience, and the role you performed in a positive manner, this will help you to display your commercial awareness and other skills in an effective way, which will impress graduate recruiters.

For example, your experiences may have enhanced your awareness of customer needs and expectations. Were you ever given the task of checking stock levels? Did you improve the stock replenishing and orders system? Did you have to liase with the merchandisers at head office? If so, how did you go about it, what factors did you have to take into consideration? You may have learnt about the importance of budgeting, sales forecasting, financial planning and marketing, all of which are buzz words which make your application form stand out, and increase your chances of getting an interview. At the interview you can spend time discussing your experience of working in the business, and go into further detail to demonstrate your understanding of the mechanics of business.

CASE STUDY: *We know a trainee solicitor who spent their summer working in the local pub. She gained an excellent insight into the commercial reality of running a profit-making business, and tied the experience to leadership, working as part of team and dealing with demanding (often inebriated) customers. She was able to market her experience and transferable skills effectively to land a training contract offer at a leading commercial firm.*

Look back at your weekend or part-time jobs and consider how useful they were in terms of your personal development. Think about the following factors;

- ➢ the products and services offered,
- ➢ the customer base,
- ➢ the importance of good, well-trained staff,
- ➢ the marketing initiatives used to maintain customer loyalty and reach its target audience,
- ➢ culture and ethos of the company,
- ➢ What new skills did you develop?
    - Sales and communication skills in a customer-facing environment,
    - Did this increase your understanding of customer care, the competitors, suppliers, and the reputation of this Company?

Law firms place tremendous value in candidates who have commercial experience, because it provides exposure to business activities. Gaining work experience (whether paid or voluntary work) is a vital part of planning your future legal career. If you manage to secure work experience during your holidays, use this as an opportunity to learn as much as possible about how a commercial enterprise works. Your work experience will help to improve your commerciality, as it is valued by City law firms as it shows a commitment to a career as a City lawyer, and proves you are coming to the law with your eyes wide open and sufficiently informed about your future career.

When it comes to work experience, anything you do that is supplementary to studying shows you are a well rounded individual who has maximised their time at university, and are willing to learn new things and put yourself out there. It can also show team work, organisational skills and that you are a worthwhile person to have on board. If you are unable to secure legal work experience, try to find work experience elsewhere, in a commercial environment to give you an insight into business and the office environment will provide you with transferable skills, such as interpersonal skills, and analytical skills, which are required to become a good lawyer. Apply for internships in other professions, such as investment banking or accountancy. There are many kinds of work experience law firms will find interesting, just make sure it has a commercial slant.

You can further enhance your prospects by securing work experience which relates to the type of work the law firms undertake. Law firms are essentially looking for people who have a keen interest in the work their clients do, and consequently, the type of work they do. For example, we know a student that wanted to work for a leading law firm that specialised in insurance litigation. She gained commercial experience by working as a paralegal at a leading insurer, a client of the law firm, and this experience was clearly valued by the law firm.

Commercial awareness is important regardless of the type of law firm you are intending to apply to. Whether you are applying to City institutions or your local firm, it is vital that you are interested in their work, the type of clients the firm works for and the sort of issues that will affect those clients, so that you will be able to relate to clients and contextualise your advice.

## What if you have no commercial experience by the time you start applying for training contracts?

If you do not manage to secure any work experience placements in a law firm then it is not the end of the world. Firms are very interested to hear of other ways that students have developed their commercial awareness.

You can display your commercial awareness through an activity you have done. For example, if you took the initiative to set up your own business? Was it profitable? What were the commercial risks involved? How did you approach this risk? What distinguished your business from others?

Remember, you still have time to get experience if you haven't already. Start now and raise your profile. Make yourself more marketable and attractive to potential employers.

**Extra curricular activities:** Get involved with activities and committees at university and law school that relate to business. Did you have a key role in any society committees at school or university? Were you given a financial role? A sales role? Have you ever ran a marathon and raised money for a charity or, secured sponsorship for an event? What process did you go through to secure the funds?

Sign up to join business games where you can increase your commercial acumen. There are organisations where entrepreneurs come together to network and exchange resources, such as **www.ukbusinessclubs.com**. There are business clubs all over the country and, by networking effectively *(chapter 8)* you will be building strong contacts with people, which will provide you with access to information and opinions that can help you to improve your commercial awareness.

Many students undertake a Young Enterprise Scheme, or become involved in committees that organise events, such as, a book sale for charity. You may have been the chair of the committee, involved in finance, sales, marketing and PR, and accounts. This would have increased your understanding of the important factors of creating a successful business.

**Travel:** Careful planning of a gap year can also increase your commercial awareness. Benefiting from international travel broadens your outlook and enables one to acquire an international perspective on issues affecting every day life. You are likely to have gained an insight into different cultures and business etiquettes from around the world. From a commercial point of view, planning your travel schedule may also develop your budgeting, financial forecasting, cost-cutting scheduling, and cash flow projections. These are all skills which are useful to running a profitable business.

## Ultimate Law Guide's Top tips on demonstrating commercial awareness during the training contract recruitment process:

**Use the application form to showcase your commercial awareness:** Commercial awareness is a key skill that any future legal employer will expect you to demonstrate during the application process.

- There are usually competency-based questions on the application form, which will look for indications of commercial awareness during your academic and work history.
- You may be asked to *"comment on a commercial transaction that you have recently followed"*. Other notoriously tough questions are:

*"Identify a current commercial issue which has attracted your attention recently, why do you consider it to be significant, who are the key stakeholders and what are the implications to those concerned?"*

*"What are the future commercial challenges for law firms over the next 5/10 years?"*

Remember that, this is your opportunity to demonstrate your interest and understanding of the current key business issues, so that your commercial awareness will resonate through your application and land you an interview for a training contract. Make sure you clearly explain why you believe this commercial transaction/challenge is a significant issue, and remember to focus on the implications for all parties involved, the particular industry and the wider economy.

If you are invited to an interview ensure you revisit your application form, because it is highly likely that you will be asked to elaborate on the points you raised in your application.

**Law firms want candidates to realise that the law can be a practical way of making money**. Law firms will be asking themselves the following questions:

> *Will this candidate be able to communicate effectively with our clients?* This will be proved through work experience or showing an interest in commercial affairs

on your CV/application form and, be put to the test in the interview "hot seat".

> *Industry knowledge*: Your awareness of current market conditions for their clients and economy in general will be challenged during the interview.
> *Can the candidate draw from their commercial experience and apply it to a set of given facts?* This will be gleaned from your application and further considered during your interview.

**Evidence your commercial awareness at the interview:** It is imperative that you have some knowledge of the broader environment in which all sorts of lawyer will have to operate, because your understanding of business will be tested, and even challenged at the interview. You should therefore know something about the top deals of the day, and how they might have an impact on the law firm's clients.

A popular question at interview is based on how you manage to keep abreast of commercial developments, which is then followed by an open question on what you have read recently, they usually take the form of the following examples;

> ✓ *"How do you keep up to date with developments in legal business?"*
> ✓ *"Tell me about a recent corporate deal you have read about?"*
> ✓ *"Tell me about what is going on in the business world right now?"*
> ✓ *"Describe a particular business story that has caught your attention recently, and why have you found it interesting?"*

Such a question gives you vast scope to showcase your knowledge and understanding of commercial awareness, which you would have hopefully built up over weeks and months before your interview. As future lawyers, when reading about deals in the press, always consider the legal implications to the commercial issues involved in that deal. This is something interviewers are particularly fond of asking about. After all, the lawyer's role is to advise the client about these legal implications.

Aspiring solicitors must start thinking about the commercial aspects of new legislation. For example, what are the likely implications of the Legal Services Act 2005 on law firms and the legal profession as a whole? Similarly, consider the commercial issues of legal advice you might give in relation to a friend setting up their own business. This should focus your mind on the kind of responses that firms will be looking for when it comes to being in the "hot seat".

## Example 1

Your client is embroiled in a legal dispute with a supplier. Is your client willing to negotiate, mediate and possibly compromise in order to reach a settlement? Or, are they determined to litigate the dispute in court? Consider the commercial implications for each option. Remember legal advisors are business advisors, and ultimately want to make or save money for their clients.

## Example 2

Your client wants to set up a business in an overseas jurisdiction. The client wants to borrow the money to do this. Is this a good idea? Write down all the advantages and disadvantages you can think of. What are the commercial implications in the decision-making process?

**Our Top Tip: An interviewer will be expecting you to demonstrate what you have read by clearly and articulately explaining the issues, and showing your own thoughts and conclusions. Think laterally.**

## Case study

At the interview you may also be given a case study to prepare before the interview. The case study will be a business scenario, and training contract applicants will be expected to prepare answers to questions on business issues facing the hypothetical company in the case study, to test their appreciation of the commercial factors within the exercise. The partners interviewing the training contract applicant may probe further to assess the depth of your understanding and analysis. Here, the law firm will be looking for you to be able to draw from your commercial experience and apply it to a set of given facts? Remember that sometimes commercial awareness simply means demonstrating that you can apply common sense to a commercial question or problem.

*When undertaking case studies, some applicants fall into the trap of thinking purely legal without grasping the elements of a client's business, and the financial implications of legal advice to a client. Many applicants simply think commercial awareness is all about reading a pink newspaper, and surprisingly many candidates, despite how badly they want the training contract, do not get it right.* **Graduate Recruitment Partner**

**Our Top Tip**: Saying you know who a firm's clients and direct competitors are will not be enough to convince a firm to offer you a training contract. Law firms want much more! You must not only keep abreast of some of their deals, which have captured your interest, but also consider the commercial implications of a deal for the client and the wider industry. This is the only way to show firms that you are able to think commercially. Avoid commerciality at your peril!

If you are not commercially aware, you will only show a massive weakness in your application. Follow the steps outlined above, read the articles on our Commercial Awareness Forum, and this will help you become commercially aware. Success at your training contract interview depends on it!

## COMMERCIALITY TEST

Commerciality is the key! Test your commercial awareness by seeing how many questions you can answer correctly. You may not be able to answer all of these questions fully, but at least you'll have an appreciation of what you need to do to reach the level law firms will expect of you.

1.  What is AIM?

2.  Give two reasons why a company would want to list on AIM as opposed to the main market on the LSE.

3.  What is a bond?

4.  Give one reason why a company would want to issue a bond as opposed to issuing shares.

5.  Which media giant recently invested in ITV for nearly 1bn?

6.  What is the difference between a cash offer and a shares offer?

7.  What is the relevance of competition law in a corporate acquisition?

8.  What do you know about stocks and shares?

9.  Where would you invest £100,000?

10. Where would you open a new office?

11. Appreciate the city environment – Apply this to a law firm of your choice.
a.  What type of clients does the firm target?
b.  What clients should we target?
c.  Who are our competitors?

12. The economy
a.  How can law firms sustain healthy profits?
b.  How can law firms overcome a downturn in the economy?

13. What are the three main attributes of an excellent legal advisor?

14. What are the key challenges facing the legal profession today and in the future?

(*See Appendix 2 for answers*).

## The City of London

During the course of writing our guide, we encountered many students who asked us to explain exactly what "the City" is, and the kind of business that takes place there. As a background to commerciality, it is important to have an idea about the way in which the City of London works.

The City is essentially a large market place of opportunity and entrepreneurship, mostly contained in one square mile, and now the City also extends to Canary Wharf in London. Part of the attraction of the City is the huge scale of opportunity that it creates.

## The square mile and law as a business

In case you have ever wondered why the majority of investment banks, law firms and insurance companies are located in the heart of London, you should be aware that the City has been at the forefront of the world's economy for hundreds of years, and has grown over the centuries at the heart of world finance, capital markets and trading. The City of London is conveniently situated between two important global business centres and time zones - New York and Tokyo - and therefore provides the integral link between the three most vital global financial centres.

## Interesting facts and figures about the City of London:

✓ There are over 500,000 people working in the City.
✓ The amount of money that moves through the City is phenomenal. Well over two-thirds of the leading global companies have an office base in the square mile.
✓ Almost 20 per cent of the world's bank lending is from the City, and around £2,500 billion of assets are managed and $650 billion in foreign exchange is traded every day.
✓ There are 450 foreign companies listed on the Stock Exchange - more than any other exchange in the world.
✓ Only the US and Japan have bigger domestic equity markets.
✓ Half of the world's shipping is brokered through London.
✓ The city has 30 per cent of the world's aviation insurance, and 22 per cent of its maritime insurance. The City of

London is unique; it even has its own local government which is different from those in other parts of the UK.

It's easy to see then why most City law firms are firmly rooted in corporate and finance related work. The amount of money which passes through the City is the reason why City law firms are able to use the law as a vehicle for making huge amounts of money. The firms charge the companies they advise according to the time they spend giving expert legal advice on their clients account.

## An illustrative example

The product the City deals in is money, and the market operates under business principles of supply and demand. The City is where Company X, wishes to raise money for its business. The Company searches for suitable lenders and investors, i.e. investment banks, private equity houses or venture capitalists. The organizations that lend money do so with an assumption of risk that the borrower might default on the terms of the loan agreement. The risk of this happening is safeguarded by the terms (covenants) of the loan agreement, which is drafted by lawyers, and signed between the borrower and the lenders. The terms of the deal may also include taking security in the form of a charge over particular assets of Company X, in case things go wrong. The borrower will also charge interest on the loan as a way of receiving a commercial return from the loan deal.

With the advent of globalisation, economies around the world have become integrated and international ties are constantly formed. Companies are merging and streamlining their businesses by selling off various parts of their operations. The opening of national borders and markets has also paved the way for companies to set-up several bases around the world. Law firms keen to take advantage of this global phenomenon have followed the emergence of new economies and taken traditional City firms to markets where they can, in essence, win new business and increase profits. Over the past few years places like the Far East and Asian sub-continent have experienced huge growth in their economies, faster than much of the developed world. India looks like it will follow the example of the Far Eastern countries once its stringent business and foreign investment regulations are relaxed, many law firms will be seeking to establish themselves there. The global network allows the biggest deals to be done cross-border very quickly.

**Emerging markets**

So what type of business can law firms do in emerging market economies? Law firms will be able to set up new companies and restructure the constitution of state-owned companies and assets. They will set up joint ventures, partnerships, and wholly-owned companies. There is also a good prospect for project finance, building new infrastructures, and taking on board energy projects for the country in question. With the deregulation soon to take place in countries like India, foreign banks will be looking to explore structured finance markets, for example, derivatives. Law firms will be on hand to provide advice about the legal aspects of these deals. This is where it becomes important to do your research about where the firms you apply to do business.

## Getting to grips with commercial awareness

Most law firms talk about the need for prospective trainees to display commercial awareness, but what on earth does this mean and how does someone display commercial awareness? In this chapter, we have not only demystified and clarified the concept of commercial awareness for you, but also given you a detailed explanation about what will be expected from you in relation to your commercial knowledge. We have explained that how to become commercially aware by giving you:

- Hints and tips on how to think commercially
- Ways in which you can build up your commercial nous
- Ways in which to show off your commercial awareness
- Our own unique commerciality test to pit your wits against

## What do I have to do to show commercial awareness?

1. Develop general and current business knowledge and understand the basics. For example, read up on any recent corporate merger and acquisition.
2. Familiarise yourself with business jargon, e.g. what is the difference between debt finance and equity finance?
3. Find out how markets work, e.g. FTSE 100, AIM.
4. Think about newsworthy current transactions, and keep clips of any interesting articles and commentary.
5. Read the business section of *The Times* and *FT* on a daily basis at least three weeks before the interview.
6. Attend talks on commercial issues at your university or law school.
7. Be enthusiastic when talking about commercial issues. This will allow you to show you have a genuine interest.

Chapter Ten

## Improving your CV and Covering Letter

It is time to start refining your choice of firm and to begin shaping the way you will present yourself to potential employers. For firms which require this method of application from you, an excellent CV and covering letter will be invaluable in making the right impression. In the attempt to recruit the right candidates it seems there is no limit to the range of skills and potential that law firms look for. Make sure your CV and covering letter do justice to your skills and experiences.

### Covering letters – make yourself impressive

A CV is a useful marketing tool, a summary of the qualities and key attributes that will market you to your target audience. Alone, it is incomplete and needs a covering letter to focus the reader's attention and highlight the points which will "sell your skills" most effectively. Covering letters are notoriously difficult to get right. In essence, the letter should make the employer really look forward to reading your CV and ultimately invite you to interview.

The covering letter is the first information potential employers read about you and provides the opportunity for your personality and individuality to shine through. Always aim to strike a balance between showing a genuine interest in the firm and keeping the letter concise. The key to any good letter is to ensure a balance between what you are looking for in an employer and what you can offer to that employer.

A fantastic letter will never transform a weak CV into a strong one, whereas a badly written letter will detract from an otherwise good CV.

A covering letter should be restricted to a maximum of one side of A4, and produced on the same type of paper as your CV. It should be laid out as a formal business letter showing both your address and the name and address of the recipient. Use a consistent font that is professional and easy to read such as Times New Roman, Arial or Garamond. Avoid using text that resembles an old typewriter.

Ensure your writing style is simple and direct. In this way, you will save space and get your message across easily and in a succinct manner. Always aim to give your letter a personal touch. Recruiters can spot a mass produced letter at a glance.

Always write to a specific person unless told otherwise. It is a good sign if a candidate makes the effort to find the right person to apply to. Use their title and surname only, e.g. Dear Mrs Ferguson.

Avoid using any superfluous language, keep it simple and avoid dressing your letter with flowery adjectives. Type your letter wherever possible, unless otherwise instructed. Word processed letters are easier to read and more economical on space. If in doubt, check the firm's website/vacancy advert or contact the firm directly.

It is very important to tailor your covering letter to the firm to which you are applying, making sure to point out why you believe you will be successful at the firm and fit in well. How you describe, present and sell yourself will decide the outcome of any application. Prospective employers receiving your cover letter will need to be sure that you are making an effort to target them specifically and will be judging your skills, experience, track record and personality against many other applicants, leave the recruiter without any doubt that you have what it takes to succeed.

Always tailor the covering letter to a specific job. Employers will know that you are applying for more than one job but ideally they need to be made to feel that you are only applying to them!

## Structure your covering Letter

Your paragraphs should be clearly laid out and bring out the following points:

✓ **Who are you?** Your first paragraph should be used to set the scene. Clarify what you are applying for. You could also include the reason for your interest in the firm. For example, *I am writing further to our conversation at the graduate careers fair in London*.

✓ **Why are you applying?** What aspects of the firm's work interest you? The second paragraph should address why you are applying to that particular firm. Why is that firm special? This is where many students fall short as they use general covering letters that are not tailored specifically to individual firms. Think about the firm's size, location and the main practice areas of specialisation. Then state your unique reason for applying to the firm. It is integral that you display your considerable research into the firm and the practice areas that you are interested in and why, making the connection with any work experience that has enabled you to arrive at an informed decision. Avoid vague generalisations such as praising the firm's excellence and international reputation. The firm is aware of this and graduate recruitment are tired of reading about it!

✓ **What special qualities can you bring to the firm? Do you have any particular achievements of interest?** What have you done? Describe any relevant experience, achievements and interests - keep it concise. This is where you need to convince the firm that you are right for them. Expect the reader to turn to your CV for supporting credible evidence of your assertions.

✓ **Why you above anyone else?** Refer to highly relevant points on your CV that you want the reader to note, without repeating the information, e.g. more details of relevant vacation placements or other work experience, give details of extra qualifications that are relevant to the job, for example, languages, your LLM and past work experience. Finish the letter by signing off professionally and in a courteous manner, detailing your availability for interview.

✓ **Closing** – ask the firm to contact you with any queries. Thank them for reading your letter.

**Our Top Tip: Always align your skills and strengths to the requirements of the practice. For example, give examples on your covering letter of key achievements which relate to the firm's criteria. This could be the ability to multi-task, good work ethic, good time management, communication skills, excellent interpersonal skills and effectiveness as a team player. You can also use the**

**covering letter to explain away any inconsistencies in your CV, perhaps your A-level or degree results were affected by outside extenuating circumstances. If so, you can mention this in your covering letter. This may well circumvent any concerns readers have about your suitability. You can also highlight other areas of past success. If you do mention a blip on your academic record – be sure to finish on a positive note that shows you in a good light, such as improved recent academic performance.**

**Always remember to Sign "yours sincerely" if addressing a named person, "Yours faithfully" otherwise. Address your application letter to the correct person and ensure correct use of the prefix Mr or Miss. Telephone the firm if you have to: ensure you know whom to write to! Don't run the risk of rejection for basic errors. Get the name of the firm right, make sure you put your name at the bottom and do not forget to sign it.**

Here are some examples of specimen covering letters; they are in no way perfect because there is no such thing. There are no hard and fast rules about what your covering letter should look like, and similar to fashion trends, the type of covering letters law firms would like to see may change over time so it is best to make sure your approach to covering letters is not out of date. The examples below only show how covering letters can be written. They will give you ideas on how you can structure your letters although we do not recommend that you copy these letters word for word!

Example 1

27 Mill
Ealing
London,
W55ER

Mr ...........................
Graduate Recruitment Manager
Robinemps Solicitors
12-18 Good Times street
London EC3 7BS

Dear Mr ...................

20th June 2008

I am writing to apply for a training contract with Robinemps Solicitors. Enclosed is my CV for your consideration.

I would like to be considered for your 2008 trainee solicitor intake. I have just completed the second year of my LLB (honours) Law degree at [insert name] University. Having attended the firm's recent open day, I enjoyed the opportunity to discuss the benefits of your training programme with your current trainees. This left me with the impression that trainees not only receive excellent training at your firm but enjoy the work as well. My work experience during the summer in the firm's Commercial Law Department provided me with a first-hand insight into the realities of working for a leading City firm, and confirmed that I am  suited to a future at a law firm with a strong commercial bias. I worked with a partner [insert name], on a large corporate transaction with one of the firm's most important clients.

I first became interested in commercial work through a seminar on careers in law at university last year. I believe commercial law would be an ideal way to combine my skills and interests in business with problem solving and working with people. My interest was confirmed following a week shadowing an in-house commercial lawyer at [insert name]. I needed to absorb and assimilate a large amount of business and technical information in a short time in order to work as an effective member of the team and to provide our client with the quality of information and first-class service that they expected. My law degree has enabled me to develop and enhance a range of skills, in particular, analysing and interpreting complex information and presenting arguments and conclusions in a logical and evaluated way.

I am applying to Robinbemps due to the wide range of opportunities that are available from your training scheme, as shown by your Lawyers for People Award in 2006. At this stage my main long-term interest is in commercial law and I believe a thorough grounding in your practice area will be beneficial to my personal development.

I look forward to hearing from you.

Yours Sincerely

Learning Resources
Centre

Example 2
Address

[Date]
Dear Ms ……………..

I would like to apply for the position as a trainee solicitor in 2008. I have recently completed my second year at [*insert name*] University. My degree has enabled me to develop and enhance a range of skills, in particular, analysing and interpreting complex information and presenting arguments and conclusions in a logical way.

I am attracted to working in a dynamic environment in which I will be challenged on a daily basis. Firm [X] is particularly appealing to me because of your reputation in finance.

I have extensive experience in banking and finance. As you will see from my CV, my vacation placement provided me with a wide range of exposure to finance and legal deals. I have also been given the opportunity to display my leadership qualities. My work experience provided me with experience of the daily pressures and challenges that a lawyer encounters, as well as the great sense of achievement that accompanies success.

I have shown I am highly motivated by winning the Contract Law Award for two consecutive years at university. My motivation, combined with my qualifications, interests and language skills, clearly indicates that I can make a positive contribution and help to continue the firm's successful future.

In return for a training contract, I can offer a strong work ethic and drive. One of the most challenging things I have undertaken was mountain climbing: an activity which enhanced my motivation to achieve my goals. I also taught English in Africa for a year and worked for a humanity project, raising funds to help people suffering from poverty and depravation. I represented the City of London at a European student conference held at the European Courts of Justice, Luxembourg. I believe that the wide range of skills and attributes will make me an excellent candidate for your firm.

I would welcome the opportunity to discuss matters further and if you have any other questions, please feel free to contact me.

Yours Sincerely

## Curriculum Vitae (CV): Top CV tips

*There is always someone out there who wants to know who you are, what you are made of and what you are worth, before they consider doing business with you...Good CVs attract investors and build partnerships; telling employers, loud and clear, who you are.*

**Sir Alan Sugar**

A CV is essentially a life and skills evaluation of your achievements and abilities. It enables you to summarise and promote what you have achieved. It is the first piece of hard evidence on which a law firm can judge you. Many of the do's and don'ts listed above are very relevant to your CV, please bear these in mind as you compile it. You should aim for your CV to give an impression of your career history and your status and achievements in previous roles. Your CV should be business-like. The following guidelines have been designed to produce a CV that creates a positive impression.

## Essential information

Most recruiters spend a few seconds spinning through a CV. Your CV is "you at a glance" and must therefore be easy to read and should suggest areas for discussion. Give the right message and impression and allocate the relevant information in the space available for things such as education, work experience/career history.

## The CV golden rules

Allocate space in accordance with the importance of the information. Decide in advance what you are hoping to write about in the different parts of your CV - allocate more space to the more important parts. For example, if you spent three years at a weekend job but only two weeks on a vacation placement at a City law firm, while your part-time job experience is useful, your legal experience is immediately more relevant. Place strong emphasis on this aspect of your career history.
Think about your experience in terms of its relevance.

✓ People who read your CV are generally busy and often scan a CV to see whether it's worth reading. Put the most important selling material on the front page, usually your degree course or work experience.

✓ There is no such thing as a general CV when it comes to applications for a training contract. Make your CV a brochure that truly represents the skills you are offering and the attributes required, and make sure the message comes across clearly.

✓ Make it look good. Aim to fill two pages of A4: half a page of blank paper doesn't look great.

✓ Given that how your CV looks is of vital importance, ensure the presentation allows enough space. Avoid long sentences of unbroken text, use bullet points or paragraphs to break things up, use bold to highlight particular achievements.

✓ Arrange dates, titles and other factual information in columns, as if part of a table, so it looks well structured.

✓ Ensure your CV is produced on good quality paper and make sure there are no spelling mistakes.

✓ As with your covering letter, get a friend or colleagues to check           it           for           you.

## Layout of your CV

The structure and presentation of a CV can help or hinder the reader to focus on the essential information. Think carefully about how you enter your details and how quickly you can read the information. The use of bullet points can help to keep information concise and guide the eye around the page. Look at each section critically and use the best format for the specific points you are making.

There is no standard format but two pages are sufficient, as recruiters do not like receiving excessively long applications.

**Our Top Tip: Build up your profile by giving the highest priority to the best and most relevant examples of your ability to do the specific job and put them on the first page. Highlight the key skills that make you most attractive to the potential employer. Be positive, direct and concise. Be selective, space is limited. Only use the information that will count towards helping your application.**

Your CV should reflect your strengths: - bear in mind employers look for evidence of teamwork, commercial acumen, sound judgment, attention to detail and academic prowess and achievement. Many students fall into the trap of thinking that once their CV is drafted it is ready for the world and ideal for each and every application. Do not make this assumption. We can not emphasise enough that it is crucial that you tailor your application accordingly to shape and match your prospective employer.

It is important to use positive language and a confident tone when concentrating on your achievements and responsibilities. Make relevant qualifications, skills and experience prominent, stating in detail exactly what you did and what skills you developed from it. Bullet points break up a CV well and each bullet point should provide the reader with a feel for the types of tasks and responsibilities that you have handled.

Once again, do not make false claims: honesty is always the best policy. If the interviewer identifies inconsistencies between your CV and what you say at interview you will not be successful.

## Structure of your CV

Every CV should contain clear sections of material, which will market you most effectively. Remember, there is no single correct format. You should think about including the following sections:

✓ Personal Details
✓ Education and Training
✓ Legal Work Experience
✓ Achievements and Awards
✓ Hobbies, Interests and Activities (other skills)
✓ Voluntary (pro bono) Work
✓ Referees

**Chronological order** - start with your most recent position and work backwards. Keep details to a minimum. Cover any periods unaccounted for and make sure there are no gaps as it creates the impression that you are trying to hide something. Include any striking or unusual interests and awards. Do not e-mail or fax an application without also sending application via post. If you do, at least follow up with a telephone call to double-check that your application has been received.

Be sure to use punchy, potent action words for detailing your achievements, e.g. achieved, won, supported etc. Be consistent with whatever tense you use, whether past or present.

**Personal details** – include only what is needed for clarity, i.e. name, address, telephone numbers, date of birth. Details of nationality can be important if you require a work permit.

**Education** – present current details first and work chronologically. Selectors are most interested in recent study; be brief in your mention of earlier exams and, if relevant, elaborate on your degree modules. Give most prominence to the most important qualification (usually your highest and most recent).

**Employment / legal work experience** – concentrate on showing relevant and transferable skills drawn from all your work experience. If you have not had directly relevant experience, think about the skills your part-time job has taught you.

**Other skills** – highlight any additional skills or proficiencies such as, IT competencies. Do you have any extra achievements, or awards?

**Interests and activities** – concentrate on activities that can demonstrate your transferable skills and show additional abilities, which you can discuss at interview. Use buzz words, e.g. created, organised, initiated.

**Referees** – two referees are customary: one academic and one work or character related. Remember to use reliable people and check first that they are happy to be referees. It might be helpful to send a copy of your application to your referees so that they know how best to support your application.

It may take 3-4 drafts to develop the right presentation style. When you have got it right, get a second opinion on the structure and presentation.

**Timing** is everything – if the closing date has passed, then you are simply too late and your chances of being considered are extremely slim to none. Check the closing date before you apply.

**Our Top Tip: Send in applications as early as possible before the firm has started interviewing. Your application will be given careful consideration as opposed to the quick glance when there is pressure to short-list near an impending deadline. Time all your applications accordingly. If you leave things until the last minute, the mistakes you make from rushing are likely to show in some aspects of your application.**

## Problem areas

**A lack of legal work experience**: If you have limited experience, you still have options available to you. Obtain voluntary work which you can present as you would any work experience. Voluntary work can be a real asset for law firms in terms of legal research and client contact, especially in smaller legal practices where the community is the focus of the work.

If the only work experience you have is in retail. This may appear somewhat irrelevant to your chosen legal career, gaining such experience should still be seen as a positive part of your background. Dealing with difficult customers, being a member of a team, managing expectations, stock control, communication and organisational skills, are all elements which have helped you develop into a well-rounded individual.

**Gaps in your CV.** Recruiters are pedantic as they will notice if you fail to account for any time gaps on your CV, and may jump to negative conclusions. If you have spent time living abroad or travelling around the world after university, always be positive about your experiences, detailing the skills and benefits you gained, such as adaptability, confidence and language skills.

## Mature students

Age should never be viewed as a barrier to gaining access into the legal profession. Most mature students have some concerns about how their application will be viewed by prospective employers. However, mature students should focus on the added skills and experience gained in a previous career, which naturally gives you a clear advantage over younger applicants.

Some of us at the Ultimate Guide trained with people who were in their 30's and 40's who had previous careers. These colleagues informed us that they had to carefully consider the decision to change careers. We found those colleagues were extremely focused on embarking on a legal career. Changing the course of your career and therefore your, and perhaps your family's, life direction is a huge decision and to consider re-training as a solicitor brings added challenges with the cost of legal training.

Our older colleagues  informed us that many firms appreciated their mature, calm and serious approach, and as a result, they were able to have extremely engaging conversations based on what they had done with their lives up to that point, because many law firms place a great deal of value in having such experience. The challenge for mature students is researching and finding out which firms are really "right" for them.

**Our Top Tip: Carefully consider a firm that will embrace your life experience and the skills gained from a previous career. Select a firm that offers a good legal career together with a flexible work/life balance. It will also be interesting to note the implications of the recent Age discrimination legislation on law firm selection of mature students.**

# JOHN LAW

42 Hardy Road, Harrow, Middlesex, HA5 3ED
Tel: 020 8866 1657   **Mobile** 07999 006 000
E-mail Training-Contract@please.com   Date of Birth 25th August 1982

**EDUCATION**

**1998 to 2001** London University
LLB (Hons) Law (2: I)

**1996 to 1998** Kensington College, London
A-Levels Sociology (A) Business Studies (A) History (B)

**1992 to 1996** South Harrow High School,
GCSEs - 9 A-C passes 5 grade As and 4 Bs including English, Mathematics, Science and French

## LEGAL WORK EXPERIENCE

**Dec 2002 to Jan 2003**

**International law firm, Singapore**
• Extensive document management, proof-reading profiles to verify the accuracy of client information, organising files into bundles and liaising with assistants and partners.

**Sept 2001 to Sept 2002**

**Magic circle firm, London, England**
Worked in communications department with data input and administrative responsibility.
• Dealing with enquiries and assisting fee earners with legal research,
• Compiling documents to track recent legislative developments that have implications for commercial lawyers.
• Managed and maintained the department's knowledge management system and updated the commercial intranet pages.
• Produced a monthly commercial law newsletter on current awareness.
• Reviewed press articles concerning transactions and key clients.

**Sept 2001**

**ABC Legal services**
• Spent three months shadowing the property partner in this medium-sized commercial firm of 20 partners.
• Attended client meetings, prepared briefings for partner in charge and liaised with clients.

**Aug 2000**
**4 weeks**

**XYZ, London**
Vacation placement - I was involved in preparation for litigation. The work involved researching various points of law to assist a solicitor draft client letters. I held client meetings and attended court for pre-judgment hearings.

## COMMERCIAL WORK EXPERIENCE

**July 2000 – Feb 20**

**LDF Food Catering Ltd - Position: Sales Consultant**
Part-time job - working for a food supplier with an annual turnover

of approximately £1.2 million.
- Co-ordination of twice yearly budgets in conjunction with sales, marketing and supply chain.
- Monitoring and maintenance of sales and stock system.
- Production of customer and product profitability information, i.e. relevant costs and revenue, pricing, and stock checking.
- Monitoring sales and marketing expenditure (£50,000 budget) and general overheads.

| | |
|---|---|
| **July 2000** | **(Name of Investment bank), New York Office (internship)** |
| | Gained experience and understanding of investment banking and capital market departments. Shadowed traders in the emerging markets division, futures and securities floors. Attended seminars on on bonds and derivatives to develop my commercial awareness. |
| **ACHIEVEMENTS/ AWARDS** | • 2001 Winner of Investors of People in History tertiary award<br>• 2000 Under 18's Amateur Tennis champion<br>[Use 2-3 examples from school, university or work. Choose more recent experience where possible and use examples that are as unique as possible.] |
| **SKILLS** | **Language**: Fluent French<br>IT skills, including use of legal databases and the internet for research, knowledge of MS Word, Excel, PowerPoint, Outlook.<br>Professional skills, interviewing, staff management, basic accounting, budgeting and sales forecast for business.<br>Driving – full licence. |
| **EXTRA CURRICULAR ACTIVITIES** | *Sport*: Football – University first team / Tennis competed in local amateur (singles and doubles tournaments), represented London Tennis foundation.<br>*Music*: Play lead guitar in a band. Often attend concerts.<br>Enjoy theatre and cinema, with interest in international filmography<br>*Mooting and Debating*: Member of debating society and law faculty mooting competitions.<br>*Travel* – Travelled widely, including; visits to Accra and Beijing. |
| **REFEREES** | Academic Title (Department)    Professional<br>Address                                      Address<br>Email/Phone number               Email/Phone number |

## More useful Do's and Don'ts

Avoid the basic errors. One in three applications gets rejected because of spelling mistakes or some other elementary error. It seems obvious but you must avoid making mistakes such as crossing outs, inaccurate spellings, missing signatures and cut and paste errors, which have been known to include references to other firms, a result of the amount of other applications the applicant has made. Remember that accuracy and attention to detail are key skills for a lawyer. Check that you have the correct name of the firm you are applying to. CV and covering letters must be well checked. You have to remember that when interviewers are short-listing candidates, they are only likely to spend a minute considering your CV, so ensure that you have had it checked over by a friend.

✓ Make your CV readable. Choose a clear format and font which is easily legible. Use clear white or cream paper.

✓ Use heading and bullet point to make the lay-out as neat as possible. However, avoid a checklist-like format. Give interesting examples and put yourself in the shoes of the reader when thinking about the way in which to set out your achievements.

✓ Another thing, do not try to be funny or claim inspiration from *Law & Order* or *Kavanagh QC* in your covering letter. It may be your intention to amuse, but unless you want the position as stand-up comedian at the firm's Christmas party, avoid it! Training contracts are in huge demand which makes choosing candidates a numbers game. If you are not serious about your CV and covering letter, law firms will not be serious about you.

✓ Avoid gimmicks. It may seem adventurous, but refrain from attempting any exciting presentational techniques. Although your CV is your personal brochure, remember you are attempting to enter the legal profession. We've heard stories of people sending out applications on luminous paper! Needless to say, they did not get called to interview

✓ Think about the impression your interests leave with the reader. Remember, not everybody will share your political, religious or social concerns.

✓ Do not send photographs of yourself unless explicitly requested.

✓ Do not lie. It may be a criminal offence and you will be sacked if your lie is subsequently discovered.

✓ Do not use worthless adjectives. Describing yourself as a dedicated team player on its own will not get you very far. Use good examples to back yourself.

✓ Pay attention to closing dates. Some firms only accept applications during the early summer window, while others are more flexible, receiving applications throughout the year. Basic information on firms that interest you should be found on their websites.

✓ It is vital that you maximise the impact of your CV and covering letter. There are no second chances in any given year to apply for a training contract. Even the most able and talented will need CVs which stand out.

✓ Avoid the scatter-gun approach, by resisting the temptation to send off scores of replica covering letters, hoping that someone will interview you. There are plenty of firms out there for you to short-list from, and there's a fair chance you will be wasting your time by shooting off loads of applications without an aim.

✓ Find the right type of firm for you (see chapter 4) and build your CV to reflect this. It is a matter of concentrating your focus on the area you are passionate about, including, tailoring your interests to suit those practice areas of the firm.

✓ Follow instructions carefully, do exactly what the firms tell you to do. There's no point sending in a CV and covering letter if the firm has asked you to apply on-line.

✓ Take advice from other people with relevant experience. Get them to look over your CV and covering letter and give you their comments then incorporate these to the extent that you can.

✓ Lastly, in your interview be prepared to justify and elaborate on the things you have mentioned on your CV and in your covering letter.

---

## Improving your CV and covering letters: Points to Ponder

Before you'll even be invited to sit in the interview hot seat, you will have to make an impression on your prospective employer. From the hundreds of applications law firms receive, your CV will have to stand out in order to avoid the recycling bin. In this chapter you have seen how to write a winning CV and covering letter including:

• how to structure your CV and covering letter

• examples of successful CV and covering letters

• the kinds of things you should be including in your CV to draw the readers interest

• top CV and covering letter tips

• how to find a winning formula for your CV and covering letter

• how to avoid the common mistakes that lead to rejection

• how to tailor your letter and CV to the job.

Chapter Eleven

## Application forms

Training contract application forms are very important as they determine whether or not you will make it to the interview stage. Application forms are one of life's necessary chores for an aspiring trainee solicitor and they cause a lot of anxiety amongst aspiring solicitors. We always thought application forms were akin to doing a piece of coursework with the time pressure of handing it in before the deadline. However, it is worth remembering that applications have to be of a very high standard in order to be invited for an interview. This is because graduate recruitment will be accountable to the partners of the law firm's business for the calibre of applicants that they put forward for the training contract selection process.

Many applicants often find these forms difficult to begin, generally because some of the questions are stretching and challenging to answer, but the majority of applicants start completing the forms before they have actually carried out a sufficient amount of research on the law firm. Research and preparation is a key part of completing top-level application forms. With only a small fraction of applicants actually reaching the interview stage means it is easy for law firms to find a reason to reject a candidate. For this precise reason, your form needs to stand out from the rest.

Many of the principles described in Chapter 10 apply to application forms. The question you should be asking yourself here is: What makes a strong application? Many applicants do not get through the first stage of selection because they have not made sufficient effort with their application form. Getting the application form spot-on is the only way you will stand any chance of getting to the interview stage.

### Getting the basics right

Before you start, check that you can meet the deadlines that most law firms set for submitting their application forms. The key to a good application form is getting all the basics spot on. We cannot emphasise this enough. Attention to detail is a pre-requisite skill for a lawyer, so spelling, punctuation or grammatical errors must be avoided. The accuracy of your written communication skills is just so important, and your application form must reflect this. Any such basic mistakes will land your form straight in the bin! If you are writing to a specific contact, spell the name correctly - an obvious point but do double-check. Don't allow your application to be binned for something this minor.

Aim to photocopy the blank form and complete a rough draft first before doing the real thing. Although you will spend longer on the form, you will reduce the chance of making major errors. You will see how the space can be maximised and it will be easier for neatness to copy from a form you have already completed.

Read through instructions twice and note any key questions. A major gripe for many law firms, are those applicants who do not follow specific instructions. Read instructions carefully, the application forms for the majority of law firms are now online, but if a firm requires you to submit a paper-based application, always use black ink. Try to remember to complete all sections of the application form, because sections can be easily overlooked. Here are some other useful tips:

- If you are asked not to send a covering letter but still do, despite all your other efforts, law firms will not be impressed by this inability to follow clear instructions.

- Read between the lines and identify exactly what the question is asking for. Note which questions overlap and look at the amount of space allowed for each question which may indicate the importance of the question to the selection criteria.

- When completing application forms try to avoid regurgitating material from a firm's brochure, and the firm's website; this will fail to impress the graduate recruiters. You will make your application shine by personalising your answers, and using specific examples in your answers that will evidence the vast research you would have invested when preparing your application. Remember that, graduate recruiters will judge each application on its own merits.

- List the skills criteria required and ensure you include examples that demonstrated these skills. Choose examples from the last three years to make your answers as relevant as possible; it's also easier to remember the details.

- Be yourself and let your personality resonate through your application form. Avoid using humour because not everybody will share your sense of humour.

- Do not use abbreviations or any jargon.

- Always keep a photocopy of the completed form to refer to if you get an interview, and also for future reference purposes.

- Carefully select your referees. It is vital that they are people who will provide glowing accounts of your strengths and potential to be a top lawyer. Ask your referees' permission before you give their details.

**Our Top Tip: From our experience, you will have an advantage if you send the application forms to the firms as early as possible. Law firms start scheduling interview dates as and when the forms reach them. It is harder to get an interview in the closing stages of a recruitment drive when graduate recruiters have hundreds upon hundreds of forms in front of them and there are only a handful of interviews. Every firm is different, but as a guideline look to start applying as soon as the firm opens its applications process.**

**Things you might think about researching before tackling your application form:**

✓   The firm's key selection criteria

✓   The firm's values, culture and mission statement
✓   Areas of law the firm practises

✓   Who are the firm's clients?

✓   What does day-to-day work involve?

✓   Will the firm require commercial work experience?

✓ Any deals or topical issues relating to the firm that you can discuss coherently.

## Tackling the application form

Never start an application form before you are properly equipped to start it. This means:

✓ Firstly doing your research and preparation on the firm as described above. Vast amounts of research is required when completing top-level application forms, and you must consider precisely what type of candidate the firm is looking for.

✓ Thinking about presentation.

✓ Examining your life and your relevant experiences.

✓ Having a clear idea of the information you want to get across.

✓ Analysing your own qualities and drafting answers which best fit the questions you are being asked.

✓ Taking your time - a good application form may take days to complete. You may have to leave the form and come back to it with fresh eyes.

✓ Watching for deadlines – get your form in as early as possible.

✓ Keeping a photocopy of every application you make.

## Researching a firm

There are many ways to research a firm. Your careers service would be a very good start. Do not take this service for granted. There is a wealth of information and resources to be gleaned from it. Most have helpful leaflets crammed full of hints and tips which just might help you through the application process. You can even book an appointment to have your form looked over by an experienced careers adviser. Some careers services provide access to students who have recently been successful in applying for jobs at your chosen firm, and you can find out how they made their application work. Ascertain what they wrote in their application forms in order to get the interview, then mirror their positive techniques coupled with your unique selling points. Even if you have left university recently, you should still be able to gain access to your former careers service.

A law firm's website will give you lots of important information and in particular an indication of the firm's entry criteria. Also, bear in mind that further hints are often found in the trainee profiles and in the kind of work that the firm specialises in. You might also want to look in general directories such as Chambers and Partners or the Training Contract Handbook. These books can be used for general reference and will give you an insight, sometimes from a trainee's perspective, about a particular firm.

## Presentation

Presentation is another key factor: The application form should be neat. Online applications should use a consistent font, which is professional and the text should be justified. On paper based applications - practise writing the form so you can avoid using tip-ex or crossing out words, and endeavour to keep your answers within the space provided. Never fall into the habit of thinking you need to fill up all the blank space available. It is often more presentable to leave a small gap after the end of your last sentence.

✓ If you are given a box in which to provide your answer, never write over the lines.

✓ Achieving the desired presentation may require you to recreate the space you are given on rough paper and to tweak your answer to fit the space.

✓ Aim to encourage the reader to read your application. This does not mean filling the page with pretty doodles. Make sure the writing is legible and the spacing clear. If you know your handwriting is bad use block capitals. Nobody, including you, would bother to read 1 of 2000 applications if it is badly written.

## How to sell yourself on paper

Many firms receive thousands of applications for training contracts each year and can tell when an applicant has done their research about the firm. They look for well-rounded candidates, so although good academic results are important, students with a broad range of interests, positions of responsibility, a proficiency in foreign languages, and achievements will stand you in good stead.

A successful applicant will be able to sell themselves on paper. This will depend on your understanding of exactly what the firm look for in their selected candidates i.e. the ability to work out what employers want to see and then select those aspects of yourself and your experience that best fit with that employer. Aim to articulate the skills you learnt from it and how they relate to the role in question, how you improved your communication skills, worked under pressure, and dealt with difficult situations - skills that employers want you to have. This is not difficult to do if your application form is well thought out.

Step into the employers shoes by finding out what the firm and their lawyers are all about, and tailor your application to show how your experience and skills put you in a good position to meet their needs. Focus on what you believe you can offer the firm. The key is to use the best examples you have and talk about them in a way that shows you have considered what the question is asking. When the graduate recruitment team read your application form they look for more than just fulfilling the minimum criteria, they are looking for people who stand out. The best way you can achieve this is by analysing your own skills and becoming aware of how the firm can develop them.

Know what is happening within the firm you're applying to. A firm in a phase of expansion is likely to be a more dynamic and exciting place to work than one which is downsizing and losing clients. Search for press coverage to see if there is anything significant to note when you are in the process of completing your applications.

## Examine your life and communicate self-awareness in application forms.

*After a presentation at a career fair a Graduate Recruitment partner at a top city firm once explained to me that when applying at law firms, "there is an art to looking smart!" I asked what he meant and was swiftly told to focus on what I had learnt the most from life's experiences and what motivated me. He then proceeded to launch a combination of questions in rapid succession. Why do you want to be a lawyer? Why this firm? What work experience do you have? Why should the firm choose you? The barrage of questions was overwhelming. I felt like I'd been hit by a boxer! As I staggered up to beat the 10 count, I knew that in order to be convincing I had to understand exactly what the firms wanted from me. I knew that I would need to demonstrate these attributes and I would need to learn to do that soon.*

### Justin Deveraux – a trainee solicitor

The questions posed to Justin are just some of those that recruiters may ask during interviews, and you will be judged on your answers to these questions, alongside other elements, including whether the recruiters see you as a person who has the personal attributes that they look for in candidates.

Most application forms will be broken down into sections. Analyse your life experiences according to these sections and write down as many examples that you can. By using this method, you will be able to draw upon the best examples that you can think of. Brainstorming in this way may trigger an example that you can talk about with passion at the interview.

**A key tip to boosting your employability is to personalise your answers on your application forms.** This will make it more original, well thought out and memorable for the interviewers. Also, bear in mind that your answers must be specifically relevant to a future trainee solicitor's role. Recruiters are looking for good candidates who can express themselves articulately. They get rather bored with the same old generic responses lifted from form to form so it is important to make yourself standout with personalised answers.

### What is your greatest achievement: (brain storm method)
✓ Teaching English in Cambodia
✓ Planning a group trip across seven continents
✓ Setting up my own pro bono initiative

✓   Winning mooting competition at university
✓   Setting up my own music events management company

The essential thing is to pick an example that you can make sound exciting and extraordinary. Imagine your best example as something very few other people would have done.

*The best examples I could think of were the ones that were most unique to my life experiences. I analysed myself and spent time analysing the firm I was applying to and used experiences which I felt were unlikely to be matched by other people. When I was confronted with a question that asked for examples of teamwork, I used the brainstorming method. I noted down three examples of my teamwork ability.*

- *A project while on a vacation scheme at a law firm*
- *A team assault course on an adventure weekend*
- *Working on a construction project in West Africa*

*In my answer, I chose to talk about working on the construction project in West Africa. Although I could have used the other examples, when I expanded on what they actually involved, this example most highlighted the difficulties we faced working as a team and how we solved these problems, which brings other skills into play. Although the firm had asked me to talk about teamwork specifically, I knew I could also relate this experience to other skills which were relevant to a trainee's role. Every team needs a leader, an organiser, etc. I knew this would be easy to talk about at interview and I would be able to talk about it enthusiastically as it was a very exciting project. The great thing about this approach is that no matter what question you're asked you already have a rough idea of what you might say.*            **K.O.B, trained at magic circle law firm**

One step on from this is to use a Mind Map and write lists of things which best describe each category, e.g. your strengths and achievements. Expand on this by thinking about which ones can provide a unique selling point or which ones are most zany or more interesting. Identify areas among these sections where you have really excelled. This way you will be able to select the best examples to fit, rather than merely putting down your initial thoughts. Also consider the skills the firms look for as discussed above, use buzz words like budgeting, forecasting, initiative, negotiate and this will help you come across well in your application form.

Here is a list of adjectives, verbs and a noun which will help you to brainstorm and organise your thoughts about the buzz words to use in your applications:

Appraised   Achieved   Assessed   Balanced   Budgeted

Communicate   Co-ordinated   Creative   Commercial

Determined   Driven   Dedicated   Delegated

Evaluated   Exceeded   Established   Experienced

Formulated   Implemented   Initiated   Involved

Liaised   Managed   Meetings   Motivated

Negotiated   Organised   Oversaw   Planned

Prioritised   Persuaded   Promoted   Scheduled

Succeeded   Strategise   Time-management

The table below may help you to remember and list things which you can later put down on your application form. The areas where you rate yourself less than 8 out of 10 are the areas you should be focusing on and working to improve:

| MY LIFE | My rating out of 10 | Examples | What I learned from the experience? How to improve? | Outcome success Achievement |
|---------|---------------------|----------|-----------------------------------------------------|------------------------------|
| Academic Profile | | | | |
| Personal achievement/ Positions responsibility | | | | |
| Teamwork | | | | |
| Personal qualities/ attributes (communication leadership skills) | | | | |
| Activities and interests (social) | | | | |
| Work experience /Jobs | | | | |
| Career aspirations Why are you applying? Short/medium /long-term goals. | | | | |
| Commercial awareness | | | | |
| Travel | | | | |

## Making the application easy to read

Aim to make your past experiences and achievements sound interesting. Avoid wordiness and be as succinct as possible. Remember you have limited space so every sentence must be crucial to your answer. Why waste five lines talking about something you could have dealt with in a sentence?

Use key words – do not seek to tell the reader what their criteria are or use the same adjectives found on their website without backing yourself up with concrete examples. The best examples are always those where you talk about specific incidents and relate it them to the given criteria.

Before you let your form leave your sight, have someone read it over for you. They may be able to spot mistakes you may have missed or advise you on how to phrase something better, including any over-elaborate use of language (which is another common reason for applications being discarded). Ask your tutor, and careers advisor or even friend for advice. No matter how pleased we were with our application forms, a fresh pair of eyes always helped us to improve our efforts.

## On-line applications

A growing number of firms are moving towards a centralised system for on-line applications. They are quicker and easier for the firm, but may not be easier for you in the sense that on-line applications require just as much preparation and thought as paper ones.

Download the application and draft it off-line in Word before you go on-line to send it, the security of having saved drafts will prevent losing hours of work and you can also cut and paste your answers from Word. Do not rush your application form even if you are pressed to meet an impending deadline, it is a recipe for making errors, only click to submit when you are fully happy.

**Our Top Tip: Use language cautiously. Be sure to incorporate those key buzz words in to the application forms, i.e skills which employers are looking for. You should know this from your extensive research. It has been suggested that some employers use software**

**packages, which scan applications for words and phrases they consider most relevant.**

## A note of caution when completing your application forms

One word of warning before you get going: graduate recruitment managers frequently inform us of their dislike of seeing applications which seem too general and not specific to their particular firm. One cause of this is students thinking they can complete more applications by using the same bog-standard answers and merely substituting one firm's name with another. Applicants often make the mistake of using a standard application and not changing the name of the firm which they previously applied to. This invariably results in an instant rejection, and is clearly not the way to achieve interview success! Graduate recruitment departments read so many applications they become easily able to detect naïve and ill-prepared students who adopt this approach to filling in their forms, without taking the time to ensure their answers are sufficiently tailored to each respective firm.

Ensure you display your extensive research into the firm on your application. You will have a better chance of gaining an interview by applying to a smaller number of select firms and spending time devising your answers to the questions. Aim to make the most of every application. It is important to remember that each application form is unique. Rather than making blanket applications as to hundreds of firms, we advise that you decide on what kind of firm you want to train with and then focus your applications to those firms in the same group, or similar strength in areas of expertise that really interest you.

## Finding your own formula

Filling out applications will prove a learning process for most students. After a few applications, your forms will become more finely-tuned. Once we began to receive offers for interviews we realised what worked for us, and what did not. Below, we take you through some typical questions you may find on application forms and provide some suggested answers to make this process a little easier for you.

It is your job to show the firm that you match if not exceed their criteria. Armed with your new list of skills and experiences from brainstorming and mind mapping, this should now be so much easier. However, be realistic. If there are requirements you do not match up to, for example, you have fewer UCAS points than required, you may be wasting your time by sending the application. However, if you have mitigating circumstances or are very strong on other areas why not pick up the phone and give graduate recruitment a call? Our research shows that HR departments are honest about your chances of gaining an interview if you fall short on certain criteria. Naturally some firms are more flexible than others.

If you haven't seen any application forms yet, here are examples of the type of questions you will come across. Start mind mapping, brainstorming and making those lists!

✓ What has been your biggest personal achievement?

✓ How have you approached your career choice?

✓ What has made you apply to the firm? How well have you researched our firm?

✓ What attracts you to a career as a solicitor? Are you committed to law?

✓ Why do you want to work for [XYZ firm]?

✓ Why do you believe you will be a good solicitor?

✓ How do you think the role of a solicitor has changed over the last five years?

✓ Describe an occasion where you worked in a group to achieve a goal. What was your role? Are you a team player?

✓ What is your proudest moment to date and why?

✓ Which film role would you most like to have played and why?

✓ How would you market the firm to a potential client?

Describe a major challenge you have faced, how you responded to overcome the challenge and what you learned from it?

✓     If you could introduce one change to the law, to make a difference in society, what legislation would it be and why?

✓     What three words would your friends use to best describe you and why?

✓     What qualities do you possess and how would these qualities assist you to become a successful lawyer?

## Structuring your answer

1.     Put the example into context by jotting down the reason you believe the firm are asking that particular question and the skills they might be looking for.

*Read and re-read the questions asking yourself: What is the firm really asking me?, so you answer the question being asked and use examples to illustrate your points? Sometimes you have to demonstrate your skills of analysis in actually deciphering the question by reading behind what the question appears to be asking you. Consider the law firms skills criteria and what this particular question relates to. Carefully consider the question and plan your answers carefully and logically. Remember the job of a lawyer is to draft professional documents of an accurate and high standard. The only evidence the recruiter will have to judge this skill is, in your application form.*

2.     Construct an answer detailing what tasks you actually undertook, including the challenges you faced and overcame. How did overcoming this problem enable you to achieve/ convince / overcome / organise? You must be clear in referring your answer to the specific question. Outline the key skills you want to get across, such as your willingness to lead the group and motivate others.

3.     What was the outcome? Whatever the example is, make sure you <u>achieved</u> something so you can discuss your experiences at the interview.

4.     Do not just list activities indicate how you used your skills portfolio during your personal experiences: teamwork,

organisation, communication and interpersonal skills, commercial savvy, enthusiasm, common sense and sense of humour to deliver positive results for the team.

5.    Finally, proof-read your answer, and edit your draft where necessary. You can make it punchy by using numbered headings and sub-headings to make it easier for graduate recruitment to read your answers. This will also show you already think like a lawyer in being able to communicate your thoughts clearly and effectively.

Look at the following examples of how you could structure your answers and notice the difference between the examples likely to get a rejection and those likely to win an interview:

**Q. Describe a recent team working experience, what role did you play and why?**

*Answer likely to get a rejection:* I helped shelve books in the departmental library. I organised the categorising of books and completed the task in half the time I had been allocated.

*Answer likely to win an interview:*
As the Academic Officer of my university Law Society, my role was to organise events for the law students in our faculty. This position entailed participating in many team work situations, including; the organisation and co-ordination of a second hand book sale. This was a real challenge for the team, as we had to persuade students' to firstly look for books they no longer used and secondly, bring them into university for the book sale. I appointed 5 salespeople and they proved successful in managing to encourage people to part with their books. I suggested that if students realised the money generated by the book sale would be going to a good cause ie to X charity? They would see the bigger picture and the philanthropic nature of our project would convince them to be charitable.

I was willing to accept the responsibility of being team leader. I adopted this role because I am passionate about the value books can bring to the lives of others, and I had been determined to motivate others in helping to organise the collection of books, the actual sale and all the jobs to complete the process after the sale. The event was marketed in a multitude of ways including; e-mails, posters, promotional cards and announcements at lectures. I chaired meetings to brainstorm ideas with the rest of the team. I delegated tasks and liaised with other members of the team to ensure everything was going according to plan. I set up room bookings, created spread sheets for data collection and calculated how much money was due to each student. I single-handedly set up a plan of action, and allocated roles for each team member. I was the first point of contact for students as well as team members when queries arose. I continually liaised with the head of the Law faculty to keep her updated on the progress of our collective effort at all times.

*The Skills I developed (showcase all your skills – use buzzwords).* This experience developed my team working skills, enhanced my time management and interpersonal skills, by ensuring each team member had been involved and felt they were contributing to a significant cause. This helped each member of the team deliver their duties within the deadline set. I enjoyed budgeting, prioritising, and taking initiative to help drive the project from conception to completion. I also demonstrated an entrepreneurial attitude in persuading many of the students to give their books for free or at a nominal price. During the book sale, I managed to sell 1,000 books which enhanced my communication skills. We made a profit of £2,768 and it would not have been possible without the whole team's involvement.

**Our Top Tip:**
✓ **Describe your achievements.**
✓ **Do not just state what you do.**

**Q. What is you main extra-curricular activity?**

This question is looking for an insight into your personality, and is also analysing your ability to provide a clear and well-structured answer.

***Answer likely to get a rejection:*** I enjoy playing football very much and used to be captain of the school side.

***Answer more likely to win an interview:*** I am extremely passionate about sport which enables me to display my determination to succeed. I captained the university football team for four years and led them to an unprecedented 11/11 wins. We retained the Borough Cup and we won the league on two occasions. As a result we were sponsored by X to go on tour to Toronto, Canada for an international tournament. My role as team leader enhanced my communication, organisation, influencing and motivation skills. It also helped me to keep fit and have some fun during a demanding degree course.

## Q. Why do you want to work for us?

***Answer likely to get a rejection:*** I read somewhere that the firm is top in its field.

***Answer likely to win an interview:*** I would to spend my future career with [XYZ firm] for the following reasons: I attended a talk at my university given by John Greene, the senior partner from your corporate department. I was impressed by the firm's incredible achievements in 2008, in what was a downturn in most markets. This led me to carry out further research into the firm's reputation on Legal 500, The Lawyer and Vault. I was interested to read that the firm has been acting for X Co. a major client in its recent high-profile acquisition of Y Co. The commercial implications of this deal are far-reaching for the company and the wider telecommunications industry.

I also thoroughly enjoyed my vacation placement at the firm. This led me to believe that a career with [XYZ firm] will provide high quality training with broad-based work. I will be working with and learning from excellent solicitors. I will also be working in a culture that is friendly, and supportive. This will foster a learning environment which is conducive to having a successful, interesting and rewarding career.

## Our Top Tip:
✓ **Show that you came to the decision in a logical and carefully planned way.**
✓ **Demonstrate your strong interest for working at that particular law firm. You can do this by raising a matter about the firm which you have researched, e.g. recent transactions their major clients have been involved in.**
✓ **Highlight any activities you have done which support your application to a specific firm.**

✓ **Have you met anyone from the firm? Perhaps mention this on the application.**

**Q. What has been your biggest personal achievement?**

***Answer likely to get a rejection:*** I set up my own business making model aeroplanes. The experience was extremely satisfying.

***Answer likely to win an interview:*** After rigorous research I was able to exploit a gap in the market and set up my own business, making model aeroplanes. From an initial investment of £10 I had a turnover of £1,800 in one year.

**Our Top Tip:**

✓ **Use facts and figures to show the extent of your achievement.**
✓ **Use appropriate examples, e.g. gaining a scholarship to read law at university:**
✓ **Did you organise an event? How many people attended? Did you set up your own business? How much money did you make? Did you start your own pro bono initiative?**

**Examples**

Below are a few examples demonstrating how we would go about answering questions on an application form. You will need to consider how succinct you need to be given the spacing on the application form.

**Q. Describe an interesting situation, apart from a formal moot or debate, in which you had to persuade others of your point of view in order to achieve an objective**.

As the commercial director of a Young Enterprise Business scheme, I persuaded team members to take on board innovative ideas for marketing our product on MySpace. This proved a difficult task as there was disparity in the group. The group had split into two opposing camps in line with their views as to the most effective marketing strategy for the project. I handled this situation by asking the group to consider the bigger picture, because I was very conscious that our target deadline was fast approaching.

I analysed the situation carefully and considered that the best way forward was to approach the opposing two sides of the camp separately in order to ascertain their thoughts on the project. This enabled me to prepare cogent reasons for the methods I believed would work successfully. I then called an emergency meeting in order for the matter to be resolved. I allotted time for each individual to express their views, and the team as a whole discussed the advantages and disadvantages of each separate marketing strategy. I managed to persuade the team to adopt my point of view, because I had listened intently to the views of each member of the group and incorporated some of their excellent ideas where possible and thought through every suggestion which had been put forward beforehand. As a direct result, each member felt their input was recognised, valued and respected. We met our deadline and enjoyed success at the company's trade fair by managing to make our product very popular, and also generated a healthy commercial return on our initial investment.

**Comment: This answer was well structured. It outlines clearly the applicant's leadership role by influencing other team members through a commercial decision-making process and careful consideration of the impending deadline and the bottom-line of a commercial return on their original investment.**

### Q. What do you do best? Give some examples and explain why.

I have often been described as determined, and I believe I am best at setting myself goals and achieving them. In school, I was determined to excel in sport and worked hard towards this. From 1993 to1995, I captained the football team and was awarded a trophy for rugby player of the year. In this season I was also selected for the Middlesex County Rugby trials.

I had always wanted to speak a modern language and chose German. My determination to be fluent in the language combined with my strong interest in the legal profession took me on an international legal work placement to a law firm in

Cologne, Germany. This experience not only gave me greater aptitude for the language, but I was also able to appreciate the workings of another legal system, and provided a useful insight into a European office environment.

I have set myself the goal of achieving in public speaking and have so far managed to attain a grade 5. I was runner-up in the Northwood and Ruislip competition 2006. At university, I frequently participated in debating and mooting and I am proud of being on the winning side of every moot that I have participated in. I was also selected to sit as a judge in the university debating final, where I had to give a report along with my final decision on the winner.

**Comment: This is a sound answer as the applicant promotes their strengths and provides examples to support their skills-set through their sporting activities, proficiency in foreign languages and developing their capabilities in public speaking. The applicant discusses their achievements which will undoubtedly appeal to the firm.**

**Q. Please give a recent example of a team in which you have been involved. What was your role? What challenges did you face?**

At Pike Solicitors, I was a team member of a Know-how Management task force. In January 2007, I was selected to travel alone to Milan, to represent the London office as part of the firm's ongoing process of sharing its wealth of knowledge and information. My job was to convey the benefits of having a Know-how database and encourage lawyers to submit new material. I encountered two challenges; firstly, that Italian was often spoken in the office, and secondly, having to adapt to the different office culture. I overcame this by utilising my A-level Italian, being versatile and utilising my interpersonal skills.

**Comment: Prospective trainees who display an ability to work effectively as a team are the applicants most likely to impress recruiters. It is interesting that this candidate comments so honestly on the factors that hindered her personal effectiveness and how she overcame them. The**

role she describes is very relevant to the job she is applying for.

**Q. Describe a recent situation (from beyond your academic experience) where you have demonstrated motivation and initiative.**

Three years ago I set up an events management organisation. The biggest event I have staged to date was a New Year's event in London, which attracted 3000 revellers. I head a team of four which I put together at university to organise and co-ordinate weekly events in London. After only two events we recovered our initial investment. On average we made £500 profit weekly. Running the day-to-day activities of the business proved challenging and fulfilling work. I have recently merged my organisation with a fellow events organiser, allowing us to diversify into other music genres. My legal background helped me draft the agreement. I am teaching myself Microsoft Front Page in order to construct the company's website.

**Comment: This candidate displays commercial nous in abundance as well as the motivation to complete tasks to the best of their ability. They also state initiative by describing how they managed to set up the business. Recruiters are impressed by students who use their extra-curricular time constructively.**

**Q. Describe an experience when you have been faced with a challenging situation. Explain how you dealt with it.**

In the first year of university, I joined the mooting club and debating society to overcome my fear of speaking in public. I wanted to plan an approach to overcoming the challenge and work with others who had experienced this fear. We generated some creative ideas and I implemented some innovative techniques to approach the challenge, which instilled self-confidence in communicating to a large audience. Debating and thinking quickly on my feet to formulate an argument while remaining poised and determined ensured that I managed to achieve my aims.

**Comment: A strong answer that focuses attention on key skills of a lawyer, thinking quickly on your feet and public speaking. This is a very honest answer as public speaking is a major challenge for most people, although not everybody admits it.**

**Our Top Tip: Be as succinct as possible in your answer. Use your natural writing style so the readers get an impression of you.**

## Application Record

Record the firms you have applied to for a training contract. Also track and monitor the stage/progress of each application in order to effectively manage your pursuit of that elusive training contract and to prevent yourself applying to the same place twice! When you have made 30-40 applications it is only too easy to forget about some of the firms you have applied to.

By devising a table such as the one below to monitor the progress of your applications, you will be able to maintain a clear idea of the progress of each application that you have made. You have to take ownership over the management of your career. An important first step is to keep a paper trail of all your applications.

| Date Applied | Name of firm (Size of firm) | Name of Graduate Recruitment or personal contact | Practice Areas | Outcome | Follow-up action required |
|---|---|---|---|---|---|
| 10.02.06 | Jimi's & co (Medium) | Mr Jimmy Greaves | Commercial | Interview date | Preparation |
| 17.02.06 | Brim & Brim (Large city) | Ms Kathy Black | Commercial Corp | Interview date | Preparation |
| 19.02.06 | Robemps (Medium) | Mr Bobby Best | Commercial Media | Reapply next year | Diarise |
| 26.02.06 | Mobile & Co (Large City) | Mrs Jane June | Commercial Corporate | Interview date | Preparation |
| 27.02.06 | Brewers (Medium) | Mr. Jim Jones | Commercial | Vacancies filled | Telephone contact at the firm |
| 13.03.06 | Thorpe & Co (Small) | Mr. Tony Thorpe | Media / Commercial | Interview date | Preparation |
| 20.04.06 | Barnes & Baines (Medium) | Miss Sarah Bain | Commercial | Rejection | Feedback- why rejection letter? |

If you receive any sort of positive response from a law firm, such as "re-apply next year or not currently recruiting trainees this year", you should utilise this response by asking whether the firm would be willing to consider offering you paid or unpaid work experience. This may well provide an opportunity to get your foot in the door. With so many prospective trainees competing for places, sometimes you have to think laterally and demonstrate a willingness to go that extra mile to secure training contract success.

## Rejection Letters

It can be a soul-destroying experience when you receive rejection letters from law firms. Do not take it too personally as there are many other talented aspiring solicitors receiving the very same letters as you – you're not alone!

## Interview feedback is vital

Different firms look for different attributes when selecting their trainee solicitors. If you have attended an interview, always try to contact the firm to find out why your application was unsuccessful. Continue to ask yourself which type of firms you are interested in and whether your skills match with what those particular firms look for in candidates. Be honest with yourself and evaluate where you went wrong, do not lose focus, continue to believe in yourself and get ready for the next interview opportunity. The more interviews you have, you invariably become better and more confident at performing better whilst in the hot seat.

## Perseverance

If your application did not make it to the interview stage, try and put it into perspective, you are one of many hundreds of talented applicants who have faced this hurdle. Review your applications and consider objectively whether you could improve them. The important thing is to take lessons from each rejection letter. The process will start by looking at the application form again, section by section, and asking the following questions:

✓ With hindsight, did you answer each section adequately? Is there anything in each section you can improve?

✓ Do you feel you need more work experience? For example, will your application be strengthened by finding commercial work then re-applying? Work experience is vital on an application, but is your experience really relevant to the firm to which you are applying? Working at your local law centre, for example, is very valuable experience but, if you are applying to a City firm it does not necessarily demonstrate your commitment to working in the City or that you have the requisite commercial acumen. Carefully consider how you present your work experience so that you make it relevant to the firm to which you are applying. What transferable skills did you gain from your work experience and how did it help you decide which firm you would ultimately like to work for?

✓  Were you being realistic when you applied to this firm? Should you be targeting firms with less stringent entry criteria? Should you cast your net further afield in terms of the type and location of firms you are applying to? Possibly apply to smaller firms or other firms where there is less competition for training contracts. You always have the option of moving to another firm after your training contract. Gone are the days when all lawyers spend their entire career at one firm.

✓  Do you need to seek professional advice with your applications? During your degree or CPE/LPC utilise your contacts by consulting your tutors to see if they are willing to evaluate your CV, covering letter and application forms. Your tutors may well be qualified solicitors themselves and will possess a great deal of experience and know-how to assist you in this vital stage of your career.

Finally, the key is to become **rejection-proof** and almost be indifferent to receiving rejections. Try not to get too hung up on those rejections letters as rejections and ultimately disappointment are part and parcel of life at the end of the day. We know that the road to training contract success is never easy but one must never give up trying. None of us are strangers to rejection letters from law firms. We recognise that rejection letters are difficult to accept after all the hard work you have put into striving to secure a training contract, but remember that, with perseverance, determination, dedication, focussed and effort all it takes is for one letter to arrive offering you a training contract – and you are there! Achieving a training contract is a momentous milestone in your career, so keep this thought and the hope that your day will soon come at the forefront of your mind.

You must continue to remind yourself what you have accomplished in your life, and how much of an asset you will be to your future firm! Try to control the emotional highs and lows that are inevitable in the process of searching for job in such a competitive profession. You must continue to believe in your ability and constantly look for ways of improving the level of your applications. Be confident in who you are and what you are offering, and you will eventually be successful in your pursuit of a training contract.

---

## Application Forms: Points to Ponder

As with your CV and covering letter, your application form needs to hit the right note. Thousands of applications are rejected simply on the basis that the applicant hasn't paid enough attention to getting the basics right. The application is slightly trickier because you are always given specific questions to write about and in answering these questions you need to be clear on the kind of skills law firms are asking you to display.

Essentially, you want to do three things (i) capture the reader's interest (ii) hold the reader's interest and (iii) display the skills they are looking for while remaining succinct in your answer. This chapter discusses in detail:

- Getting the basics right
- How to research firms and use the right information on your form
- When to start the form
- Focus on your life experiences and achievements
- The best way to tackle application forms
- Figuring out what the firm is really asking you
- Selling your best skills and attributes
- Thinking through the question and planning your answers carefully and logically
- Examples of how to de-code questions, answer questions and comment on the quality of the answers
- The common mistakes that often lead to rejection
- How to deal with rejection and following-up for feedback

---

Chapter Twelve

## **Succeeding at the interview**

Well done! Your application form or CV hits the spot and you are invited for an interview. Now what? Now it's time to prepare for the interview performance of your life! Interviews are often thought of as the most nerve-wracking part of the recruitment process but if you are well prepared, they can end up being quite enjoyable.

Before you get totally freaked out by the idea of being grilled by one or two of the firm's partners, bear in mind that the training contract interview is a two-way process. It is an opportunity for the firm to find out more about you but also for you to decide whether or not that firm is the one you want to work for. The fact that the firm has decided to interview you should give you a positive message – you have definitely impressed them on paper. You should use this fact to bolster your confidence but remember that the job is yours to lose if you do not demonstrate in the flesh the wonderful attributes you have described so well in your application from or on your CV.

### **"Preparation is the key - he who fails to prepare, prepares to fail"**

A good candidate will have done their homework before an interview. The better prepared you are, the higher your chances of receiving a job offer; we cannot stress enough the importance of thorough preparation. It makes a significant difference to your chances of landing the training contract. Behind your preparation should be two principles: (i) being able to get to the bottom of the skills that each firm is looking for in its prospective trainees, and (ii) realising that at the interview, by your actions and your words, you must promote your cause and sell yourself as the ideal prospective trainee. This will help you to prepare your attitude and positive approach to interviewing for a training contract.

We suggest that the first step in your preparation should be to revisit your application form and/or CV. It was this form which sparked the firm's interest in you so, go back to them and review exactly what it was that you said. Ensure that you know your CV and application form inside out. We're not talking here about memorising the names and addresses of your referees but focusing on the main areas, for example academic life, work experience and extra-curricular activities. Interviewers are likely to use your CV as a basic structure for the interview, so spend some time looking for clues to questions you may be asked.

*Those who are blessed with the best talent don't necessarily out-perform everyone else, it's the people with follow through who excel.*
**Mary Kay Ash (U.S. Business woman and Fundraiser)**

## Know yourself inside out

One of the keys to success at any interview is to know yourself inside out. Who doesn't know themselves, you may ask? You'd be surprised! Can you express succinctly and articulately your personal views on topical issues or even the things that you enjoy the most?

It sounds straightforward, doesn't it? However, having spoken to a number of interviewers when writing this guide, the number of candidates who stumble on seemingly straightforward personal questions is remarkable. Too many candidates do not take enough time before the interview to actually prepare for such questions, and are left floundering when the interview comes around and they are asked specific questions. In your training contract interview expect to be grilled on fundamental issues such as what motivates you as a person and what drives you to be successful.

Imagine you're 25 minutes into an interview, it's going extremely well, you've answered all the questions with aplomb so far, then all of a sudden the interviewer drops a question that you have never taken time to consider. For example:

*Mr Smith, you've told us what you like about the law and why you want to become a lawyer, Is there anything you don't like about the law?*

Do you panic? Obviously you need to appear calm, poised and unflappable, by saying something that is intelligent and well thought out, while making sure the answer doesn't contradict something you've said previously. Indeed, the last thing you want to mutter is something which may bring into question your dedication to work in a commercial firm.

Although many of you will be able to think quickly on your feet, how convincing and well-structured is the answer likely to be? You really don't want to blurt out the first thing that comes to mind then end up trying to defend a weak answer.

This reflects the importance of knowing yourself inside out. Had you gathered your thoughts on a particular topic before the interview, you would simply have rattled off your answer giving appropriate examples. However, because you may not have properly considered a topic, a potentially simple question becomes a tricky one which could throw your confidence and affect the rest of your performance.

In your interview you will be expected to answer straightforward questions about your likes, dislikes and the reasons behind these; all of which can be considered well in advance. You want to sound thoughtful and analytical when you give answers to this type of question because often these will be the least difficult ones you will face. If you answer such questions extremely well, your confidence to tackle the more difficult questions will increase dramatically.

**How to do it**

Look through your CV and application form and consider the types of questions you could face about the various stages of your educational attainment. Here are some examples:

Consider and analyse:

- ✓ What you liked / disliked about each stage
- ✓ Your favourite / least favourite subjects at each stage
- ✓ Your greatest personal achievement
- ✓ Your reasons for choosing a particular university
- ✓ Your reasons for not doing company law as a final year elective
- ✓ What you got out of playing chess for your school
- ✓ Why did you choose to take a gap year and teach English abroad?
- ✓ Where do you see your career heading in the next 5 or 10 years?
- ✓ What are your personal career goals?

Ask yourself why you made the choices you did. What have you gained from your experiences in terms of skills and personal development? Would you have done anything differently with the benefit of hindsight? An interviewer will almost certainly want to discuss in more depth those aspects of your application which they found most interesting.

Finally, when reading articles in newspapers about interesting transactions in the press or changes to legislation, after considering the mass of information: constantly ask yourself "Is this a good or bad thing?" followed by: "Why?" This method will assist you in organising your thoughts and coming to a reasoned conclusion, rather than attempting to do this during the interview.

## Background research for the interview

Before you go into any training contract interview, you will need to know a great deal about the firm. This means more than simply skimming the firm's website. The thorough research needed is something which can easily be prepared in advance and getting this right will mark you out as being an enthusiastic, diligent and conscientious candidate. The aim is to demonstrate that you have a very good idea of what the firm actually do, the clients the firm advises, recent deals involving those clients, the importance of those deals, and your views on why they were significant for the clients.

As part of your research you may want to find out who you will be interviewed by. Some HR departments will be willing to give you these names, and this may help you in your preparation. You'll have an indication of the type of personality you will be facing and may be able to anticipate some of the questions. Furthermore, if you find out that you have similar hobbies to the person interviewing you, this may help to establish a rapport during the interview.

The first steps in your research should be to look at the firm's website, which will contain lots of information, and follow this up by viewing websites such as Legal Week and the Lawyer (*see chapter 19 for website details*) which will highlight any interesting news about the firm in the weeks preceding your big day. Make notes on any points of interest. In terms of researching your interviewers, the website of Legal 500 contains a database of some of the partners at the leading law firms, which includes a brief biography. When thinking about the type of information you need to know about a firm, think about the following:

✓ What type of work does the firm specialise in?
✓ What type of work, if any, is the firm highly regarded in and why?
✓ What type of clients does the firm attract?
✓ Has anything major happened in the last few months that you can talk about at the interview?
✓ Has the firm won any awards?

Chambers and Partners have a ranking system on their website which gives an overview of what the firms does. Look for interesting articles on the firm. On this note, it is best to delve deeply and perhaps use more obscure examples. At the interview, these examples will set you apart from other candidates.

The second step is to find people who have either managed to secure training contracts at the firm or, even better, people who work there. These people will be able to provide you with an insight into the recruitment process. Find out if recent graduates from your university have been offered training contracts with the firm. If so, go that extra mile and make contact with them, because utilising your contacts and gaining an insight from their experiences could well prove an essential ingredient for your training contract success.

Maximise all your available resources. Check whether your university has links to any law firms from which you can get the advice of people who are trainees or associates there. Consult our useful website section (*see chapter 19*). Some of the websites we mention have regular features on various law firms which are often very informative and helpful to your career planning.

**Our Top Tip: If you know anybody at the firm you are interviewing with, get in contact and ask them to provide an insight into their experiences working for the firm. Aim to gain some background information on the people interviewing you. If you find out that the partner interviewing you is passionate about tennis and you play**

tennis, it could be a useful conversational tool to build up a rapport with the interviewer, make a connection and create a more lasting impression.

## What your prospective employer wants

Recruitment processes are built around selection criteria. There is a range of criteria that interviewers will be grading you against – the absence of even one or two of these could mean almost inevitable rejection. You can learn what your firm's skills profile might include by reading their brochure and website. Draw up a list of 7 - 10 skills you think the firm might be looking for and think about how you can demonstrate in your interview that you can bring these skills to a firm. For each of these skills, think of as many examples as you can to substantiate your attributes and be prepared to discuss them. You may have done this when preparing your application form so don't re-invent the wheel, simply build on what you already have. You may want to think about the following:

✓ **Commercial awareness** – All law firms view commercial awareness as one of the most sought after qualities in a prospective trainee solicitor. Demonstrating an understanding of the business context in which legal advice is provided will therefore prove a vital ingredient to training contract success. Candidates must also display common sense, sound judgment, maturity of thought and the ability to form a well-reasoned and cogent argument.

✓ **Good communication / interpersonal skills** are considered essential by most recruiters. Graduate recruitment tend to look for candidates who are bright, animated, friendly, lively, personable and able to articulate their thoughts in a clear and concise manner, communicating effectively as well as listening actively by asking appropriate questions. No matter how intelligent a candidate is, if they are unable to communicate coherently and confidently with people, they will be no good in front of clients and will not be given a training contract.

✓ **Leadership and teamwork skills** – It is important that you demonstrate that you are an effective team player yet are equally adept at working autonomously and independently.

✓ **Drive** – During the interview your answers should reflect your enthusiasm to work for the firm, your high energy levels, motivation, determination, stamina and dedication to succeed.

✓ There are many other personal qualities that are perceived as essential to success in the selection process, such a sense of humour, initiative, a vibrant personality, not taking yourself too seriously and establishing rapport with your interviewer.

## What the interviewers want to hear

Each time you are asked to discuss one of these skills areas, interviewers want your answer to include real concrete example, which highlight this skill. In view of this, an integral part of your preparation for an interview should be to draw up your own list of the criterion and examples from your past experiences that clearly highlight and match these personal qualities.

Interviewers are likely to find out how you feel about your career success to date, e.g. how you have handled particular situations in the past, as this will be a clear indicator of your character and how you are likely to respond to challenging situations in the future. For example, if the candidate's application form mentions leading a team, the interviewer may ask them about the easiest and most difficult aspects of that endeavour. (Preparing for easiest/hardest questions should be part of your interview preparation.)

Interviewers may be interested to know what you would do differently if you had to perform the task again. If you are a member of a rather unique club or society, or you travelled during your gap year, then you might reasonably expect the interviewer to pick up on these points and ask you further questions on these parts of your life. Even if you feel that you haven't done anything wildly exciting, something on your application form has clearly interested the law firm enough to invite you to interview. What was it? Have a go at predicting some of the questions you might be asked and carefully consider how you might be likely to respond to those questions.

One of the things you can confidently expect the interviewer to want to know is why you have decided on a career in law and what made you choose to apply to that particular firm, so research the firm thoroughly. They will only expect you to know information that is available to you, so you will impress them with your incisiveness if you have done further research.

If you are trying to convince an interviewer that you are genuinely interested in a career in law, it is important that you take time over the summer to read the newspapers, particularly the law sections, to keep up with current events in your chosen field and consider some of the issues. No interviewer will ever go for anything too obscure but they might reasonably expect you to be interested enough to follow major stories in the press. You need to be able to demonstrate that you understand what a solicitor actually does (*see chapter 2*) and that you have considered the different practice areas (*see chapter5*). For example, if you are applying to a commercial law firm, do you know what the role of the solicitor is and can you show that you are commercially aware? In summary, preparation, preparation, preparation is the key to interview success and there is really no substitute for it whatsoever. One of the most common reasons cited for a candidate's failure at interview is a lack of thorough preparation:

- ✓ Be ready to expand on any decisions you've made regarding your education and previous career moves.
- ✓ Be self-assured and confident when discussing your key achievements.
- ✓ Research the firm in great depth.
- ✓ Pay attention to the finer details of your application, because these are surely some of the intriguing features that tend to prompt questioning and a closer examination by interviewers.
- ✓ Similarly, ensure you fully understand what the role of a trainee entails.

With more experience of interviews you invariably become better equipped to handle the type of questions you will be asked, but there is always that element of surprise, so be sharp and ready!

By taking some time to consider these preparatory tips, you can approach an interview with self-conviction and let your bubbly personality do the rest. Bear in mind that no matter how well you prepare and give excellent answers, you will not build a rapport at the interview unless you exude an engaging personality.

## Practical tips for pre-interview

By far the most important thing you can do if you want to make a good impression is to look the part. Prepare your interview outfit in advance. A good tip is to choose clothes that are one step smarter than you would expect to wear if you got the job. Ensure your appearance is both smart and comfortable. Law is a conservative profession, so you need to dress accordingly.

## Dress to Impress

Dress to impress! Dress in a way which you believe will appear credible to a client. Pay attention to your grooming: The final part of your preparation should be to give some thought to what you are going to wear. You do not need to rush out to the Armani store but you do need to present yourselves as a prospective future lawyer – so you need to look the part. Your outward appearance is important to convey a positive and professional image.

Aim to look business-like and play it safe. Guys wear a dark-coloured suit, black, dark grey or navy. Make sure your hair is neat and tidy, get a trim if required. Check that your nails are clean and shoes are shining. Ladies should also wear a dark suit. Try to avoid anything too eye-catching or patterned. Shoes should be comfortable and not too high and you should not wear anything resembling sandals. Make-up is fine but keep it moderate and be understated by keeping jewellery to a minimum.

*Our Top Tip: Dress to impress! You never get a second chance to make a favourable first impression!* **Before your interview, find out what the interview process involves, if you haven't already been made aware of it. For example, find out the format of the interview. Who will be conducting the interviews? How many interviews will there be? Will you be required to undertake any psychometric testing?**

## The handshake

A handshake is the only element of physical contact that you will have. A strong but not over-bearing handshake and a natural smile complete a positive picture. The pressure of your handshake should match the interviewer's. Do not give a weak handshake even if the interviewer does, and always accompany this with eye-contact. As your interviewer introduces themselves, reciprocate by repeating their name with a greeting like: "Pleased to meet you, Ms Jenkins," and do not forget to smile. A simple acknowledgement has a large impact. If you are really nervous before your interview, hold a handkerchief to avoid proffering a clammy hand.

## Different types of interviews

**Two-to-One:** The traditional format of training contract interviews involves meeting with two partners or, one partner, and the graduate recruitment manager. This is the most typical type of interview format. The interviewers may play a good cop, bad cop routine where one will be perfectly friendly to you and the other might not say much and might ask particularly difficult questions so be aware of this possibility and don't let it faze you. Stay alert and polite, ready for the next question.

**Panel Interview:** An interview which involves more than two interviewers. The panel size is usually between 3-5 interviewers. The key difference between a panel and two-to-one interview is the balancing act of trying to maintain eye-contact with all your interviewers. Our advice is to direct your answer to the person who asked the question while "taking in" the rest of the panel. The trick is to look at the person talking to you and shift your glance from that person to the others. Not every member of the panel will be looking at you; some may be taking notes, others may seem switched off. Do not allow this to affect your confidence. Remain poised and continue to direct your attention to each panel member.

Do not expect a logical and chronological order of questioning - you may even be asked the same question more than once.

**Telephone interviews:** This type of interview is mostly used for screening purposes as a precursor to the one-to-one meeting. Be clear and precise in your answers and use plenty of intonation, you can only use your voice to be expressive. Plan and ensure you are ready for the phone call. If you are not prepared or, in the right frame of mind, to do yourself justice, re-arrange the time of the phone call. You might want to wear a suit or smart clothes which will help to get you in the right frame of mind, as opposed to rolling out of bed and doing the interview in your pyjamas!

## Double-check the interview details

On the day before the interview, double-check the date, time, and ensure you know the location of your interview. Doing a "dummy run" beforehand can often provide peace of mind and assurance before the anxious moments just prior to an interview. Make sure you know where the interview is taking place and allow yourself plenty of time to get there. Familiarise yourself with the journey to the location, to ensure you arrive in plenty of time. If driving leave early and consider any unexpected traffic. Check timetables and book train tickets in advance. Anticipate delays, especially on unknown routes. If you are going to be unavoidably delayed on the day, contact your interviewer swiftly and let them know. Ensure you familiarise yourself with the name and title of the interviewer.

Remember that you are being assessed constantly from the time you arrive at reception to the time you leave, so it is important not to let your guard down. If a current trainee at the firm is showing you around, it might not be wise to confide in them things you would not say to the interviewer. If you are offered lunch with other candidates and trainees, be careful what you say and avoid drinking excessively any alcohol that is offered. You need a clear head to be successful!

Finally, before you arrive at your interview bear in mind that you must be pleasant to everybody you meet on your interview. Any impolite or unprofessional behaviour towards any support staff, although unknown to you, may be reported to your interviewer and you may lose the job despite all your brilliant answers. Nobody wants to work with someone who lacks respect for staff members.

## The hot seat

The interview is the beginning of the real business of selection. On the day of the interview, have a read of a quality newspaper to ensure you have covered any pertinent issues that may have come to light. Allow plenty of time to get to your interview and aim to get there at least 15 minutes before so that you have time to gather your thoughts. There is nothing more likely to cause panic and anxiety than the fear that you are going to be late. Ten minutes spent in Reception will give you time to collect your thoughts and a chance to read the firm's brochures or study recent press releases. Leave yourself enough time to visit the toilet and tidy up if necessary. Use your time waiting in the Reception area to get a feel for the culture. Interviews are central to the selection process and therefore interview performance will be the deciding factor. This makes the face-to-face meeting a critical part of the recruitment process and you will need to impress from the start. It is natural for the firm to want to meet people that they may be working closely with, just as you will need to feel comfortable that you are joining a firm that is right for you.

We stress that although the training contract interviews cannot be taken lightly they should not be feared. Tough interviews can be made enjoyable with the right attitude and correct amount of preparation. The training contract interview will usually consist of two interviews. The first is typically a screening interview with graduate recruitment, and the second is usually with one or two partners, with the latter likely to be more challenging in terms of the range of questions and topics covered. At interviews candidates are expected to confirm the favourable impression that they have already made on their application form.

**"The words we choose are just 7% of the message - the content. The other 93% is made up of tone of voice, breathing, pronunciation, movement, expression and gesture."**

Research shows that recruiters form a firm impression about candidates within the first few seconds of meeting with them. First impressions largely derive from how we communicate through our body language. It is vital that you spend some time considering how you want to come across at the interview, as well as thinking of your responses to the interviewer's questions. No matter how well qualified for a job you were "on paper", the interviewer will be interested to see evidence of your personality.

Interviewers usually commence on a relaxed note, asking the candidate various warm-up questions. This is your opportunity to get rid of your nerves and build up a little rapport with the interviewer before the tough questioning starts. Questions about your journey to the interview, how your university course is going, will go towards shaping the firm's impression of you. Answer these questions well and you will feel more relaxed and comfortable.

## Confidence

Confidence and self-belief go a very long way. Many candidates will be nervous and the interviewer will try to see through this, but exuding a degree of confidence in the interview situation will enable you to stand out in the interviewer's mind. Expect a challenging interview but do not enter the room like a victim. The good news is that most of the competition has fallen by the wayside. Your academic ability is not going to be challenged (unless there are discrepancies in the consistency of your grades) and the hard part of getting your foot in the door is over. The focus is now on the whole range of personal attributes and skills that will be assessed at the interview.

Although demonstrating self-confidence is an important ingredient of training contract success, one word of warning: there is a fine line between confidence and arrogance - cross it at your peril! Confidence is the self-belief that you are talented enough to get the job. Arrogance is displaying an innate view that you are not only the one for the job but the job is already in the bag!

The key to success at the interview is recognising the deeply subjective nature of your meeting and turning this to your advantage. Your approach should mirror the strategies taught in How to win Friends and Influence People **by Dale Carnegie** – be as charming as you possibly can and avoid saying anything which could be construed as arrogant. The interviewer is not looking for ways to catch you out; they want to like you, so be prepared to talk about whatever they are interested in. It is not in their interest to give you too harsh a time because news of unfair and unreasonable interviewing practices spreads quickly.

## Interview nerves

You wouldn't be human if you didn't feel a little nervous and anxious before your time in the hot seat, but this can work in your favour. When the adrenalin is pumping it can make you sharper. However, excessive anxiety has the potential to affect the nerves of even the most competent of interviewees, and interviews are not naturally the most relaxed of activities. But as long as you do enough preparation you should be confident of being able to deliver, and do yourself justice and really increase your chances of being identified as the best applicant for the job. If you have prepared thoroughly for an interview, it shouldn't be too nerve-wracking when you get to the interview itself. Here are some tips that have helped us to combat interview nerves in the past.

## Get a good night's sleep

Try to follow your normal routine before your interview to ensure a decent night's kip, whether that means soaking yourself in a hot bath, reading yourself to sleep or going to sleep with your favourite childhood toy by your side. Listening to your favourite music can help relax, keep you positive and uplifted. Going for a run or doing half an hour of physical exercise is also a good way to relax and facilitate a good night of rest before an important meeting.

## Positive visualisation

Describe in detail how you want to come across in your interview and repeat this over in your mind. For example, "I see myself sitting in a chair, smiling, relaxed and answering question after question with aplomb. My bright personality is shining through and the interviewers are clearly enjoying interviewing me." You'll have to believe it to achieve it! You know you can actually do this because of the amount of preparation time you have put in. It is now time to put this preparation into action. Do not worry, worrying never helps, it just acts as a negative energy-sapper which will inhibit you from enabling your bright personality to resonate at the interview. Positive thinking should help to combat your nerves.

## Minimise the reasons to get stressed

Iron your shirt the night before the interview, check the travel directions, set out everything you need to take with you with. Re-read your application or, your CV. Pack any requested certificates, references, a spare CV and a notepad and pen. Do not arrive over-laden with belongings. A mobile phone is always useful. However, ensure it is turned off or on silent before arriving at Reception. If you need to make a checklist and tick everything off before you go to bed, do this. Then you can simply forget about it.

## The crib sheet

The culmination of weeks of preparation will give you an idea of the key messages and key skills you want to get across during your interview. List this down on one A4 sheet of paper. Also list things you have found difficult to remember or anything else you are likely to forget. Consult the list before you go to sleep the day before your interview and again on the actual morning. In this way you are ensuring that key messages remain at the forefront of your mind.

## Smile

The single best way to relax yourself before going into your interview is to smile. Smiling releases natural endorphins, which are the body's natural antidote to stress. A smile is also the universal greeting by people around the world. When you smile, it encourages people to smile back and will help the interviewers to warm to you. Remember to ensure you keep smiling throughout your interview. Even as you make your way to the interview, practise your smile; smile when you go into the corner shop to buy your newspaper or when you buy your ticket at the station or, even when you catch an attractive person admiring your sharp suit and brand new shoes.

If you notice your nerves creeping up on you just before you are called into your interview take a deep breath in, breathe out slowly and smile! You'll feel the difference. The dreaded nerves means many candidates who are strong on paper let themselves down in the interview. Some people will get tongue-tied, whilst some talk too much. If you feel this may describe you then take action now and practise your delivery tone and pitch for the purposes of your interview.

The delivery of your answers in interviews is vital. If you think you might have a problem with this, get someone you trust to interview you and invite them to constructively assess your answers. Practice is the key to improving your interview technique. Book an appointment or mock interview with a careers advisor and allow them to assess your performance. Take on board any pointers you are given in terms of content, tone, volume and clarity of speech, and work on them until you feel comfortable that you have them mastered.

It is often the case that the interviewer is just as nervous as you are. Try to make your interviewer feel at ease and to build up a rapport with them, by leaning slightly forward when answering a question, showing your enthusiasm coupled with a smile!

**Our Top Tip: Aim to convert your interview nerves into positive energy by having positive thoughts and thinking of your greatest achievement and how that success made you feel about yourself. That's the attitude you need to take into your interview!**

### Interview technique

A standard interview will generally start with an introductory chat: *How was your journey? Tell us about yourself? What have you been up to over the summer?* The interview is then likely to move on to questions specific to your application and experience, followed by scenario-based questions and/or commercial awareness questions. The interviewer may then give you some general information about the firm and the role, and finish with an opportunity for you to ask your own questions.

### LISTEN – PAUSE – THINK – SPEAK
An area where students often stumble is in responding too quickly to a question, without taking time to pause and think it through. When answering, listen and pay attention to the interviewer. Think for a second to avoid blurting out rubbish, and then answer the question that is being asked of you, and not the one you wish they had asked. It is so important that **put your brain in gear before you put your mouth in motion**.

Think about your answer to the question and then illustrate it concisely, by giving positive and apt examples from your experiences to date.

Avoid irrelevant detail and one-word answers. You will have prepared yourself in advance for some of the most likely questions so use your ready prepared structure to guide you. The trick is to sound as natural as possible and come across as real as if you are having any regular conversation. Remember that the interview is a two-way process, so it is important to have a conversation with your interviewer to discover whether this law firm fulfils your specific requirements. The interviewer will set the course of that conversation but don't make it hard work for them. Have an open and enquiring mind and convey your enthusiasm in your answers like you do when you are catching up with a friend about what you got up to during your exciting gap year travelling around South America.

It is important not to get so carried away when giving your answer that the interviewer finds it hard to get a word in. Be enthusiastic about what you have achieved, be interesting to talk to and be prepared to express an opinion in a discussion but don't defend it to the death – the interviewer is not trying to trip you up - show instead that you can listen to the views of others.

## Effective Communication

All firms want lawyers who can communicate effectively at all levels, you can do this by delivering clear and concise answers, a consistent tone of voice and effective use of pauses and silence to construct arguments. Make eye-contact and listen carefully and actively to demonstrate your interest in what is being said.

Make sure you sit comfortably so that you are not perched on the edge of your chair or slouched down. Your body language will say a lot about your confidence. Posture is very important. Relaxed shoulders present an open and confident manner. Aim for a style of talking that is conversational and natural – using positive language is important, while use of humour must be subtle.

Repeat key words and phrases if you believe you need to get the interviewer back on track. Once you have answered the question, keep quiet and never feel the need to carry on talking.

Silence in interviews has the purpose of providing you with more time to think and construct your answer. Do not allow silence to make you uncomfortable. The most important thing is to remember that you can use silence as a tool to buy yourself time to think. Silence is a normal part of conversation. Keep your body language relaxed and avoid using unfilled time to fiddle. If you feel the interviewer is waiting for you to say more, you can always ask whether there are any further details the interviewer would like you to add.

Many people worry about how to deal with difficult or unexpected questions. It is perfectly acceptable to take a minute to fully consider your answer to a question, although we would advise against allowing long silences to develop. You can recognise these questions as they usually begin with "What if" or "What would you do if…..". Firms look for evidence of qualities such as lateral thinking and generating ideas and solutions quickly, and expect you to think about your responses. These questions are challenging in content and style. You must think about what you would say and how you would say it.

**Our Top Tip: If you do not know the answer to a technical question, say so, and state that you would like to go away and research that area before you are in a position to offer an informed and reasoned opinion. You will do much worse if you try to bluff your way through an answer and talk nonsense. Some questions may seem as if they are designed to catch the candidate off-guard. Think about how you will react to a question you might not have anticipated. It is how you answer these types of questions as well as what you say that is important. If your answer is delivered in a cool, calm and well thought out manner, the interviewer will be impressed.**

**Another Top Tip: Even the best lawyers don't know the answer to every legal question. The secret is to learn the way you disguise your uncertainty. This can be achieved by remaining poised and appearing to retain your confidence, which demonstrates you are a person who is calm, unflappable, and able to think laterally when put**

**under pressure and faced with challenging and intractable situations.**

## Eye-contact

Not enough eye-contact gives the impression that you feel dominated or uninterested, whilst too much eye-contact could be construed as threatening. Try to face your interviewer directly, sit with an open and relaxed pose, which is professional and comfortable, to create the best environment so you can be yourself.

## Gesticulation

Some people use their hands as part of their communication tools. Your objective is to be yourself in an unnatural setting. Always refrain from doing something that you would not usually do. It is much more important that you remain focused and natural.

## Commercial interview: How to talk about a deal

✓ State the deal.
✓ Which area of law did it cover and which practice groups were involved?
✓ What was the significance of the deal? What is impressive about the deal, for example, did it involve a multitude of lawyers working in various jurisdictions?
✓ What interested you about the deal and why?
✓ Are there any other interesting legal / commercial implications for the client and wider industry?

## General interview tips

Every interviewer has their own style of interviewing: Interviews usually last between 30 to 45 minutes but sometimes you may be left feeling that all your careful preparation has been for nothing. It has been known for a keen rugby fan to spend the entire interview discussing this sport with a candidate or, for an interviewer to pick on one topic for discussion and to base the whole interview on it. The point we are making here is that you need to be fluid, versatile and prepared to adapt and go with the flow of the interviewer.

The interview is your opportunity to shine and show that you are the right fit for their particular firm. As well as showing that you are cut out for a training contract at the firm, you need to give them something to remember you by. This is where your level of enthusiasm comes into play. Do not let your interviewer form the impression that you are treating this as just another interview on the list. And above all, always remain poised! Remember that you are discussing a subject you know most about – you!

Throughout an interview, your interviewer will be trying to assess how good you will be with clients.

✓ Will you make a client confident in your ability as a lawyer or will you leave your client feeling unconvinced and in need of reassurance?
✓ Does the candidate interest us?
✓ Does the candidate have the kind of personality that will compliment people at the firm?

A business is only as good as the people that constitute it. The best firms of solicitors look for candidates with the total package of skills, those lawyers that will benefit the firm, be the future of the firm, and have partnership potential. This is a key issue in any law firm and it is therefore very important that you demonstrate an appropriate level of confidence at your interview. Do not let yourself be intimidated. Interviewers want to know whether you can do the job, whether you will be motivated to do the job and whether you will fit in with colleagues.

*Some of this may seem obvious and straightforward but when faced with nerves and the burning desire to receive an offer, even the simplest of things are forgotten.*

## Uncertain questions

If you are unsure about what the interviewer is asking you, don't be afraid to ask them to re-phrase the question, explain, elaborate upon or clarify the particular question, as this will serve to prevent an incorrect interpretation of the question and therefore an irrelevant answer. Remember the key messages from your crib sheet? Listen for opportunities to get your messages across in your answer.

A good interviewer will allow you to do this with open questions; otherwise you must simply take the opening when it arrives. If the appropriate time doesn't arrive, the interviewer will normally give you an opportunity to talk about anything additional. You can simply state that you believe there are one or two things you would like to mention that would be of interest to them. Make sure your points are absolutely relevant.

**Our Top Tip: You can often lead the interviewer to talk about things that you are most comfortable talking about. Drop hints to lead the interviewer to your own prepared territory: your greatest achievements highlighting your strengths and outstanding qualities. You may be asked an open-ended commercial question such as "What have you read in the papers recently?" This is your opportunity to wax lyrical on your best topics. Aim to nail this by delivering well-structured, meaningful and detailed answers that have a profound impact on the interviewer.**

### Asking questions and finishing the interview

What you ask is as important as what you say. Keep a list of 3-4 intelligent questions to ask at the end of the interview, as this demonstrates your interest in the firm and shows your sound understanding of pertinent issues facing the firm and legal market at large. Do not ask basic questions about matters that you could easily find out from research. For example, which countries does the firm operate in? *See chapter 13 for examples of questions you might want to ask the interviewer.*

When the interview is over, use your best professional etiquette and thank the interviewer for seeing you. At all times, stay polite and formal. Make sure you find out what the next step will be, e.g. when the second interview will take place or when you will hear back from the firm.

Finally, remember you are effectively "on show" until after you have left the building.

## Post- interview

Think honestly about how things went. Consider what you did well, what you didn't do so well and write down all the questions you can remember being asked. Don't dwell on any mistakes you may have made.

Follow up by asking your careers adviser for advice if you identify any particular issues of concern. Discuss your performance at the interview with others but always rely on your natural instinct and overall impression of the day and whether you feel the firm is right for you. Did you enjoy it? If so, it probably went very well. We hope you get the offer.

## Interview feedback

If you are unsuccessful, obtain as much feedback as possible about your performance. Ask where you went wrong, how you can improve for next time. Learning from your experiences will enhance your future performance.

Too many candidates do not seek feedback from their interviews. If you do not get the job, it is only fair that the firm tells you why. It is paramount that you ask for advice that will help you perform better and aid your personal development for your future career. Try to contact the interviewer personally, otherwise obtain feedback from graduate recruitment.

Questions you should be asking the firm are as follows:

- ✓ What impressions did they form of you?
- ✓ How can you manage these more effectively in the future?
- ✓ Did you answer the questions well?
- ✓ Did you appear interested enough? What characteristics were lacking?
- ✓ Were you rejected because you did not reach the required standard, or were other candidates better qualified or experienced?

Open a file detailing these and then take action to remedy any faults. This is all part of your evaluation, development and progress. Seek the opinions of close colleagues and friends whose views you value and trust. Ask them how they see you and how you could improve the image and message you wish to project. Listen carefully to their comments and criticisms, and endeavour to view these as constructive and helpful rather than damaging to your ego or reducing your self-confidence.

**Our Top Tip: Write a hand-written letter to the firm thanking them for meeting you. It adds significant value and differentiates your approach from other candidates. Recruiters will perceive this as evidence of potential client service skills.**

---

### Succeeding at interview: Points to Ponder

Research shows that recruiters make their mind up about people within the first few minutes of meeting them. First impressions derive from a combination of what we say and the way we communicate with our body language. It is vital you spend time considering how you would like to come across and the kind of image you would like to present. The key to success at interviews is recognising the deeply subjective nature of your meeting and turning this to your advantage. In this chapter we discuss:

- Thorough preparation for a training contract interview is required. Remember "He who fails to prepare, prepares to fail".
- Knowing yourself inside out for the purposes of the interview - here we present simple techniques which when mastered will help you come across well.
- There are different types of interviews and interview techniques to consider.
- How to handle interview nerves.
- The things that really impress interviewers.
- How to handle rejection after interview and following up for feedback to facilitate improvement in your future career development and progress to becoming a successful lawyer.

---

Chapter Thirteen

## How to answer those tough training contract interview questions

Many prospective trainee solicitors feel overwhelmed by the unlimited range of questions that could be asked during training contract interviews. However, the good news is that many of these questions can be anticipated and considered well in advance.

The following section is designed to help you prepare answers for these interview questions. The responses are not model answers, but serve as suggested approaches to successfully answering both expected and unexpected questions.

Our **golden rules** for answering questions are:

✓ Listen carefully and make sure you understand the meaning of the question you are being asked. Consider the intonation and tone of the interviewer and deliver your response appropriately. Look attentive and concentrate.

✓ Be honest and open: do not try to give the answer you think the interviewer wants to hear – the only right answer is the truthful one. Avoid sounding as if you have rehearsed your responses, aim to have a pleasant conversation.

✓ Keep your answers coherent, full and succinct and do not waffle.

✓ Tailor your answers by always taking into account the needs and expectations (criteria) of the firm interviewing you, ascertained from your research.

✓ Take your time to answer and do not worry too much about silences. Are there any further details that can be added?

✓ Lastly, think before you speak. Always put your brain in gear before you put your mouth in motion!

Take time to consider the questions you are likely to face and think about how you might respond. Prepare a brief career overview in response to that ever popular kick-off question: "Tell me a bit about yourself". Be ready with plenty of examples to illustrate your skills and how you could contribute to the firm.

Here are some of the most frequent questions you may be asked when attending an interview, with brief guidelines on what your response may be. Try to be original. Think about the key messages you would like to get across. It is your interview!

## What are your strengths and weaknesses?

Be positive, illustrate your strengths and tell how you have turned any weaknesses into strengths. Always end your answer on a positive note.

## Why did you apply here?

Deciding whether to join a law firm is a really big decision, so you have to spend a lot of time considering it! By undertaking work placements you will have a better impression of the work solicitors carry out and whether that will suit you. Consider why this firm is particularly appealing.

## Why should we employ you?

Think of how your strengths relate to the job, don't be too modest, but don't be arrogant. Body language is important here!

## Where do you see yourself in five years time?

Give a realistic idea of what you want to achieve in terms of responsibility rather than position.

If an interviewer is not fully certain about your suitability for the job you will not be offered a training contract. You have to provide full, well-thought out and excellent answers to circumvent any doubts arising. Most interviewers believe past performance is an indicator of future potential, so you must have structured examples of past work and particular successes in life and career.

Here is a valuable insight into the world of interview questions and the techniques best used to answer them. There are some questions that are asked frequently in interviews and you should consider your thoughts and possible response beforehand. Another method you can use when thinking about how to answer interview questions is the **STAR** method. Done properly it should enable you to nail those tough competency-based interview questions.

**S**ituation – Set the scene for your response

**T**ask – What was the problem YOU were tackling

**A**ction – How did you deal with the problem?

**R**esult – What was the result and outcome? Aim to demonstrate that a measurable impact and positive contribution was achieved.

If you are faced with a difficult question, make sure you stay calm, don't get defensive, and take a moment to think about your response before you answer. Try to personalise your response as much as possible. Remember, the responses below are only suggestions,

## Q. Tell me about yourself

This is a difficult question to answer, as it is so open-ended! This is often used as a gentle opening question for the interviewer to see what sort of person you are. The interviewer is really saying "I want to hear you talk." Note that first impressions are often formed here, so it is imperative to have a strong well thought out introduction highlighting some of your strengths and achievements. It is intended to give the interviewer an overview of you as a candidate.

**A.** Identify some of your main attributes and have them memorised. Describe your qualifications, career history and range of skills, emphasizing those skills relevant to the job on offer and your fit and suitability to the firm. Give an account of your working life, and extra-curricular activities, focusing only on what is relevant to why you are applying, gradually giving more detail as you come up to the present day. The key to answering these questions is to show your compatibility with potential employers. Think about your skills, qualities and experiences that support these points. Finish off with a short statement about your life outside study or work to show you are a balanced and well-rounded person.

## Q. What have your achievements been to date?

**A.** Select an achievement that is work-related and fairly recent. Identify the skills you used in the achievement and quantify the benefit it had to the company. For example: "My greatest achievement has been to design and implement a new sales ledger system, completing it ahead of time and improving our debtors' position significantly, saving the company £50,000 per month in interest".

## Q. Why have you applied to us?

**A.** The interviewer wants to know why you specifically want to work for that firm above all its competitors. To respond by saying that the firm has a good culture, good work and clients and a friendly work environment is not enough. That answer can apply to many firms. You need to remember what led your genuine interest into this particular firm. Does the firm do an area of law that you are particularly interested in? Have you met anybody at the firm? Where is the firm positioned in terms of the marketplace and its business strategy, and why do you find this interesting? Why does this particular firm stand out from its rivals? This information can be located in a firm's marketing brochures. It is very easy to research the firm, and the individuals within it.

## Q. Are you happy with your career to date?

**A.** This question is really about your self-esteem, confidence and career aspirations. We're sure the answer will be 'yes' and you'll obviously follow up with a brief explanation as to what it is about your career so far that has made you happy. If the answer is, genuinely no, think of a tactful way to explain why. No interviewer wants to hear any kind of negativity. If you have hit a career plateau, or you feel you are moving too slowly, you might qualify your answer by explaining that although you are not satisfied with your career progress so far you have gained good experience and that you firmly believe your best is yet to come.

## Q. What is the most difficult situation you have had to face and how did you tackle it?

**A.** The purpose of this question is to find out what your definition of difficult is and whether you are able to overcome adversity. The options here are endless. You can tell the interviewer about the time you skied off-piste alone late one evening and managed to find your way back to base camp through a blizzard. You can even select a challenging work situation which can be quickly described in a few sentences. Explain how you defined the problem, what the options available to you were, why you selected a particular course of action and what the outcome was. Always end your answer on a positive note. See the STAR method above.

## Q. What do you like about your degree / university?

**A.** This is a straightforward question. All you have to do is make sure that your "likes" correspond in some way to the skills required for the job on offer. If you choose to talk about academic subjects, there is no point telling your criminal lawyer interviewer that you like the fact that your university provides a specialist M&A course.

## Q. What do you dislike about your degree/university?

**A.** Be cautious with this answer. Avoid the trap of using negative comments about your studies, your university or a lecturer. For questions like this, controversial answers are best avoided.

## Q. What has been the toughest part of your degree so far?

**A.** Employers will be interested in hearing you talk intelligently about your course in some depth. The best answer here is to think about the challenges you have faced as an undergraduate. You should be careful to avoid highlighting your weaknesses as this isn't what is being asked of you. Give an example of a demanding project but avoid obvious ones such as your dissertation – the vast majority of students do one, what was so hard about yours? Demonstrate how you handled the difficulties by using careful consideration and planning.

## Q. What do you see as your key strengths?

**A.** Why is this question asked? Essentially to see if your strengths match the skills the firm is looking for. To answer the question you must evidence what you say with concrete positive examples. This is one question that you must anticipate being asked so there is no excuse for being unprepared. Concentrate on discussing your main strengths and matching these with the firm's selection criteria and specific skills. List three or four proficiencies, e.g. your ability to learn quickly, determination to succeed, positive attitude, and your ability to relate to people, and back these up with solid examples. <u>The key is to work out how these strengths could benefit the firm</u>. Avoid stock answers or rhetorical ones, just give examples by drawing on past experiences. Use the STAR method if you are explaining a particular strength in detail.

## Q. What is your greatest weakness?

**A.** This is a question geared to assessing your self-awareness. The worst thing you can possibly say, as one of our mates did, is that you don't have any - this will give the impression that you lack self-insight and honesty. This rather tough question is not intended to make you slip up! You have two options: give an example of a weakness that will not be detrimental to your job prospects. While you will be reluctant to identify your shortfalls, think about mentioning things that do not come naturally to you, such as public speaking to large audiences. You might mention how you have overcome this through practice and training. The second option is to describe a professional weakness that could also be interpreted as strength. An example would be: "I know my team think I'm too demanding at times. I tend to drive them pretty hard but I'm getting much better at supporting others to meet the team's expectations through regular meetings."

The only weaknesses that are safe to admit to are those which do not impair your ability to get things done, like being too punctual or the shame associated with supporting a particular football Club! You can also add a positive spin by saying how you intend to work on the chink in your armour.

## Q. Is there anything you would have preferred to do differently, if you could?

**A.** Why asked? Again, interviewers are looking for your awareness of limitations. You are being asked to identify examples of poor performance. Give an example from when you were young, something that did not go well, e.g. an idea being criticised; an example that can be put down to a lack of experience rather than low skill or poor judgment. This is an opportunity to show how you can learn from your mistakes.

## Q. What would your friends say are your best qualities?

**A.** This is a question that gives you scope to outline your skills, such as teamwork, interpersonal and communication skills. Always aim to provide solid concrete examples to support each of your qualities.

## Q. Describe a mistake you made at work and how you responded to criticism?

**A.** Our advice is to use an example from the beginning of your career when you were much less experienced. Set out the circumstances and, importantly, stress that you have learnt from the scenario, and finish on something positive, such as what you would do differently in the future.

## Q. Do you work well under pressure?

**A.** Why asked? Yes, you work well under pressure (it would be foolish to admit not to). However, to stand out from the crowd you need to demonstrate one or two clear examples of how you have worked very well in a pressurised working environment. A law firm is a dynamic working environment where pressure and tight deadlines are part of your daily routine, so it is important to show you can handle stress and working in demanding conditions. There are differing types of pressure: time constraints, demands from a partner, responsibility and lack of support. You may ask what the interviewer considers an acceptable level of pressure, and what they mean by it, in order for you to find the best example.

**Q. How would you deal with a situation where you disagreed with your boss on a work-related issue?**
**Q. How would you handle a client making unreasonable demands?**

**A.** Why asked? These types of hypothetical scenarios are given where you have to think on your feet and describe what you would do. Questions like these are asked to see how the candidate would handle a potential conflict situation. You need to show maturity of thought when answering such questions. Diplomacy is the key in situations like this. Take your time to think through the conflict being presented and listen to your own sense of integrity before giving your answer. This is the one time you should aim to give the interviewer the type of answer they want to hear. It is a good idea to draw on your own experience whenever possible by giving examples of how you have effectively managed a similar situation in the past and are therefore capable of handling a problem as effectively in the future. The key is to show you are aware of the parameters of your responsibility and the inherent risks involved in the high level work you will become involved in.

**Q. Can you give me an example of any work experience / teamwork /leadership?**

**A.** This is a common competency question asked because it is a good indicator of future performance. Draw from your portfolio of examples which cover your career history and experience, and make sure you cover the different and varied activities that you have been involved with. Commit these to memory in the **STAR** format described above and be ready to select from them as appropriate.

**Q. Give me an example when you failed to persuade someone of your point of view.**

**A.** Always put a positive spin on your answer. The selector wants to see your logical thinking and how well you deal with situations that don't go your way. Give examples of your adaptability and problem solving.

**Q. I am concerned that you do not have the amount of legal work experience we expect for the role of trainee solicitor.**

**A.** Why asked? Most firms will be comparing you not only against the criteria for training contract selection but also against the answers of other candidates. You have to demonstrate that you have the qualities required to be a successful solicitor. Your objective self-assessment during your preparation will assist you in identifying shortcomings in your experience, and you will have also prepared ways to counter these. Always focus on the positive points, i.e. the experience that you have got, even when the question is framed in a negative way.

**Q. Why might you not accept this position if it were offered to you?**

**A.** This is a tricky question testing your openness and integrity. It is usually posed for those candidates with more than one offer. It is asking you to expand on exactly what you are looking for from the firm that you join, in terms of training and career development. It tends to be a winding-down question near the end of the interview. (It is a good sign; they have probably decided they would like to take things further.) Being honest is the key. You will be clear in your mind about what you are expecting in terms of the firm's culture, level of responsibility, client contact and future prospects of partnership.

**Q. Why did you leave your previous place of employment?**

**A.** The most diplomatic way of answering this is to state that you were looking for a new challenge, more responsibility, experience and a change of environment. Do not be negative in your reasons for leaving.

**Q. Where do you see yourself in five years time?**

**A.** Why asked? To see how quickly you expect to move up the career ladder. This question seeks to gauge how ambitious you are; and how realistic you are in terms of achieving your career goals. Focus on your medium-term plans. Explain how you see your training at the firm fitting into your plan to be a qualified lawyer at their firm. Aim not to give specific time references about when you think success will happen. This is an opportunity to talk about career development and display your ambition.

**Q. Tell me about a time where you gave excellent standard of service to somebody and solved a complex and challenging problem. What processes did you use and how did you ensure you achieved the correct outcome?**

**A.** This is a three-part question, so dissect it and plan your answer in the same logical format, as a structure is more likely to help remember the layout of the question. Focus on the situation and set the scene – tell a story about what you did, e.g. client care, handling pressure and the analytical skills you used in problem solving. Explain the result, the action you took to assess the level of client satisfaction. Although you will use examples from the past, you might mention what you would do in the future.

**Q. Why did you take a gap year?**

**A.** To answer well, you need to show your career decisions are carefully planned, assessed and analysed. Discuss your gap year in terms of your overall personal development.

**Q. What will you do if you are not successful at this interview?**

**A.** This question is a way of testing your commitment to being a lawyer. When answering the question you have to perform a balancing act of appearing to want to work for that firm rather than one of their competitors. It would also show whether you are the kind of person who develops contingency plans.

**Our Top Tip – You might face off-the-wall questions that you might not have anticipated and could not possibly prepare for. Use a logical approach because this is where your quick thinking comes into play. Take your time to answer these questions. One such question we have heard asked is How would you go about organising changing England from driving on the left to the right?" Think logically and set out the steps. All you have to do is**

provide an answer which is well-reasoned and considered - there is often no right or wrong answer.

## Commercial awareness questions

When seeking to impress at interview it is important to demonstrate you are commercially aware and understand the commercial area in which the law firm is operating in. Is it competing with the top 20 firms? Is it a market leader in a particular practice area? Who are the firm's clients? Comment on a current deal relevant to the marketplace or a recent event in the news, to show you appreciate the local and global market conditions. Casting a keen eye over the pages of the financial press and keeping up-to-date with current affairs will help to develop awareness and knowledge of the commercial world. A common commercial awareness question takes the form of "Talk me through anything that you have recently read in the press". What aspects interested you? This provides an open question to really demonstrate your thorough preparation (*refer to chapter 9 on commercial awareness.*)

### Q. How would you go about establishing a business abroad or a new office in Barcelona?

**A.** As it is a global company they have contacts and/or offices around the world. You could contact one of the new offices opened and check their previous approach or get in touch with another member of the team based in another jurisdiction that has recently opened a new office and gain their views. You might then write a strategy on how the new office would operate in terms of staffing, work and how it would pitch for clients. With commercial questions of this nature, you can afford to be creative.

## Legal questions

Although your academic background is usually proven by the time you get to this stage, some firms still like to ask the occasional question on the law: *What is a tort? Tell me any case that has interested you? If you could pass any legislation what would it be? Should trial by jury be banned?* It is worthwhile brushing up on knowledge of the main areas of law, together with any particular areas that you have focused on, for example, in a dissertation.

## Leading questions

Leading questions can be used to confirm a view from reading your application, e.g. *You haven't done very well at land law, have you?* Your average candidate might be tempted to respond with a monosyllabic answer which may appear to suffice, while his head drops to the floor. Your excellent candidate will contest the interviewer's train of thought, will think of an excellent way to counteract this question, deliver the message they want to get across and finish on a positive note: *"Although I found the law of property challenging I still achieved a good result compared to the rest of my year. The lecturer even noted that this year's paper was set to a much higher standard than in previous years. This is why I am very proud of my grade and my overall academic achievement."* These types of question can be challenging, - the key is to appear calm and self-assured.

Often leading and unexpected questions give you the opportunity to steer the ship and get the interview back on track, controlling the conversation in the way you want, providing evidence of your personal qualities, which you fear may have been overlooked by the interviewer.

## Competency questions

As you have seen above, these questions are designed to generate concrete evidence of certain skills in the form of specific examples. They focus on a particular time or occasion – *Tell me about a time when you. Give me an example of your organisational skills. Describe your actions and your role in the project? Tell me about a time where you solved a complex and challenging problem? What did you do?* In an interview it is important to listen carefully to the question and pick out exactly what competencies are being asked of you. If you can nail the skills they are looking for, you are more likely to come up with an excellent answer. Again the STAR method will help you here.

## Other questions you might consider:

- ✓ How do you feel about working long hours and/or weekends?
- ✓ How would you improve the firm?
- ✓ Tell me more about project X that you worked on?
- ✓ What has been your biggest challenge to date?

- ✓ What experience of working in a team have you had?
- ✓ How do you organise your study and extra-curricular activities?
- ✓ If you could invite anyone for a dinner party whether past, present or fictional, who would it be and why?
- ✓ If you could give a speech, what subject would it be and why?
- ✓ What do you enjoy about the legal profession?
- ✓ Give an example of when you have worked under pressure.
- ✓ Give an example of when your work was criticised.
- ✓ Give an example of when you have felt anger at work. How did you cope and did you still perform a good job?
- ✓ What kind of people do you find it difficult to work with?
- ✓ Give me an example of when you have had to face a conflict of interest at work.
- ✓ Tell me about the last time you disagreed with your boss.
- ✓ Give an example of when you haven't got on with others.
- ✓ Do you prefer to work alone or in a group? Why?
- ✓ Which other firms have you applied to?
- ✓ Why do you want to work in this location?
- ✓ This organisation is very different to your current employer. How do you think you are going to fit in?
- ✓ What are you looking for in a company?
- ✓ How do you measure your own performance?
- ✓ What kind of pressures have you encountered at work?
- ✓ Are you a self-starter? Give me examples to demonstrate this.
- ✓ Give me an example of when you have been out of your depth.
- ✓ What have you failed to achieve to date?
- ✓ Tell me something about yourself.
- ✓ Why would you like to work for this firm in particular?
- ✓ What attracts you to this role?
- ✓ Describe two major achievements in your career.
- ✓ If you could change anything about your career so far, what would it be?
- ✓ How would members of your team describe you?
- ✓ What important points came out of your last appraisal?
- ✓ Describe your management style.
- ✓ What do you look for in a manager?
- ✓ Describe your toughest client.
- ✓ What do you want from your next role?
- ✓ What does success mean to you?

✓ If you won a million pounds on the lottery what would you spend it on and would you still work as a lawyer? If not what type of work would you do?
✓ What are the key things that drive or motivate you?
✓ What really winds you up in the workplace?
✓ Describe your greatest challenge so far.
✓ Describe a difficult work scenario and how you managed it.
✓ Where do you see yourself in two to five years' time?
✓ What are your career aspirations?
✓ What would you say about your current and last employers?
✓ If you weren't applying to be a lawyer, what alternative career would you choose?

Training contract interview questions will really test your mettle. Interviewers will be assessing how you answer for evidence of how you handle the unexpected and are able to think on your feet. Always take your time, acknowledge the question. If necessary, ask for a minute to collect your thoughts, ask the interview to clarify if you need to and then clearly set out your answer.

## Your questions answered

Now that you have been grilled by the interviewer and survived, it is now time to ask a few questions of your own. Asking good questions can demonstrate your understanding and knowledge of the profession, and your research into the firm itself. Be careful - it is all too easy to give the impression that you have not done enough research into the firm, if you don't ask the right type of question.

As part of your research before interview, prepare a list of questions you would like to ask your interviewers. It is advisable that you do ask at least one question, to show you are interested in the firm and that you are not lacking in imagination. Firms will be more than a little surprised if you have no questions at all. During the interview, you may have additional questions. You might want to know more about the choice of training seats, or you might want to know the basis upon which they decide to retain their trainees at the firm after qualification. Think about this before the interview rather than during it! Be ready to ask questions that you have prepared beforehand. This can demonstrate you have thought about the role and done some research on the organisation. Ensure they are open questions so you can discuss them with your interviewer. Those which invite thought and comment are more memorable to the interviewer than those which request specific detail. The questions also give you a chance to show your enthusiasm for the role.

## Some possible questions to ask

✓ How do the different groups at the firm view their trainees as a general group resource?
✓ How will my progress be monitored?
✓ How are trainees measured in terms of performance?
✓ What direction does the firm see itself going over the next 5 to 10 years?
✓ What is the next stage of selection and when can I expect to hear back?
✓ How would you describe the firm/company culture?
✓ What do you see as the key challenges of the role of a trainee?
✓ How do you differentiate yourselves from your competitors?
✓ What are the firm's major business objectives in the coming year?
✓ What processes exist to support employees in their career development?
✓ How would you describe the firm/company's values?
✓ What are the major issues currently facing the firm in view of [insert as appropriate]?

## INTERVIEW QUESTIONS

You may be wondering what type of questions you will be asked at the interview. From our own experience and following research with dozens of law interview candidates we have compiled a briefcase of the various questions you may be faced with. Not only that, we show you the rationale behind these questions and how to respond to them in ways which will impress the interviewer and help you come across as an interesting, sharp and articulate candidate.

At interviews it is important to work out how your strengths could benefit the firm and aim to convey these points in your answers.

- How to deal with commercial, legal and competency questions
- Follow the STAR method of answering questions.
- Listen carefully and make sure you understand the meaning of the question being asked.
- Be honest and open. Avoid sounding as if you have rehearsed your responses, aim to have a pleasant conversation.
- Keep your answers coherent and succinct.

Chapter Fourteen

## Selection Centres/Assessment Days

Although assessment centres are more commonly seen in the selection process for banks or accountancy firms, this method of selection is now being increasingly used by law firms. Here are some of the kind of assessment you may be asked to do.

### Group exercises

Teamwork is essential for success in the workplace. One of the ways this quality will be tested is in the group exercise scenario. You will normally be required to complete a discussion-based exercise. Some candidates will feel uncomfortable being observed while discussing a topic. However, it is important that you do not blow the difficulty of this task out of proportion as this will seriously affect your confidence and may hinder your performance. You will need to be relaxed in order to do well.

In any group exercise the recruiters will be looking for certain skills from every candidate. They may not be expecting you to tick every single box. However, there will be core competencies that they are looking for. Here are some of those qualities:

- ✓ **Leadership** - Can you influence and guide the group to a solution?

- ✓ **Interpersonal skills** - How well do you interact with all members?

- ✓ **Time management skills** - Are you conscious of the time given for the exercise?

- ✓ **Problem solving** - Do you understand the issues involved and can you unravel issues to reach a solution?

- ✓ **Creativity** - Can you think logically and laterally and suggest innovative solutions? Are your ideas original?

✓ **Decisiveness** - Have you demonstrated your ability to respond quickly to alternative and possibly opposing arguments?

✓ **Business awareness** - Did you show an awareness of the potential problems arising from the solutions that were put forward? You will often need to detail practical solutions, which will be pragmatically implemented.

✓ **Good interpersonal skills** - How receptive are you to other personality types? Are you able to bring out the best in others?

✓ **Persuasiveness** - Are your ideas consistently taken on by the group to help the overall objectives of the exercise?

✓ **Communication** - How clearly and effectively can you get your message across? Is there sufficient clarity in your answers?

✓ **Teamwork** – Some exercises will be designed to see how well you work with others. Get stuck in, make a contribution and don't stand back.

Your contribution must help the group to complete the task. At the same time you must be seeking to promote yourself. The best thing you can do is to get this balance right, showing off your strengths and demonstrating the fact that you were instrumental in helping the group itself reach a solution. Bear in mind that the assessors will normally be looking to see how the group reaches a solution rather than the solution.

## Our Top Tip

✓ **Read the brief several times**
✓ **Pay close attention to time deadlines**
✓ **Play a part but by no means boss the group**
✓ **Be diplomatic**
✓ **Never be too verbose or put down another candidate - you will only make yourself look bad**
✓ **Be prepared to argue your point and defend your views**
✓ **Be prepared to compromise**

✓ **Don't be the person who manifests any type of anti-social behaviour**

## Various roles

Although everyone should be seeking to contribute original ideas, people may fall into various roles. Here are some examples:

✓ **Leader** - Is usually the person who chairs the group, the leader will normally take responsibility for guiding it. The leader will direct the discussion and perhaps will be the most dominant personality or the most vocal member of the group. If you do assume this role, make sure you listen to others and avoid being too authoritative.

✓ **Organiser** - Along with the leader, this person will help to allocate roles to group members if necessary. The organiser will encourage others who have made good points and will invite feedback from everyone. The organiser will help to move things along when the group is unable to reach a conclusion on any aspect of the discussion.

✓ **Summariser** – This is the person who sums up the decisions that the group has made. This normally saves time during the discussion and prompts the discussion of points which have yet to be decided. The summariser might be heard to say:

*"Before we carry on, can I quickly run through the decisions we have made so far?"*

✓ **Time-keeper** - This person will be very conscious of time throughout the discussion. It's amazing how quickly time elapses during the discussion, and somebody needs to stop the group getting carried away. Volunteer for this role early on; keep an eye on the time and feedback to the group on how time is progressing. Write down the times the exercise starts and is due to finish. The timekeeper might be heard to say:

*"I'm very conscious that time is against us, can we move on to the next point?"*

*"We currently have 10 minutes left to complete the task. Shall we deal with the next issue?"*

**Our Top Tip: Do not think that assuming any one of these roles alone will win you the job, but if you establish yourself as one of the key players in the group you are likely to make relevant and necessary contributions. With every role you undertake, strive to ensure you are involved throughout the decision-making process. Be confident but never aggressive in defending or asserting your views. A frequent reason for candidates doing badly during these tasks is losing sight of the ultimate goal – to complete the task successfully.**

## Strategy

Think about how your personality fits in to the afore-mentioned roles and play to your strengths. Try to join in the discussion as early as possible and contribute to the discussion regularly. In order to make an impression you will have to talk consistently.

*I wanted to be one of the first people to speak. I knew this would allow me to establish myself as part of the group. I knew if I suggested that all the group members took turns to put forward their views on each issue it would show that I was a team player and considerate to all members. I also suggested that in order to come to a decision, the group should put each issue to the vote. Everyone agreed with me. I established myself in the group and showed that once again I wanted all members to be involved.*

**Omer Maroof, Solicitor at SJ Berwin**

## Give good reasons

Candidates often tend to blurt out the first thing that comes to mind: do not say anything unless you can substantiate it. Every time you make a point, try to back it up with three reasons. Most candidates hardly ever do this but it will, ensure that you are heard. It would be very rude if the group members didn't allow you to explain all of your reasons. It will show the assessors that you are thinking logically and are focused on the task. It will also help to influence the other candidates. They will swiftly avoid opposing your views and will tend to agree and listen when you make further points. It will also come across well to those observing. It is rare that anyone will be able to counter all three of your reasons, as they might do if you use only simple rhetoric to make your points.

If somebody is dominating the group, suggest that the group should hear from everyone, and invite everyone to contribute, particularly people who have not had the opportunity to contribute much to the group discussion. Perhaps make a suggestion and ask other members whether they agree. This will give others a chance to talk and take the focus from the dominating member of the group, which will make you will look like a fantastic team player. It will also allow quieter members to get their voices heard.

The worst thing you can do in a group exercise is to say nothing. You will not show the assessors any of the qualities they are looking for and therefore cannot win the job. Always join in. If there are four of you, perhaps try making every fourth comment. Be clear when you speak and maintain eye-contact with all group members.

It's the quality of what you say that counts. Nervousness plays tricks on all of us; the resulting adrenalin may make you talk relentlessly but be conscious not to do this. Talking too much may lose you the job as quickly as not saying anything.

Don't feel the need to repeat or reiterate a point somebody has made. Because of time pressure, most of the points you make should be trying to move the discussion forward.

Some people have a tendency when faced with anxiety to think of points to discuss and then forget them just as quickly. Make sure you jot down a quick note of any crucial points you think of. The time at which the point comes to mind may not be the most appropriate time to bring it to the discussion. Write a quick bullet point and raise it when it becomes relevant.

Do not be afraid to compromise, this does not reflect badly on you. If you do have to concede you might not want to do so immediately, in which case make your counter argument strongly and back it up with reasons, e.g. "I have three reasons for maintaining this view…" Saying something like this will force the group to hear you out. If you find that your arguments are not accepted by the rest of the group, concede in a graceful manner and move on. You will be judged on your contribution and will probably have impressed the assessors with your logic and maturity.

Any candidates demonstrating a distinct lack of interpersonal skills will almost certainly face rejection. Again do not be one of them. Respect for group members is a must. Keep in mind the need for diplomacy and never put anybody down, even if you are confronted with the most obnoxious of group members. You do not have to have a heated argument to prove your point. The assessors will have noticed anti-social character types and will be assessing the rest of the group on how they deal with them.

Do not lose concentration - follow the conversation and move with the group. There is no point raising issues that have been decided and concluded or talking about one issue when the group has moved on to something else. You need to be sharp. Stay alert! Finally, remember to acknowledge everyone by name.

## How can I improve?

Think of diplomatic ways to express yourself beforehand. Think of phrases you could use. In the heat of the moment you don't just want to say the first thing that comes to mind.

Practise with friends in a group. Discuss a topic and be conscious of (i) the amount of your contribution, (ii) how well you articulate your viewpoint and (iii) backing up what you say with reasons. Ask your friends for feedback.

**Our Top Tip: Remember, in the group exercise you are not competing against the others so don't view it as a battle. It is possible that every individual in the group could be selected because you are being marked against the firm's standards, not how well you perform compared to your peers. Therefore avoid super competitive behaviour.**

### Tackling the case study

A case study is sometimes given to candidates in order to test their analytical skills and ability to assimilate a mass of information and pick out key aspects as well as to test their communication skills.

A candidate will sometimes be given a bundle of documents or a document containing information and will have a short amount of time to assimilate the information, read the case study and then present it to the interviewer. When you are presenting the case study, you should ensure you have read all the documents through before you write anything. Annotate your thoughts onto the paper as you are going through, remembering that time is of the essence and ensure you check that the pages are not double-sided.

The golden rule to tackling the case study is to apply logic and common sense. There are many ways to structure the way you present information to the interviewer. In our experience, the actual case study question often provides you with a ready-made structure so why not apply common sense and use that structure, i.e. follow the order dealing with each question in turn? You will save yourself time and much anxiety during the preparation stage. For example, the case study may ask you to consider three aspects in your report/presentation. When giving your feedback, comment on these aspects in the order given. Your interviewer will follow your train of thought more easily.

Write down as much as you can on the case study. Sometimes adrenaline will make people talk faster than they normally do, and it's amazing in this situation how quickly you may get through what you have written. Remember to pace yourself and not to rush through. There is less chance of getting stuck or being unsure of what to say next when you are presenting. Although extremely difficult in time-pressured situations, write neat orderly notes. The worst thing that can happen is that you get in the room and are unable to read your own writing or cannot follow your argument through because you have scribbled down random words. Give the interviewer time to assimilate the information you are delivering.

During your reading of the case study try to anticipate any questions which may be asked, and quickly run through how you would answer them if they were posed during your discussion with the interviewer.

Try not to race straight into the case study. Introduce it by firmly establishing your understanding of what you are being asked to do. Tell the interviewer how you are going to approach the case study. Once you begin, it is very important to break the case study down as much as possible. Do not immediately rush to conclusions.

Stick to the crucial issues and introduce and outline these one by one. There may be question marks, grey areas, or more information needed in relation to the case study, - do not be afraid to tell the interviewer this. Even in the face of ambiguous information, make an educated guess, backed up with solid reasoning to show the interviewer that you are thinking like a lawyer. Listen closely to any questions you are being asked. If you had already anticipated these, as advised above, they shouldn't present too much of a problem. If not, be as confident with the answer as you have been throughout the presentation. If you are unsure, do not try and bluff your way through an answer. If you do not know the answer, be honest and say so. However, the key to doing this is perhaps to state you are happy to go away and research this point further in order to offer a more informed view on the matter, and provide a definitive answer. After all, that's what you may have to do as a trainee.

Never be afraid to state the obvious as long as it is relevant. Try to think as laterally as possible: What do the issues in the case study link to? You may be asked, for example, who you would seek advice from about a certain issue Analyse how the role of other professionals would help to solve the issues.

If you make a mistake or give false facts or figures, apologise quickly and do not dwell on it or allow a mistake to affect your body language and composure. The interviewer is also testing you on how you are able to handle pressure.

When you're presenting the case study, there is nothing wrong with thinking aloud. However, do not do this continually. Remember that thinking aloud may cause you to mutter, which will definitely not impress the interviewer.

Do not forget to conclude. Let the interviewer know that you have finished presenting your case study. Ask him/her if there is anything additional they would like to know, to show you are conscious that you may have left something out.

Say as much about the case study as possible. It is likely there is a checklist of various points that the interviewer is expecting candidates to cover. It goes without saying that the more you say the more boxes they are likely to tick.

There is no right or wrong answer in the majority of these types of case study. Obviously questions such a: "How can we raise finance?" have specific answers to hand. The case study is essentially a demonstration of your potential to analyse a scenario and report on it in a logical, confident and clear manner. The interviewer will be looking to see how many of the key issues you can spot and how effective you will be when put before a client.

Lastly, it is important that you really get into the role and convince the interviewer to believe in your approach.

## Effective presentations for training contract interviews

Presentations may form part of an assessment day. You are not alone if you feel apprehensive about giving one. If you are asked to do a presentation you may be able to select a topic and prepare in advance, or you may be given a list of topics on the day and asked to select and prepare one in a given amount of time.

All lawyers are expected to present information and pitch ideas to clients and colleagues in a way that is persuasive and easy to understand. Whether presenting to a small group or a large room, the prospect can be enough to make most people's legs turn to jelly. Some of the things you can practise before any presentation are your delivery, positioning and body language. The successful delivery of information in a viable manner can be an empowering way to influence people. Once you are fully comfortable with your own style, the actual presentation should become less daunting. You can then concentrate on using your personality and charisma to deliver the message. Even if you do feel nervous, remember that nerves give you the energy to display enthusiasm and should help you think quickly. Good preparation creates confidence, which will enable you to control your nerves. The presentation for the training contract might last between 5 to 10 minutes and you may be required to make group presentations.

## Tips for presenting (where no prior preparation is allowed)

For this type of presentation you will usually be given 20-30 minutes to choose a topic to prepare, and you will be given scrap paper and prompt cards. When you are asked to choose a topic, don't always go for the most obvious one. Take time to gather your thoughts, and consider which topic you could deliver most effectively. You should aim to use the first five minutes brainstorming and drawing mind maps on scrap paper, but bear in mind that the time will elapse very quickly so you shouldn't spend too long on this. Once you have an idea of what you want to talk about, write your presentation straight onto the prompt cards in a logical, easy to follow fashion, using bullet points.

## Choosing a topic (prior preparation)

If you are allowed to choose a topic for your presentation, aim to choose an original subject that you know extremely well and have direct experience of. This will allow you to sound knowledgeable and enthusiastic, and you will easily deal with any questions which are posed. If you do it well it may be the case that your audience will be learning something new. This will naturally allow you to hold their attention as you spark their curiosity.

Think about the likelihood of anyone else choosing a similar topic. Try to stay away from general topics such as university life, school days, etc. Try more unusual topics, perhaps something cultural: Do you have any experience of Indian Weddings or Bar Mitzvahs, for example? Have you been on any unusual adventures? Do you have any wacky hobbies? If so, find an interesting angle from which to deliver your presentation. If it's something you are enthusiastic about this will be visible in your delivery.

## General tips

### *Prepare, plan, practise, and perform...*

Thorough preparation is vital to delivering a successful presentation. Excellent speaking involves organisational skills in relation to control, language and effective delivery. It is not always what you say but how you say it!

If you are given a time limit, you will need to prepare the presentation and then practise it to ensure you are within the time limit. Use an audience of friends or family members or practise in front of a mirror. Over-running a presentation in this type of assessment will make you look extremely disorganised and ill-prepared. Do not reduce your chances of landing a training contract by making this basic error.

Always follow a structure. Even if you get lost or forget what you are supposed to say, the structure should help to bring you back on track in a way that those observing will not notice. Do not attempt to write a script, as this will make your presentation sound extremely stifled. Instead, write down key words. As you mention these they should trigger your thought process.

If you have the opportunity to prepare for the presentation, aim to use effective visual aids. Using diagrams and pictures where possible will simplify and break up your presentation in addition to helping to maintain the attention of the audience. In order to attain maximum impact, keep your presentation simple.

Good structure to your presentation is crucial. Follow the Ultimate Guide 5 W's.

- ✓ WHY – What is your aim for the presentation, and why is the audience there?
- ✓ WHO – What is the knowledge level of the audience? What information do they need to go away with?
- ✓ WHAT material have you prepared for your audience to take away with from your presentation? Prepare Handouts.
- ✓ WHEN – At what point in the day is your presentation? For example, if immediately after lunch, think about how long your presentation will last for and how to hold audience attention.
- ✓ WHERE – What is the location of the presentation?

**Our Top Tip: Think of a logical structure and aim for a fluid delivery. Most people like to see visual images as aids, such as illustrations and pictures. Never read your presentation from a script, you will sound stifled and unnatural. Research thoroughly and prepare properly. The more you practice the better your presentation will be. Aim to keep your talk short and simple!**

### Introduction

- ✓ It may be appropriate to introduce yourself. Always smile, say hello and welcome! A warm, enthusiastic and confident greeting creates a good first impression with your audience.
- ✓ A good opening remark sets the scene. The audience want to know what to expect - so tell them. You need to make your audience believe in you and want to listen - highlight the objective of the talk
- ✓ Aim to build up a rapport with the audience. You need to be enthusiastic from the start, using varied intonation and facial expressions.

### Main body

The structure of your presentation should follow the structure you have outlined in your introduction. This should form the substance of your presentation.

- ✓ Keep your objectives in mind
- ✓ Do not forget about the audience, keep them interested
- ✓ Identify the main points in a logical order and link them to your message

✓ Use examples to illustrate your point wherever possible
✓ Break down any great mass of information
✓ Talk concisely in short sentences
✓ Use effective phrasing if you want a particular point to hit home

Never say too much. Keep your presentation to a maximum of three key points and give your audience a reason to listen. If you include too much information the listeners tend to switch off and the effect of your presentation will be lost.

## Conclusion

✓ End on a positive note
✓ Repeat the key points and emphasize those points which are most important and that you wish to get across
✓ Draw all the threads together and end firmly on your key message
✓ Lastly, thank your audience for listening

## Body language

Your body language needs to demonstrate that you are confident and comfortable in front of your audience.

✓ Avoid holding large pieces of paper if you have shaky hands, instead use prompt cards.
✓ Do not speak in a monotone. Speak as you would in a conversation, using the appropriate intonation. The sound of your voice must be controlled.
✓ Try to look at all of your audience - engage in periods of eye-contact, this will enable them to feel involved and they will be more receptive to you.
✓ Most of us have nervous habits. Try to reduce these by taking preventive measures. If you tend to fidget try instead to keep your hands by your side or behind your back as you talk.
✓ Resist the temptation to fiddle with any objects
✓ If you do move around during your presentation, make it as natural as possible and make any movement purposeful. Do not confuse your audience by pacing up and down unnecessarily.

*I once went into an interview where I had to give a presentation halfway through. I have a tendency to speak a little too quickly when I am nervous. As I had time to prepare the interview before hand, I wrote PAUSE – take your time in big letters between each point. Following this instruction helped me to sound more natural and slowed the pace and volume of my speech.* **K.O.B., trained at magic circle law firm**

## Questions anyone?

Lastly, when preparing for the interview, it is always useful to bear in mind potential questions which may be asked. This obviously allows you to think in advance. Once you have concluded your presentation never forget to offer to answer any questions the audience may have. When answering the questions, maintain the same level of self-assuredness and confidence. If you're not sure how to answer a question, be honest about this to ensure that your presentation maintains its credibility. A useful technique to employ if you are unsure of an answer, is to say you will need to go away and research that point, or that you will be happy to discuss later over a coffee! The last thing you want to do at this stage is to ruin your presentation by trying to bluff an answer. Do yourself justice!

---

### Selection centres / Assessment days: Points to ponder

We have covered in this chapter assessment days and selection centres and given you hints and tips on how to come across well. Remember:

**Group exercises** - Teamwork is essential for success in the workplace. A group exercise is a method of testing your teamwork, communication and interpersonal skills.

**Case studies** – The golden rule in case studies is to apply your logic and common sense to the documentation you are analysing. Remember you are being tested on your ability to assimilate and evaluate large amounts of information and form a coherent, well thought out view on the documentation.

**Presentations** – Remember a presentation has a beginning, middle and a conclusion. Prepare, plan, practise and perform.

---

Chapter Fifteen

## How do you decide between two training contract offers?

Well done on receiving your training contract offers! Choosing which firm is right for you are essentially a personal judgment, and what is right for you may not be a good option for someone else. The last thing you want is to go through all that effort of getting a training contract only to find out that you have chosen a firm that is not right for you. Our suggestion is that you do your best to find people who can talk to you more in depth about a firm, particularly current trainees. When speaking to them consider the factors below, some of which you may have covered when deciding to apply to the firm in the first place (ensure you review your old notes).

### Factors which may influence your choice of firm

✓ DOES THE FIRM HAVE A WELL-ORGANISED AND STRUCTURED TRAINING PROGRAMME? This will enable you to gain effective, practical and comprehensive training as a lawyer.

✓ CLIENT CONTACT: Are the trainee solicitors at the firm given early responsibility, do they attend client meetings and report directly back to clients?

✓ WHAT LEVEL OF WORK WILL YOU BE DOING? Do trainees actually undertake real quality work, such as drafting commercial contracts, and correspondence to clients? Do trainees attend client meetings with the firm's partners?

✓ HOW MANY training contracts are available? Are you suited to a large intake or are you the kind of person who would prefer being part of a select handful of trainees?

✓ ARE TRAINEES AT THE FIRM VALUED? Following your communication with current trainees or junior lawyers at each firm, look to secondary sources such as Roll on Friday, Lawyer2B, lawcareers.net and Chambers and Partners student directory which are all valuable sources of information to provide an insight into the experiences of trainees at each firm.

✓ CHANNELS OF COMMUNICTAION - Is there a good training framework – a supervisor monitoring and appraising your progress?

✓ CULTURE - Does the firm have a good management culture, friendly working environment and ethos?

✓ REPUTATION OF FIRM - How important is it for you to work for a firm which has a strong reputation and is in the top 20 law firms? It also worth considering the reputation of the particular practice area that you are interested in qualifying into at the end of your training,

✓ WHAT IS THE RETENTION RATE? What is the likelihood of you being kept on once you qualify at the firm? It is a good sign if there is a track record of trainees remaining at the firm, and also a number of trainees that have gone on to become partners. What are your chances of qualifying into your desired practice area?

✓ A WORK/LIFE BALANCE? Despite what your contract may say, the job of a lawyer is simply not 9-5. However, a work/life balance is integral to your well-being; continually doing late nights at any firm will naturally impact on this. Are you prepared for it?

✓ SALARY: At the time of writing this edition, law firm salaries are a hot topic with some firms now paying an annual salary of over £65,000 to newly qualified solicitors. How much is money a motivating factor for you? Conversely, will your salary be in line with the Law Society's minimum wage requirements?

✓ FUNDING. Will the firm pay all your law school course fees and living expenses? This will save on the amount of your student debt.

✓ BENEFITS AND PERKS. How much does the law firm value its people? Think fringe benefits and corporate discounts. Is there a possibility for you to take leave after qualification? What kind of bonuses are on offer? How many days holiday do you get?

✓ PRO BONO WORK. Is there an opportunity to do work for charity and put something back into the community? Is this important to you?

✓ VACATION SCHEME. Did you do a vacation scheme at the firm? Think back to your vacation scheme. What was your experience like? Did this experience match your expectations? Do you still have any contacts at the firm whom you could talk to?

*I chose my firm based on a gut feeling. It's hard to tell one outfit from another especially at the big City firms, you have to look at where you feel most comfortable. I chose a firm that had a very friendly working environment more so than other firms I had visited previously. I had done a vacation scheme there so knew some of the people. The HR representatives were all very bubbly people and the partners who interviewed me were very positive about the training I would receive at the firm. I could tell that the firm appreciated individuality. On the tour of the office, I could see that everyone I was introduced to seemed to enjoy working at the firm. This wasn't the case at all the firms I visited.*

**A 3rd Year university Student, at Kings College, London.**

It is important to remember that you cannot hold more than two offers before accepting an offer of a training contract in writing. If you do receive any further offers, the Law Society permits you to turn down any offer that you do not really consider seriously.

Some firms, upon making you an offer, will invite you back to try and convince you to join their firm. They will normally take you out for a meal. Take advantage of this. You will get the opportunity to meet current trainees and you can ask all the questions you want without feeling any pressure.

Never sell yourself short - any firm should feel lucky to have you! Joining a firm should be a two-way process. From the firm's perspective they have managed to secure a talented leading lawyer of tomorrow, and from your perspective you will be working for a law firm that recognises your talent and is willing to invest their money and time in training you. (*See Chapter 17: Meet our Friends, where our friends discuss why and how they chose their firms.*)

## Choosing between two or more firms: Points to Ponder

How do you ensure you choose the right firm if you are successful in obtaining more than one offer. Remember that joining a law firm should be a two-way process. You have successfully matched their training contract selection criteria. How well does each firm fulfil your selection criteria? The following non-exhaustive quick summary of factors may help you decide which firm to choose:

1. The structure and organisation of the firm's training programme.

2. Are you likely to get direct contact with the firm's clients?

3. Will you be involved in quality and interesting work?

4. Will you be one of many trainees or part of a select few?

5. Does the firm have a good reputation?

6. Will the culture of the firm suit you?

7. Will you receive a good salary?

8. Is the firm offering you sponsorship to fund your legal training?

9. Will you be able to maintain a healthy work/life balance?

Chapter Sixteen

# What if I complete my legal studies without a training contract?

There are currently more places on the LPC than there are training contracts available, which makes the market place extremely competitive (*see Introduction for specific facts and figures*). You may find yourself in a position where you have successfully completed your legal studies without the security of a training contract and may be wondering what to do next if you find yourself in this position.

For some people the route to qualification as a solicitor will be fairly straightforward to the extent that they may not be aware of some of the difficulties we describe in this guide. For others the route will be more difficult and longer than anticipated, but there are a wealth of opportunities in the legal market where you can build up your skills until you find a training contract.

Our advice to any students who have made up their mind to pursue a career in law would be to continue the process of applying while building up legal experience in their particular area of interest.

Consider your next step carefully and remain positive. While writing this guide, we met many students who had become downbeat about the training contract application process. The frustration for some was that they had got to interview stage at firms but had unfortunately been unsuccessful. The other group of students we spoke to were those who had difficulty even getting to interview stage.

Our advice to these students was to focus of what they considered their area of weakness. If you have made numerous applications previously, you will need to try and establish (preferably with the help of careers advisors, colleagues and friends) the reason you have been unsuccessful so far, then act on this as best you can.

## Case Studies

### Student X

One student we met had excellent credentials but was not very confident in her ability. Student X was extremely determined to succeed and after using some of the Ultimate Guide's top tips, managed to improve the way she came across at interviews, her confidence gradually increased and after another round of applications, she was offered a training contract.

### Student Y

Another student we spoke to wanted to work for a City firm but had no legal experience. Our advice to student Y was to build upon his commercial experience. If you do have aspirations to work for a City firm, the firms you wish to apply to will want evidence of your commercial drive. Student Y had spent 6 months working at the Free Representation Unit (FRU). Whilst this is very good experience, it did not fit in with his City aspirations. Student Y was interested in finance work and applied for paralegal positions at investment banks and law firms with excellent reputations in the finance sector. It is important to demonstrate your commitment in the area of practice that interests you the most. Student Y spent 8 months working at an investment bank while continuing to apply for training contracts and eventually secured one at a leading firm.

The examples above have been provided to show that there are ways in which you can improve your prospects if you don't manage to secure a training contract by the time you expect to.

### Transferable skills

Remember that transferable skills gained from your legal studies will also be highly valued in other sectors of the employment market. After gaining good experience and progressing well in some of these fields, your application to a law firm is more likely to stand out from the rest.

The Law Society may award reductions for trainees who have significant prior legal work experience, which they can offset by up to six months "time to count". An increasing number of people take the LPC part-time while working, usually due to family or financial commitments.

## What options are available to you?

### Paralegal

Paralegals are employed on either temporary or permanent contracts. Paralegals often undertake a wide range of tasks and are normally recruited into specific departments. This work can vary from legal research to proofreading legal documents, drafting and preparing agreements and organising trial bundles. Paralegals at some firms will do similar work to trainees, but much of the work will revolve around document management, involving heavy administrative duties and logistical tasks, such as filing documents, photocopying, generally facilitating efficiency and assisting in transactions.

Becoming a paralegal is a good way of getting the type of legal experience that will add value to your application form. Students who do not manage to secure a training contract by the end of their studies should consider working as paralegals. You may consider this as a way to use and develop your legal skills and find out whether you really enjoy a particular area of the law.

It is not uncommon for people who have worked as paralegals to be subsequently offered training contracts at the law firm where they work. At some of the largest city firms, we came across a number of trainees and associates who managed to get themselves noticed by impressing some of the partners they had undertaken work for while working as paralegals.

If you decide to apply to a firm you are paralegalling for, the firm will still require you to apply through the standard channels, i.e. application form and interview.

A word of warning; becoming a paralegal is a not a guaranteed way of securing a training contract. We spoke to some paralegals that had been rejected for trainee positions at their firms, due to a policy of not recruiting paralegals from within the firm's ranks. The onus on the student wanting to apply for a training contract through paralegal work experience is to research the prospect of eventually becoming a trainee, so that accepting a job offer does not frustrate your ambition to qualify as a solicitor.

Some people enjoy their role as paralegals a great deal and decide to make it their long-term career. Paralegals in large City and US firms earn good salaries and have good opportunities to work overtime at an increased rate of pay. Should you decide to paralegal as a possible career option, The National Association of Paralegals offers a post graduate diploma in paralegal practice.

**Our Top Tip: You can apply to firms who take on paralegals through speculative applications or through recruitment agencies. If you decide to make speculative applications, ensure that you find out the name of the person who deals with paralegal recruitment before writing in. In addition, there are numerous paralegal agencies who will register suitable candidates.** (*See the list of some recruitment agencies in Chapter 19.*)

## Outdoor Clerk

The work of an Outdoor Clerk involves assisting lawyers by preparing court documents and delivering them to court, attending hearings and visiting clients. Much of the work is litigation-based, so is a possible means for future litigation lawyers to gain experience clerking. You can normally secure these positions through legal recruitment agencies.

## Institute of Legal Executives (ILEX) route to becoming a legal executive

The training and qualifications are different to conventional solicitors, although in many respects their jobs can be very much similar. Qualified legal executives provide support to solicitors and do work that is charged to clients. They can work in private practice, local government or in-house positions, and normally specialise in conveyancing, civil and criminal litigation, family law and probate.

One benefit of choosing the ILEX qualification is that you can earn while learning. You do not require a degree to become a legal executive, but to progress as a legal executive you have to pass the ILEX examinations. The qualification is recognised throughout England & Wales, and law graduates are exempt from the academic parts of the ILEX professional training and qualification. You will need to complete a qualifying employment period of a minimum of five years in order to qualify. Also see ILEX's website for further details on this route into the legal profession (*see Chapter 19 for details*).

## Civil Service Fast Stream

This is the Civil Service's accelerated development programme. Fast streamers normally move through a series of roles within the Civil Service and gain a very broad experience. Day-to-day tasks will include briefings or even writing speeches for ministers and other seniors. There are various specialised departments for which a law degree will be seen as particularly useful, for example:

✓ Department for Culture, Media and Sport
✓ Department for Environment, Food and Rural Affairs
✓ Department for Transport
✓ Department for Work & Pensions
✓ Department of Trade and Industry
✓ Foreign and Commonwealth Office
✓ HM Customs and Excise
✓ Home Office
✓ National Assembly for Wales
✓ Office of Telecommunications

To find out more about recruitment, check out
**www.careers.civil-service.uk**

## Company Secretary

The title is often mistaken for a clerical role as opposed to a managerial or professional role. A Company Secretary will help the company to implement the developments and new legislation in company law and will deal with much of the corporate filings in relation to the company. They will be responsible for making sure directors comply with their obligations and that shareholders are kept updated. It is generally a varied role which will involve corporate governance, insurance arrangements and executive share schemes and also dealing with confidential information. This role will provide valuable commercial exposure. In order to progress to a successful career you will be required to pass the ISCA exams to get chartered status.

For more information check out the website of the Chartered Institute of Company Secretaries: **www.icsa.org.uk**

## Accountancy and Tax

If you have done the LPC, you will have no doubt enjoyed studying the various tax and accounts modules! One option may be to put what you have learnt into a practical context while developing any interest you may have in finance. Accountancy will require numeric skills and these will be put to the test during the interview process. The nature of tax is challenging, with constant changes in legislation. This will provide a career that will test your intellectual ability and will be a constant challenge as well as allowing you to stay close to the law.

Both roles will involve working closely with companies in an advisory and compliance capacity. Audit will involve looking at companies internal accounts and writing reports based on your findings. Tax will involve finding innovative strategies to enable companies to operate in the most tax efficient manner, and anticipating at an early stage the tax implications which may affect a business. Both accountancy and tax will involve taking professional qualifications, normally through ICAEW (Institute of Chartered Accountants in England and Wales).

## Finance

There is an outstanding range of business opportunities and a broad selection of specialist areas, which will require your transferable analytical and logical thinking ability. Bear in mind that, getting a graduate position at a financial institution is equally as competitive as landing a training contract. Nearly all the City banks have an international presence and you may have opportunities to travel. The work, although demanding, is also very financially rewarding. There is a wealth of information out there about these jobs (*see chapter 19*).

## New York (NY) and Californian Bar

If you are thinking about undertaking one of these qualifications in order to work in the US, bear in mind that the US legal market is just as competitive as that in the UK. Passing the NY or Californian Bar exam does not in most cases lead to instant job success overseas, although upon passing the exams you will technically be a qualified attorney. Interestingly, we know of one friend who successfully passed the New York Bar and was able to get a job with a New York law firm in London practising as a New York Attorney. Our friend, who studied at an English university, will be taking the QLTT in order to become dual qualified in England and Wales.

Bear in mind that whilst gaining additional qualifications will add an extra string to your bow, it will add little to the rest of your academics and experiences if these do not meet law firms' stringent criteria. That said, - it is a qualification which will no doubt enhance your all-round portfolio of skills. The people we spoke to took the exams for a variety of reasons, some were looking to make a permanent move overseas, and for others it was purely for academic purposes, while the majority of people were looking for the qualification to enhance their career prospects.

If you are determined to work overseas, do not be discouraged by the competition. Do your research and find what types of opportunities are available. New York, for example, has lots of paralegal agencies, and paralegals are paid more by way of remuneration than in the UK If you do decide to take the exams you will have to travel to the US. The exams for the NY Bar take place twice a year in Albany, the State Capital, which is approximately two hours on the train from New York City.

## Research and analysis

Law graduates are looked on favourably for this type of work. All those laborious hours spent doing practical legal research at university and law school will come in extremely handy for this. Companies such as Deveraux and Deloitte are keen to employ law students to undertake essay writing and research assignments, which is a great way to earn some extra money.

## Recruitment Consultant

Getting a job in legal recruitment in particular presents an opportunity to make numerous contacts in the field. This role encompasses being on the phone, corresponding via e-mail and dealing with various clients and different personalities. You will generally enjoy some autonomy in your role as you will essentially be an agent, "the middle person" between the companies and the people you are aiming to place. If you are successful you can build effective business relationships with your clients. If you fancy the chance of getting to know people and remaining connected to the profession, this may be the job for you. You will tend to work in a fast-paced and dynamic environment. This will involve lots of negotiating and organising, it will require a high level of interpersonal skills and you may even get to travel to exotic locations to meet clients if you're lucky. Developing contacts may allow you to make an impression in the right places in order to fulfil your ambition of qualifying as a solicitor.

## Postgraduate study

After graduating, going back to the books to pursue postgraduate study is a popular option, but ensure your decision is for the right reasons:

## Does an LLM/Master's in Law increase your employability?

Many students are uncertain about what they want to do once they have completed the LLB. Some opt to do an LLM Master's, to use an extra year to enhance their employability or decide whether they would like to commit their future to the law. A Master's programme is structured around 12 months full-time or 2 two years part-time, and the course is usually taught in a similar way to the undergraduate course by a combination of seminars, lectures and a final research paper.

The LLM allows you to focus on a wide range of subjects in much greater detail. For example, if corporate law appealed to you while at university, the Master's programme offers the perfect opportunity to explore the subject. Indeed, if you decide to apply to a corporate law firm, enrolling in a relevant Master's programme will show employers that you have a genuine interest in this area. During the Master's programme you will develop your analytical skills and improve your written skills, and you can sell these on your application forms. You will be studying an area of your particular interest meaning that you enjoy your Master's programme more than the undergraduate course.

Given that the job market is extremely competitive, a respected postgraduate course may make you more appealing to potential employers but not all employers value the qualification as much as they do your first degree.

For some students an LLM may lead to a career in academia, and because the LLM is taught largely by research this will offer you an appropriate way to this career path.

## International

International LLMs are generally considered impressive to have on your CV by some recruiters. There are lots of courses available and it may take some time-plan your study. In the US, and Europe, application processes can be rigorous and complex. In addition you may want to identify any possible sources of funding. Postgraduate study abroad is costly, and more and more students are doing courses from home, using the internet and e-mail to cover the material.

**Our Top Tip; an LLM is not a magic wand that will automatically further your career. A postgraduate qualification may well equip you with a competitive advantage but an LLM does necessarily increase your prospects of securing a training contract. Choose your course and your institution through research. Enrol on a course that you are genuinely interested in. The year is difficult enough and will only be made easier if you have a keen and genuine interest in this area of the law. You must be able to promote the value of any postgraduate study to any law firm that you apply to, by showing how your qualification makes you an asset. Find out from any employers you are interested in how well they regard the extra qualification. Ultimately, only undertake the LLM if it is something that you are personally interested in doing.**

## Useful locators of funding sources:

Charities and Trusts – see Law Society and Postgraduate Study & Research (AGCAS)
University funds – awards to students continuing in same institution from undergraduate level
Bank loan – student loan / career development loan
Government sources – **www.dfes.gov.uk**
International students – contact the British Council
Research Council awards – research board and councils
Useful website – **www.lifelonglearning.co.uk**

---

### What happens if I complete my legal studies without having secured a training contract? Points to Ponder

Many students find themselves in the difficult predicament of finishing their legal studies without first having secured a training contract. It may be sensible to carefully review your training contract applications. Are you spending enough time researching the firm, drafting your applications, checking for minor errors? Are you failing at interview? It is a good idea to ask colleagues who have managed to secure training contracts to assess your CV, covering letters and applications in order to suggest ways that you can improve.

There are many options and different career alternatives available for students without a training contract. The first step, assuming you want to remain in the law, is to contact agencies to find out more about any roles that are available in the recruitment market and also write directly to law firms to see if they would consider offering you a role as a paralegal. For those aspiring solicitors wanting to continue studying, look at the range of universities which offer good options for postgraduate study.

Finally, even if you are yet to experience training contract success, remember, there are still many ways that aspiring solicitors can build their skills and make themselves more attractive to law firms. Remember for many students the journey to becoming a solicitor is sometimes more akin to a marathon than a sprint. Gaining further legal experience will develop your knowledge, experience and contacts which will surely increase your chances of landing a training contract.

Chapter Seventeen

## **Meet our friends**

This section profiles some of our friends who have managed to secure training contracts. They have very kindly agreed to offer their own unique hints and tips about the recruitment process and describe from an individual perspective the key factors that helped them become successful in securing a training contract. A common theme that spans across their experiences is the amount of effort and preparation needed to get the elusive training contract offer.

### **GRAHAM CUTTS**

Graham is a solicitor with Lovells. He trained as a solicitor with Penningtons, in London. He studied law at Durham University.

In my opinion, prepare for an interview from the perspective that you are selling yourself to the firm. After all, that is all the interview is: a sales pitch. Your CV has secured the interview, let your personality do the rest. Try and judge the sort of character they are looking for. You may need to adjust your approach (and presentation at the interview) accordingly.

Here follows, a few basics: Be up-to-date on current affairs, political in particular - (the opening question at my interview was whether Mr Hoon, former Defence Secretary, should resign, legal developments and business movements, (you needn't read the FT from cover to cover, but be alive to a variety of angles the interviewer could take). This all depends, at least from a commercial awareness perspective, on the particular firm.

Be polite from the moment you walk through the door, to receptionists, etc. I've been told that the interviewer will often ask how the individual approached the firm's front desk. Smile. Show them you are personable.

Dress smartly but understated - always better than the other way round. Be confident without being arrogant, and competent in your reply without rambling. Keep eye-contact at all times, (some people find this very difficult: Practise! Imagine a triangle around the eyes and nose - focus on that area and you can't go wrong).

The most difficult part of the application is the application form itself. Select the right firm according to your interests and tailor your answers to each individual question - never cut and paste; they spot it a mile off. Take your time on the form, no spelling errors / mistakes – this goes without saying. This is the document that must catch their eye out of thousands, hence the difficulty! Just take your time, proof-read several times and get others to do the same.

I chose Penningtons from the Training Contract handbook. The firm appeared to offer a broad base of practice areas - this for me was the most important aspect of the firm. If money drives you then apply for the top firms, but be aware that the top salaries may come at a price - often long hours and sometimes little client contact (because of the sheer size of the firm you could be a small cog in a big wheel). Smaller to medium-sized firms are likely to throw you in at the deep end - judge whether this is for you. Look for a firm that suits your character. This can only ever be subjectively assessed - try to find out as much as possible about where, potentially, you will spend the rest of your working life!

My key piece of advice: work hard at law school - (the LPC/GDL is easily failed, though not conceptually difficult, some struggle with the sheer volume of work); research into the firm and their clients (as law is a client driven business, find out as much as you can about the firms/individuals that will ultimately pay your wages!); perfect your written and analytical skills.

You need: good attention to detail, ability to prioritise tasks effectively, good people skills, ability to digest information and assimilate with task in hand, meet your deadlines and finally KNOW THE LAW!!!

## NOREEN AHMED

Noreen is a trainee solicitor at a magic circle law firm in London. She studied law at UCL.

### The application form

Put plenty of time aside to present a good form. Research the firm so you can highlight the qualities they are looking for in their trainees in order to answer the often obscure questions. This will be much easier if you're genuinely interested in the firm you're applying to. Chambers Student is great for information on the different firms and practice areas, so should help you gauge where you'd be best suited. Speaking to trainees and lawyers at the firm will also give you an idea of the working environment and level of responsibility given.

Tailor your answers to the particular question – cut and paste jobs don't always work! Check for spelling mistakes and make sure you stick to any word limits. Read the form out loud as it's a good way to ensure you're not waffling. Ask others to read it too so it makes sense. Your college careers service is also invaluable for advice on form filling so do use them.

### Before the interview

Preparation is the key. Your application has suggested to the firm that you have the skills and qualities they require, but you need to prove that you have them. You must sell yourself in the best possible light, and with sufficient grounding you can pre-empt their questions.

Find out the format of the interview process first. If your interview is with a large firm, I would suggest that for two weeks before the interview you become as "commercially aware" (sorry to use this irritating term!) as possible. Pick out two to three current issues you find interesting, and would feel comfortable discussing at interview, from *The FT* or other quality papers such as *The Times*, every day if you can, or try to glance at key stories on the *BBC News website*. If you can discuss an issue knowledgeably you will impress the interviewer, and by reading the press regularly you will understand how deals or current news stories have unfolded, and sometimes their combined impact, e.g. how hurricane Katrina affected already rising oil prices – any intelligent person can point to that - but if you can slip in something like, "I read in *The FT* this week that petrol prices have risen faster than at any time since the 1970s," it makes your comment full, interesting and prompts a response from the interviewer, making the process more natural than an interrogation. In order to get some sound reasoning for your views read *The Economist,* which has analysis from leading experts. All this will definitely make you stand out from someone who simply picked up a paper the night before their interview!

Don't panic if you're asked a direct question such as, "What's your view on Mozambique's fiscal policy?" Rather than freaking out you could politely answer: "I'm sorry but I don't know much about that, but I read in *The Times* that fiscal policy in many countries is currently geared towards cutting taxes." Immediately you will be transformed from nervous wreck to knowledgeable news follower!

Try to read up on the firm, not just by looking at their website and brochures – everyone does that. Do a search on *The Lawyer, Lex* and other legal websites to bring up articles about the firm and its lawyers. Moreover, there are often articles comparing firms, which will help you to back up your reasons for choosing Firm X rather than Firm Y.

Try to speak to trainees and contacts at the firm. They are usually very receptive to giving you helpful advice on the sort of people the firm look for, which will help your presentation style at the interview.

## At the Interview

Dress appropriately - a dark coloured suit is usually a safe option. In terms of body language maintain eye-contact and don't fold your arms as it looks defensive. Try not to gesticulate too much as it's distracting.

Relax and smile so your personality comes through but remain alert and professional. Don't try to act in a way that is inconsistent with your character as the interviewers are experienced enough to see through a façade. In your answers be honest but positive e.g. if asked about a blip on your academic record be truthful as to why but explain that you have learnt from your mistake as reflected by your results since then. Keep your answers succinct and relevant.

In a nutshell, imagine that you're already a lawyer at the firm and that you are trying to win an important client (the interviewer).

## After the Interview

Don't dwell on it too much but do make a note of the questions you were asked and think of other possible answers to anything you found disconcerting. This will help at your next interview. Above all be positive – you're always your own harshest critic!

## OMER MAROOF

Omer trained as a solicitor at SJ Berwin. He studied law at City University, in London and completed a Masters in Corporate Law at UCL.

### How to prepare for interviews

Much will depend on the type of firm you are interviewing with. Your aim should be to try and convince the interviewers that the firm would benefit from offering you a training contract. You can go about convincing them of this in a number of ways. The first is to realise the importance of your CV/application. It goes without saying but you would be amazed at the number of people who are instantly rejected because they are unable to answer questions on their CV/application. A good way of ensuring you know your CV is to get a friend to play devil's advocate and ask you questions on your CV. The interview is an opportunity to showcase your personality and allow the interviewers the chance to see that you will fit into their firm.

Take the time to research the firm - this can entail visiting your careers service and obtaining any details of past interviews, reading online material on the firm and talking to people who have interviewed/worked at the firm. It is also very important to talk to people about interviews in general. Make a list of all questions that you/your friends have been asked at interviews and write out answers for each of them.

It is also important to be familiar with current affairs (particularly those with a legal or commercial twist). Reading the FT is not strictly necessary (although if you already do it I take my hat off to you), I feel the business section of most broadsheets is sufficient.

For the interview itself, ensure that you are smartly dressed. Always take an umbrella with you just in case the predictably unpredictable English skies open up. Try to arrive 5 to 10 minutes early. Be polite to everyone you come into contact with. Make sure that you greet your interviewers with a firm handshake. Be confident in your answers and do not be afraid to show your personality. Maintain eye-contact throughout and show an interest in what your interviewers say about the firm (ideally you will be able to use some of that information to form the basis for one of your end-of-interview questions).

## Most difficult part of the application process

The most difficult part of the application process is the initial application itself. Firm selection is so very important. You will find that spending time to research firms will substantially reduce the number of firms that you are really suited to. Although it may seem too time-consuming to do this, it is definitely worthwhile as making 20 excellent tailored applications will give you a better chance of success than making 100 identical applications. Always give yourself plenty of time to complete your application and try not to wait until the deadline before submitting it. Most firms will have a core of about four or five main skills that they are looking for in trainees. Your aim should be to deduce what these are (from your research) and then use the application form to show examples of how you possess/have used these skills in practice. Get a friend to review your application. Check and re-check to ensure that there are no typos as this will often result in your application being rejected. If you are doing an online application always print off a copy to check before sending. Cutting and pasting from previous applications should be avoided at all costs - the formatting is never the same and the firm will be able to spot it instantly and this will (again) result in your application being rejected.

## How and why did you choose SJ Berwin?

I chose SJ Berwin because of its strength in corporate law. Having completed a Masters in corporate law, it was important for me to find a firm that shared my passion for this area of law. Having spent three months as a paralegal at SJ Berwin, I was also impressed by the firm's emphasis on the importance of collegiality. Put quite simply, I found SJ Berwin's dedication to its clients, along with its commitment to professional and technical excellence, inspiring and its willingness to give early responsibility to those willing to take up the challenge refreshing. My goal was to get hands-on experience of high quality work early into my training contract and SJ Berwin have certainly given me the opportunity to do this. It is important to emphasize the need to look at whether a firm is right for you. Working for a Magic Circle firm as a trainee undoubtedly has its perks (most notably the salary) but it also has pitfalls (minimal client contact, long hours and bit-part involvement in transactions/cases). Working for small firms will mean that your salary will not be as high and a lack of professionalism may also exist but this can be off-set against the high levels of responsibility and quality of work that you are given. SJ Berwin, as a medium/top City law firm, is ideal in this regard as it provides the best of both worlds; the salary and professionalism of a Magic Circle firm together with the responsibility and quality of work provided by the smaller firms. It will be for you to decide the kind of environment you want to work in and you should try to select a firm that matches your personality/work-ethic.

## Key piece of advice

Ensure that you work diligently at both university and law school and get the best grades that you are capable of. Your academic results are one of the first things that firms will look at when deciding which students to call to interview. However, for the top firms, excellent academics are not enough. For these firms it is a given that you are intelligent - so what else can you offer? Firms are looking for evidence of students having positions of responsibility (preferably recent) and relevant work experience, if you don't have any legal experience, go and get some, even if it is on a voluntary basis at a Legal Advice Centre).

Being able to communicate in a second language is always positively received, as is having interests outside of law. Always make use of the careers service at your university. Arrange a mock-interview so that you are not overly fazed when the real thing comes round. Finally, and this is one of the most important pieces of advice I can offer, never give up (if you get rejections, ask for feedback and use it to improve your future applications) and always have confidence in yourself (if you are not confident in yourself, it will be difficult to convince a firm to have confidence in you).

## What makes a good trainee?

A good trainee should:

- be able to prioritise tasks effectively and efficiently; have good attention to detail;

- be able to deal with pressurised circumstances - you would be amazed at how many people (from partners to trainees) are unable to handle pressure - keeping your head at difficult times will set you apart from others;

- take pride in his/her work - make sure there are no silly mistakes in the work that is done (whether it be bibling or drafting) - such errors if consistently repeated reflect very poorly on a trainee and will not encourage your supervisors to give you added responsibility;

- not sulk at criticism - instead take on board whatever is said and improve your performance;

- check and re-check emails/letters before sending them out or showing them to a supervisor - it will only take a minute and can be the difference between seeming competent or careless;

- take detailed instructions before beginning a task; do not be afraid to ask questions - it is quite possible that unclear instructions were given at the outset;

- not make promises he/she cannot keep - make sure people are aware of your workload; tell someone your unhappy with the quality of work/level of responsibility you are being given, so that steps can be taken to address the issue (there is no point waiting until your end of seat appraisal to bring this up); and

- be polite to everyone at the firm as there will undoubtedly be times when you will need their help.

## MARIA CHRISTOU

Maria completed her LLB law degree at City University and is the In-House Trainee Solicitor at Motorola.

### General Advice

It is vitally important for a successful career in law to attend a university that has a renowned reputation, to carry out extra curricular activities, volunteer for positions of responsibility and have a good breadth of work experience, whether it is voluntary or paid. The realisation suddenly dawns on you when you are in your second or third year at university that there is fierce competition for a Training Contract. As a consequence, obtaining a 2:1 brings added importance and is very important to ensure that you are marketable to any prospective legal employer.

### Obtaining a Training Contract

It is all well and good to give useful tips and hints with regards to obtaining a Training Contract when you are at the early stages of your career, i.e.: at college or university. However it is often the case that students fund themselves through Law School, without a Training Contract and in most instances you might be working two or maybe even three part-time jobs to pay for fees, books and travel, resulting in limited time to study let alone time to undertake the right extra-curricular activities and work experience. Consequently the time constraints may unfortunately mean applications are omitted or placed at the bottom of your list of priorities. At this stage prospective trainees become panic stricken. What do you do in this instance?

- First and foremost do not fear - you have not missed the boat!

- The fact that you have held down a part-time job and a demanding course shows that you are dedicated to a career in law, and that speaks volumes to any prospective employer. Via working and studying you have already acquired skills that can be adapted and honed to those required by a competent solicitor. For example, effective time management, prioritising your caseload and working under pressure.

- If your heart is set on working for a mid-size or magic circle law firm, upon researching into their recruitment process, you will promptly realise that firms that fall within these categories are recruiting trainees for an intake two or three years in advance. You will have to decide whether you want to wait that long for a training contract.

- Prepare a legal CV no more than 2 pages long and try to obtain as much legal work experience (paid/unpaid) as possible. Join legal recruitment agencies, utilise your existing contacts and begin undertaking tasks that you can add to your CV to show that you are a responsible, well balanced individual. During that time, make full use of your Law School's careers database and actively search for training contracts at firms that carry out areas of law where you have a keen interest. Speak to your peers, as they may know something you don't. Often if you are working at a small law firm and you prove your competence and worth, they are likely to keep you on and offer you a training contract, beware of empty promises though! Ensure any promises are formally documented. If you are working for a magic circle or mid-size firm, you will benefit hugely by adding this experience to your CV and doors will open for you.

- Consider all your options. Training contracts are available at local authorities, and in-house too, and the start dates are far sooner than at most law firms!

## Applications for in-house training contracts

The majority of in-house training contracts tend to be in Industry and Commerce/Commercial/IT/Telecoms/Multimedia. If you are interested in working in-house, the application process can present a challenge, largely because most companies will not advertise training contracts in newspapers, on the web or with the careers services, as they do not have the time to go through thousands of applications. The majority of in-house firms will ask agencies to streamline candidates' CVs, to ensure that they have the qualifications sought, the right experience and skills. Agencies will hand over to the firm the

CVs of the best, most suitable candidates. In-house teams will take over the recruitment process. The same principles apply to applications in-house as they would to applying to a firm in private practice:

- Ensure that you have researched the firms/companies well and that your CV and covering letter are tailored to the firm/company.

- Note experiences from varied practice areas, as training in-house will often mean that you are working on numerous legal issues/practice areas at any one time.

- Highlight your competence in IT and language skills too, as they tend to carry a great deal of weight.

- Having a passion for the industry will shine through and make your application stand out from the rest.

**Interview**

Preparation is the key to training contract success. Read through the job description and ensure that you have examples of the skills and qualities required for the job. You will be asked many questions relating to your CV, so be prepared to elaborate or substantiate. Carry out research into the industry prior to interview. It is highly likely that you will be grilled on new developments in the industry and new up-coming areas of law. You will also need to show that you have a good commercial awareness, so read the news and keep up to date with current affairs in business.

It has often been stated that "it is not the best CV that lands the job, but the best interviewee", so let your personality shine through, show that you have great interpersonal/communication skills, as that is key to working in-house.

The number of interviews prior to securing a job in-house will vary from two at minimum to five at maximum, so ensure that you make a note of the questions you were asked, as it is likely you will be asked the same questions again.

## Training as a solicitor in-house

Training in-house will mean that you have a very hands-on role and you will have the opportunity to gain responsibility earlier than in private practice. A role in-house will ensure that you have a varied workload and many exciting challenges on a daily basis. Depending on the firm/company you train with, you may also have an opportunity to travel, which is quite rare for trainees in private practice. As an in-house trainee, you will have specific management areas and responsibilities (as well as having to deal with any other matter that may come your way), you will be responsible for managing business meetings and you will work closely with your client, so you will see the results of your advice first-hand. In addition you will need to adopt a commercially minded approach to problem solving, as you will be involved with the operations of the company, often making commercial as well as legal decisions. Finally internal and external people management skills are required on a daily basis.

Whether you decide to pursue a career as an in-house solicitor or follow the pathway of working in private practice, I wish you the very best of luck and a prosperous career in law.

## OLU DANSU

Olu is a trainee at Beachcroft Wansbroughs. He studied law at Coventry university and completed a Masters in Commercial and Corporate Law at UCL.

## Application Stage

One of the most difficult decisions I had to make at the application stage was trying to decide which firms to apply to. Like most applicants, I initially tried to apply to as many firms as possible by simply sending out my CV without actually spending sufficient time in researching the firms. This is the wrong approach, as the consequence is that insufficient time and effort is devoted to completing a form or researching a firm.

Eventually I decided to focus on just a handful of firms that I identified as offering seats in areas of law that I was interested in, as well as having a good record of offering support to trainees. It is therefore important to decide the area of law you are interested in and research specific firms in that area. Try to focus on a few firms at a time and designate a specific amount of time to researching and completing each application. I spent an average of one week on researching and completing each of my application before submission.

Remember that most firms receive a huge number of applications at this stage, and the competition is fierce; therefore try to do yourself justice when submitting your application by making sure it portrays your personality and qualities to anyone reading it.

## Tips:
- Decide the area of law you are interested in and focus on firms that offer seats in those areas.
- Try to apply as far in advance as possible, and try to avoid last minute applications.
- Always get a third party to proofread your completed application or CV before sending it off. It is easier for other people to spot your errors and offer suggestions.
- If there are questions on an application form that you find difficult, ask others for their opinion. If you know anyone that has a training contract already, or is a trainee, ask for

his or her opinion. Never be afraid or shy to canvass other people's views if you are stuck on a point or question.

- Before submitting any application, always take a step back and ask yourself: is this the best that I can do?

## Interview and Assessment Stage

Various firms adopt different procedures at this stage. Some will have an interview (formal and/or informal), while others will also have an assessment day. Usually, you should be told what process to expect before the day. Whatever the process, preparation is the key to training contract success.

Find out what help your careers service provide and where appropriate, make use of this facility. The College of Law's careers office, keep files containing feedback from applicants that have attended interviews and/or assessments at various firms. I found the resources in the careers office invaluable. They gave me an idea of the format of the assessment day and the type of questions to expect.

It is likely that most other careers offices will provide the same service. Try to find out about this, as they may contain helpful information about the firms you are interested in. I would strongly advise anyone to start out their preparation with the careers office, and it is also possible that they could arrange mock interviews for you, as was the case with me.

**Tips:**
- Give yourself enough time to prepare, find out what services are provided by your careers service and make use of them.
- Try to arrange a private mock interview before your appointment. The more you practise interviews, the better you become at them.
- Try to be yourself on the day of your assessment, concentrate on your own work and don't get influenced by other candidates' behaviour or approach.
- If given a written exercise, take your time and work to your own strengths. Don't panic if other applicants start writing furiously before you've even had the time to get your thoughts together.
- Follow any instruction diligently; if asked to write a two-page report, don't exceed the two pages.

- If you have a group exercise, relate to the other applicants as colleagues, not opponents or competitors. Don't be overbearing or dominating, and whatever you do, don't criticise another candidate's idea, no matter how stupid it may sound.

## AMEER MALIK

Ameer has secured a training contract at a magic circle law firm. He studied law at Durham University.

### Advice

Applying for training contracts can seem like a frustrating process but if you're persistent, realistic and prepared to put some real thought into the applications you make, you can achieve what may seem like the impossible.

In the search for a training contract I began by deciding whether or not I wanted to practise law as a solicitor. Having initially been unsure I quickly realised the decision to practise law as a solicitor is not one to be taken lightly. Not only will you be spending at least two years in the profession before becoming qualified but employers throughout the application and interview process are looking to offer contracts to those candidates with a focused desire to pursue a career as a solicitor.

Having decided that I wanted to pursue a career as a solicitor I began my search for that elusive training contract. The first thing I did was to decide on the areas of law within which I wished to practise. Although it can be difficult to decide which areas of law you might want to train in, it is important you try to make as informed a choice as possible. I used the experience I gained from my degree and subsequent work experience to direct me towards the areas of law I was most interested in.

I then proceeded to take an in-depth look at the specific qualities of those firms that specialised in the areas I wished to eventually practise in. Deciding which firms to apply to for your training contract is an important step and not one to be rushed. Every firm has a very different culture and set of values; finding the right one that will suit you takes time and research. Aim to meet as many different people as you can within a firm, whether at law fairs, presentations, open days or interviews. Ask yourself if you like the people you meet. Could you see yourself working with them? Do their practice areas interest you? Some of the things that I considered were the nature of the training programme, the overall friendliness of the firm, the firm's main areas of expertise, and the firm's overall reputation in the legal world. I also considered the trainee retention rate, its client base, and other factors such as foreign travel and language grants.

One of the things I found extremely helpful was the use of careers fairs to gain an insight into law firms and their people. Having only completed a single vacation scheme it was here that I was able to ask questions about those firms I was interested in and more importantly talk to representatives of prospective firms. Whilst talking to these representatives I took a mental note of each trainee or partner's name and used it in my applications to show I had done a bit more hands-on research than having just read up on the firm. I was also able use the answers I gained from each representative to help emphasise the points I was making e.g. having spoken to X. This proved to be extremely successful in making the firm believe that behind my application was a genuine interest to work at their firm and that I had gone that extra mile to research the firm's areas and people. Often at each interview a partner would be quite impressed by the fact that I had spoken to X trainee or Y partner.

## Making an application

Having decided on the types of firm I wanted to apply to, I began to make my applications. Applying for a training contract is a time-consuming exercise but it is essential that you take time over each application to maximise your chances of success. Although it is accepted that you will be applying to a large number of firms, recruiters will still want evidence that you know something about the firm other than what is written on the firm's brochure or website. It was no surprise when I received most response from those applications that I tailored specifically to each individual firm.

I would find it helpful to always read through the application form before starting it. This way I knew what was coming and could answer each question confidently. I preferred to make all my applications online, and found it easier to copy and paste a copy of the firm's application form into Word and complete it there. This allowed me to make use of spelling and grammar check and would also mean I would not be compelled to complete the form in a set time.

When trying to write each answer I would write my answers in such a way that firstly answered the question but was also able to demonstrate that I possessed many transferable skills that would be useful in the work place e.g. team working skills, communication skills, extra-curricular activities, and commercial awareness. I would also try to use separate examples that demonstrate the various skills I possess so as to avoid repeating myself. I would try to use each answer to express a different quality about myself. It is also essential to highlight all work experience you have had, even if it is not legally related. As well as this, try and illustrate what you gained from each role where applicable within the application form. Also ensure, if you have stated in your application that you are applying to the firm for one of their specialist areas, that you can show a genuine reason why you are interested in that area of law; preferably something beyond the fact that you studied it at university.

Having completed each form I would get someone you trust to check the form for spelling, grammar, punctuation before sending off each application. I was surprised by the number of simple mistakes I made which the computer did not pick up on. Before sending off each application I would always print off a copy of my final application so I could read over it before the interview and was not caught off guard by anything I might have written.

## The interview process

The interview process is always a mixed bag and you can never really pre-judge what type of interviewer you are going to get, but I found it helps if you know what the interview process of each firm will involve. Each firm is different but the interview process can be quite wide–ranging, including interviews, psychometric tests, written tests and group exercises. With this in mind I would always call the firm's HR department to find out what selection methods would be used so I could prepare or at least was not caught off guard.

Do research the firm before the day, and when looking over current affairs I found it was better to know two or three issues in great detail rather than being able to talk briefly about lots. This way you can talk more confidently and will not be exposed if the interviewer presses you on the issues. If you have not been reading the papers regularly I would highly recommend the publication called *The Week* which breaks down all the key issues of that week in one publication.

I would always try and prepare some searching questions to ask at the end of the interview. Make sure you try to ask genuine questions and especially ones that are not readily available on the firm's website or through-out its legal literature. This will just expose you as someone who has not done his homework.

Whatever the interview process holds in store, try to remain as relaxed and as calm as possible at all times. I found that some interviewers were often playing devil's advocate with your answers just to see how you come to your reasoning or how you simply deal with their line of questioning. I found I was most successful in answering questions by taking a few seconds to think about the question being asked then answering clearly and succinctly. This meant I would avoid rambling.

Firms are often quite quick to respond to applicants that they interview and if I was unsuccessful I then would always follow-up my rejection letter by requesting some feedback. I found this extremely helpful as it would help to iron out my flaws before the next interview.

Chapter Eighteen

**Our 10 step strategy for training contract success**

Here is a strategy summarising our methods for achieving training contract success. Securing a training contract involves focused planning, self-belief, determination, enthusiasm, persistence and becoming a student of the training contract recruitment process.

1. **Do you know the route to becoming a lawyer?** Have you thoroughly researched the legal landscape in order to understand the recruitment market and gain a realistic picture of the profession you are hoping to work in? Think carefully about your choices. Do you really want to be a lawyer or are you just attracted by the glamorous "fat cat" stories?

2. **Do you really want to be a lawyer? Have you thoroughly researched the legal profession?** Do you understand the work a solicitor undertakes? Decide which type of firm is right for you. Gain some valuable work experience in various legal practice areas. Get on the right road to choosing a firm that is right for you.

3. **Network:** Contact a lawyer for career advice, and to mentor you in order to gain an insight into the dynamics of a law firm and a further insight into how the profession works. Learn to think like a lawyer from an early stage in your career and gain an understanding of what makes a successful lawyer.

4. **Know yourself.** Assess your position through a SWOT Analysis, so that you are aware of your skills and areas that you need to improve on.

5. **Market yourself effectively.** Do you know what law firms look for when selecting trainee solicitors? Learn how to stand out from the crowd, promote your skills and network.

6. **Get to grips with the legal environment.** Focus and tailor your approach to the type of firm you want to work

for. Explore in detail the attributes law firms look for in a prospective trainee. A great deal of self-belief and self-motivation helps to maintain your momentum when searching for a training contract.

7. **Become commercially aware.** Gain a true understanding of the "business of business". Alternatively, if you want to be a non-commercial lawyer, research the relevant marketplace to develop your knowledge of your chosen practice area to increase your chances of securing a training contract with the firm of your dreams.

8. **Start applying**. Research the firms you are applying to. Send in your CV and application forms well before the deadlines. Tailor your applications; avoid the "scatter-gun approach", quality is much better than quantity.

9. **Prepare for interviews the smart way by thorough research**. Consult your careers advisors and past students who have been interviewed at these firms to gain an idea of the type of questions you could be asked.

10. **Gain more work experience and vacation placements (whether paid or unpaid.)** This will help build up your CV and make you more marketable to law firms.

Follow these strategies to get on your way to securing a training contract!

Chapter Nineteen

# Here are some useful websites and contact numbers, so make use of them!

**www.rollonfriday.com** – is a resource filled with information relevant to young lawyers, with news, views and gossip on the legal profession delivered with humour, and a healthy dose of irreverence. Roll on Friday ("ROF") are dedicated to providing accurate and up to date information, and the discussion forums are a core part of the site and are famous throughout the legal profession. The forum has specific boards for students to discuss training contracts, and qualified lawyers to discuss their careers, which is required reading throughout the online legal community.

Roll on Friday also features:
- A weekly edition featuring the latest news from the legal world, things to do at lunchtime and the next couple of weekends, not to mention their legendary Glamorous Solicitor.
- The inside track on the top City and regional law firms - includes the top firms' salaries, benefits and independent reviews. Your first call before making any application.
- "Make me An Offer" to post an anonymous CV to be reviewed by top law firms. They will contact you if they are interested in offering you a job.

**www.lawcareers.net** - This is a vital website for students: Its list of immediate vacancies is excellent for those still searching for the elusive training contract and good paralegal experience. Each week the site features articles and news on developments and aspects of the profession that will help with preparation for interviews and applications. The site also has some very good profiles of trainees who talk about their experiences. Any student who is serious about obtaining a training contract needs to know about this site.

**www.lexonthenet.com** - Website geared to lawyers of the future, students and graduates.

**www.thelawyer.co.uk/lawyer2b**- Excellent website for students and lawyers.

**www.chambersandpartners.com/chambersstudent** - This site contains a student guide which covers the very first steps on the road to a career in law up, to acceptance of a training contract offer. The site is packed full of information that any aspiring lawyer will need. It includes a calendar of events, including deadlines, a good overview of global opportunities and a review of various law firms.

**www.studentlaw.com/lexonthenet.co.uk/www.campus-legal.co.uk** - This website contains topical features; it will often provide commentary from people on the inside of the profession. It features a section on the legal market in particular "market round up" which brings you the latest deals done by the most well-known City firms - all important for that training contract interview. It also includes a section on commercial awareness and industry sectors.

**www.timesonline.co.uk/law** - This site contains news which is updated in real time and is full of analysis of various legal issues. The website details some interesting features on recent events in the legal profession.

**www.doctorjobs.com** - This website features lots of different professions. The law section has a specific discussion forum where you can pose questions to other students or indeed Doctor Job herself. Each month they feature an expert from the legal profession who is ready to answer all your questions. The site will tell you which firms are recruiting at present.

**www.lcan.org.uk** – Law Careers Advice Network. This is a website set up by the Law Society, Bar Council, Careers Advisory Service legal group and Trainee Solicitors Group (TSG). This is an excellent website dedicated to providing an information portal and guidance for students and aspiring solicitors. The website covers routes into law - qualifying, funding, recruitment, training contract, pupillages and tenancy and alternative careers. Check out the frequently asked questions section. The site is also helpful for those looking for paralegal vacancies as it includes an extensive database of paralegal employers.

**www.prospects.csu.ac.uk** - This is the UK's official graduate careers website, including all graduate careers options. It is possible to search for training contract vacancies and read a "close up" on typical work activities.

**www.legalweekstudent.com** - The site contains the latest relevant news specifically for students, and an extensive archive of student features. The archive covers *legal week, legal director, legal IT and legal week global.* Use it to research any topics which are particular to the firms you have applied.

**www.lawgazette.co.uk** - Contains law articles, news, features and opinions in the form of editorial comment and views from the profession. Site also contains a job search section.

**www.solicitorsjournal.com** - To gain full access to this site you will need a user name and password. The site contains news and features geared more towards work that non-City and regional firms specialise in, for example, crime and private clients.

**www.legal500.com** - Legal 500 is more of a directory. If you have the names of partners conducting your training contract interview, the partner directory is a good tool for researching their backgrounds and interests. You never know; you might just share the interviewing partner's interest for Tiddlywinks, which may help build up a good rapport during interview. The site also has a directory on in-house lawyers and a useful section on essential facts and figures about the top 100 law firms, including turnover and net income.

**www.lawstudents.org.uk** - The good grammar guide; may come in handy when completing all those training contract application forms. There is also a forum for students - helpful for advice on courses.

www.graduatecareers.hobsons.co.uk - General career website but gives overview of the legal profession in necessary detail.

www.gti.co.uk - Group GTI is the publisher of the TARGET series of magazines and directories and includes useful links to leading overseas careers websites for those wanting to know more about international opportunities, (e.g. Malaysia, Singapore, Ireland and Germany).

www.spr-consilio.com - This is an on-line only magazine. It often provides an alternative view on current legal issues.

www.nclg.org.uk/index.html - The National Critical Lawyers Group (CLG) describes itself as bringing together academics, practitioners and students in an explosive forum designed to extend critical thinking.

**www.venables.co.uk** - Contains general information for students, companies, individuals and lawyers. A legal resources site.

**www.traineesolicitor.co.uk** – Contains discussion forum for trainee solicitors and students where you can ask any difficult law-related questions.

Industry specific

**www.legal-technology.com** - The leading site on developments in the legal field.

**www.elsa.org** - European Law Students' Association. Offers students a chance to travel, experience new cultures and learn about alternative legal systems. Applications for these schemes are done on-line by registering your CV.

## Professional bodies

www.lawsociety.org.uk - The Law Society
www.barcouncil.org.uk - The Bar Council
www.cigroup.org.uk - Commerce & Industry Group
www.ilex.org.uk - Institute of Legal Executives
www.blacksolicitorsnetwork.co.uk - Black Solicitors' Network
www.gsdnet.org.uk - The Group for Solicitors Disabilities
www.womansolicitors.org.uk - Women Solicitors' Group
www.societyofasianlawyers.com - Society of Asian Lawyers
www.gsdnet.org.uk - Group for Solicitors with Disabilities
www.spg.uk.com - Sole Practitioners' Group
www.sfla.org.uk - Solicitors' Family Law Association
www.tsg.org.uk - Trainee Solicitors' Group
www.lawcabs.ac.uk - Central Applications Board - CPE/LPC providers
www.gls.gov.uk - Government Legal Service (Public sector lawyer recruitment)

## Employment agencies and jobs

There are many sites on the web which offer temporary and permanent jobs for students who have yet to find training contracts. These were the most helpful ones we found. Be aware that there are agencies out there that only offer positions to students who have already secured training contracts at City law firms.

www.hayslegal.com
www.badenochandclark.com
www.legalcv.com
www.simplylawjobs.com
www.totallylegal.com
www.taylorroot.com
www.totaljobs.com
www.legalweekjobs.com
www.timesonline.co.uk
www.lawnetworks.co.uk
www.deverauxdeloitte.com

## More vacancies and law articles:

www.guardian.co.uk
www.the-times.co.uk
www.independent.co.uk

## Networking

www.facebook.com
www.myspace.com
www.linkedin.com

## General jobs

www.jobs.guardian.co.uk/
www.graduate-jobs.com/gj/index.jsp
www.grb.uk.com/
www.milkround.com/s4/jobseekers/

## The legal press

The following legal publications will keep you abreast of the latest developments and any major changes in the profession.

They will also feature topical issues. You do not need to subscribe or buy these; use your careers or local library to get access to reference copies.

*The Lawyer* – published weekly
*Legal Business* – published monthly
*The Law Society Gazette* – published weekly
*Commercial Lawyer* – published monthly
*The Times*, Tuesday Edition - weekly

## Chapter Twenty

## **Diversity and Law**

We have included this chapter mainly to raise awareness of and to address the issue of under-representation of minority groups in the legal profession.

The business need for diversity has never been stronger. In recent years, public sector and private companies have been challenging law firms to provide diversity credentials when pitching for work, and many law firms in the UK are rising to this challenge. Some cynics claim this new found commitment to diversity by some law firms is nothing more than a response to the requirements set by their clients. For others, diversity is seen as searching for the most talented people, and any efforts to attract and retain applicants of the highest quality from the widest possible pool is a positive move.

Over the past 10 years, law firms have been trying to catch up with the diversity policies of major public companies and US firms. UK firms have been urged to do more to ensure that entrants into the legal profession come from diverse backgrounds and are representative of the industry and business world they serve - the profession needs to draw from a wide talent pool to reflect the widening range of global clients in the UK and abroad. Today diversity in recruitment has become a key strategic business issue for firms and lots of them have set up internal committees to address this.

For us, diversity is really about offering equality of opportunity and, the removal of barriers irrelevant to the ability of people to practise law. Diversity initiatives must filter through the whole profession and can't be an "add on" in order to make sure all the right boxes can be ticked. It is widely accepted that in a competitive legal market, the best talent should flourish regardless of background, but the issue of background still remains a concern for some students and there are many bright students out there that law firms are not able to attract because the students believe they will not be suited to working at a particular type of law firm.

Despite the significant number of talented students from non-traditional backgrounds studying law, including those from ethnic minorities, there remains a great disparity in numbers between those that go on to successfully gain training contracts and become partners at the country's top law firms. Many students from non-conventional backgrounds face particular obstacles to qualify as solicitors, often because they don't have access to the right kind of knowledge to become sufficiently informed at the all important early stages of their career. In some way, we hope that the information in this guide will help to address this problem.

It is not only ethnic minorities who may face these challenges. For others, such obstacles might relate to social, educational, financial or family circumstances or to a gender, disability, or sexuality which makes the ambition of qualifying as a lawyer an unduly difficult journey. Diversity in law will enrich firms because such applicants will be able to provide different perspectives on matters, which all go towards delivering a full seamless first-class service to the client.

**The Law Society** has been committed to playing a leading role in the elimination of discrimination and the promotion of diversity in all of its activities as a regulator, a representative body and an employer, and has launched its own diversity access scheme. The scheme aims to identify people who have the outstanding attributes of intelligence, integrity, determination, drive, and commitment required to be outstanding solicitors, and who, without support, will almost certainly not be able to realise their ambition of qualifying as solicitors.

The Diversity Access Scheme will provide support to talented people by helping them to gain relevant early work experience. It aims to put people in touch with solicitor mentors who can provide invaluable advice, and in addition, provide scholarships to enable students to complete the vocational stage of their studies.

**The College of Law** invested £1.5 million to the Pathways to Law Initiative, jointly launched with the Sutton Trust in October 2006 to help attract a more diverse spread of talent into the legal profession. The Sutton Trust will commit £10 million over the next 5 years to improve aspirations and educational opportunities among able students who are from socially disadvantaged backgrounds. Five City law firms; Allen & Overy,

DLA, Freshfields, Linklaters and Lovells also pledged more than £350,000 to help fund the programme.

Every year, the Pathways to Law Initiative targets 250 potential law students' from state schools and non-professional backgrounds who will be the first in their families to go on to university. The initiative will help students with workshops/mentoring and provide work experience within their firms. It was launched after a Sutton Trust report found that the majority of partners at the leading law firms had been educated at private schools.

We hope that we can convince any person reading this guide who may have negative perceptions about diversity, and their own prospects of succeeding in the legal profession, that they should not to be put off from applying to law firms.

There are various groups and bodies committed to offering support to aspiring solicitors from minority sections of society.

**The Association of Women Solicitors**
The Law Society, 113 Chancery Lane, London WC2A 1PL
Tel: 020 7320 5793

**The Association of African Caribbean & Asian Lawyers**
114 Chancery Lane, London, WC2A 1PQ, Tel: 020 7320 5873

**The Black Solicitors Network**
Contact: Zainab Kemsley, Policy Executive,
The Law Society, 113 Chancery Lane, London WC2A 1PL
Tel: 020 7320 5800

**The Group for solicitors with Disabilities**
Amco House, Cedar Court Office Park, Denby Dale Road, Wakefield
WF4 3BA. Tel: 01924 232 438

**Society of Asian Lawyers**
C/o: Saima Hanif, 4-5 Gray's Inn Square, Gray's Inn, London WC1R 5AH

**Law Careers Advice Network**
Student Line: 0870 606 2555

## DIVERSITY AND LAW

In a competitive marketplace the best talent should flourish regardless of background. Many students from "non-traditional backgrounds" still face particular obstacles on-route to qualifying as solicitors. Those obstacles might relate to social, educational, financial, gender, ethnicity or disability. This chapter introduces you to various groups who can help students faced with these obstacles and offer support through a network of people who may share similar experiences.

## CONCLUSION

We hope this guide has provided you with a useful insight into the process, preparation and planning involved in securing a training contract: the beginning of your illustrious legal career!

You must focus on your career as early as possible, always remembering that no matter what stage in the journey you have reached, there are things that you can do to improve your prospects. The best opportunities come up early and the best strategy is to be well organised, and to consider your future career as early as possible, in order to get ahead! Law is not an easy career choice. You must be truly committed to becoming a lawyer and realistic about what a legal career involves, if you are not, you will not enjoy it.

There is a great deal of similarity between the mental strength and discipline required to train for sporting success, and the type of discipline required when taking your first steps into law. The challenging of achieving a training contract is more like a marathon than a sprint. Research the firms you believe are best for you, seek a vacation scheme with the firm and eventually prepare to impress the firm at your training contract interview.

To succeed in law you must think like a winner! This requires drive, energy, determination and enthusiasm. You cannot give up on your goals at the first hurdle. You must be prepared to accept rejection as part and parcel of the process, so try not to be too discouraged if you receive your fair share of rejection letters.

**Our Final Top Tip: Do plenty of research as there is a lot of information available to assist you. There is no excuse for being under-prepared. Make sure you are aware of what you're getting yourself into. As it is, qualification as a solicitor is a big commitment but the hard slog is really worth it if this is your ambition. Keep your goal of securing a training contract at the forefront of your mind and never lose sight of what you are setting out to achieve. It is a good idea to apply to firms that undertake the work you have a personal interest in. The bottom line in the hunt for a training contract is to become a "student of the process" by learning and implementing effective**

**methods and building and reinforcing a personal network of contacts to help you now and in the future.**

A great first step for students entering the training contract process is to find a lawyer who can share their experiences about the profession with you. Picture yourself doing the work that they undertake. Is this something you would enjoy? Learn as much as possible about the firm's dynamics before you apply to them. Throughout our writing of this book, we met trainees who joined firms for all the wrong reasons and a few months after joining the firm, came to regret their choice. Carefully consider what you observe about a firm's culture. The best way to source this information is first hand, by undertaking vacation placements and speaking to people at those firms.

Aim to identify your outstanding qualities early and undertake a SWOT analysis (*see chapter 7)* in order to take stock of how your credentials can be improved.

Our advice is to remain patient and aim to be the best that you can be! Your attitude to becoming a **"student of the process"** is a key component to the factors that contribute to training contract success. Look at how you can add value to the law firm you are aspiring to join. Aim to create a positive impact and show that you can make a difference to the law firm that you work for. Firms will be greatly impressed by a student who demonstrates the kind of strategies outlined in this guide. Devise a plan to help you get the law job that you dream of.

If you have any further questions or require additional advice, please do not hesitate to contact us. We are happy to answer any questions and are available to provide individual and group advice to help you secure a training contract offer. Please email us at **info@ultimatelawguide.com** if you have any questions.


**The Ultimate Guide Team**

## ACKNOWLEDGMENTS

This career guide would have not been possible without the extraordinary support of a number of people.

I have to start with my wife, Jin Kyung. Not only did Jin provide the emotional support throughout writing this guide, but she understood my vision of what Ultimate Law Guide is striving to achieve and helped me arrive at many ideas that are reflected in the guide.

I must express my gratitude, and acknowledge the effort of Kofi Owusu-Bempah, whose valuable contribution has helped make this guide what it is today.

A great deal of support has been offered from the Robinson family, the Lee family, and the Owusu-Bempah family for their support and encouragement.

A special word must go to the Ultimate Law Guide's hugely talented creative designer, Nadim Antonio DeGouveia-Akhtar whose faith in this guide and whose creative gifts have helped establish Ultimate Law Guide. Nadim has gone the extra mile time and time again, and for that I am tremendously grateful. The same spirit also characterises all of our friends in Chapter 17, our colleagues, the students, the lawyers and other professionals who agreed to speak to us and who provided invaluable advice in preparing this guide.

I would also like to thank our advertising partners for seeing the unique value in this career guide.

Finally, a special thanks to our publisher, Ultimate Guides who have been continued to support the team and I with the Training Contract Success guide. I look forward to more Ultimate Guides.

**Thank you all**

**Craig Robinson**

## Appendix 1

## Training Contract

After reading so much information about training contracts, below is an example of what a Training Contract for a full-time trainee solicitor actually looks like.

**THIS CONTRACT** is made on

...................................................................................................
...........................

BETWEEN X................................................................... [the training establishment] and

...............................................................................[the trainee Solicitor]

1. The purpose of this contract is to set out the principal duties and responsibilities of the training establishment and the trainee solicitor in accordance with the Training Regulations 1990 and "Training trainee solicitors: The Law Society requirements".

2. "X" is the training establishment for the purpose of the Training Regulations 1990.

3. [The training establishment] is authorised by the Law Society and has agreed to provide training for the trainee solicitor according to the rules of the Law Society as set out in "Training trainee solicitors: The Law Society requirements".

4. The trainee solicitor agrees to be trained by [the training establishment].

5. [The training establishment] has appointed ............................................... to be its training principal who will ensure that training is given in accordance with the requirements of the Training Regulations 1990 and "Training trainee solicitors: The Law Society requirements".

## DATE OF COMMENCEMENT AND FIXED TERM

6. This contract begins on ............................................... and continues for two years, subject to the provisions for earlier termination.

## COVENANTS OF [THE TRAINING ESTABLISHMENT]
## Salary

7. [The training establishment] will:

a) pay the trainee solicitor a yearly salary of not less than £............ payable by equal monthly instalments;

b) ensure that the Trainee Solicitor's salary is never less than the minimum prescribed for trainee solicitors in the local law society area where the trainee solicitor is based.

## Training Principal

8. a)The training principal is the individual responsible for [the training
establishment's] obligations under this contract.

b) The training principal may delegate those responsibilities to others but where this is done the name of the person or persons appointed must be given to the trainee solicitor.

## Terms and Conditions

9. The trainee solicitor is employed by [the training establishment] under the terms and conditions of employment which have been supplied but if there is any conflict between those terms and this contract then the terms of this contract prevail.

## Basic Skills

10. [The training establishment] will:

a) provide the trainee solicitor with the opportunity to practise:

i) client care and practice support skills;

ii) communication skills;

iii) drafting;

iv) interviewing and advising;

v) legal research,

b) provide the trainee solicitor with the opportunity to gain experience of the
practice of:

i) advocacy and oral presentation skills;

ii) case and transaction management;

iii) dispute resolution;

iv) negotiation.

## Legal Topics

11. a) [The training establishment] will provide the trainee solicitor with proper training and experience in at least three distinct substantive areas of English law. The following examples are for information only; this list is not exhaustive:

Banking; Family;
Civil Litigation; Immigration;
Commercial Law; Insolvency;
Company Law; Insurance and Reinsurance;
Construction; Intellectual Property;
Criminal Litigation; Local Government;
Employment; Magisterial;
Environmental Law; Personal Injury;
European Community; Planning;
Property (including Trusts;
Landlord and Tenant); Welfare;
Shipping and Airways; Wills and Probate.
Tax and Financial Planning;

b) If [the training establishment] is not able to provide proper training and experience in at least three distinct substantive areas of law it must make suitable arrangements for the trainee solicitor to be seconded to an office of another solicitor or elsewhere as agreed by the Law Society to acquire the appropriate experience.

c) [The training establishment] must ensure that during the term of the training contract the trainee solicitor gains experience of both contentious and non-contentious work in accordance with the Training Contracts Skills Standards.

## Review of Experience and Appraisal of Performance

12. [The training establishment] will:

a) provide the trainee solicitor with the means to maintain a record of the trainee solicitors training;

b) ensure adequate arrangements for guidance, including access to a
supervising solicitor, on a day-to-day basis;

c) make suitable arrangements to regularly monitor the trainee solicitor's
progress and that in accordance with "Training trainee solicitors: The Law Society requirements" a minimum of three appropriately timed compulsory appraisals take place during the two years;

d) make prompt and adequate arrangements to deal with any personnel
concerns in respect of the trainee solicitor.

## Law Society Requirements

13. [The training establishment] will:

a) i) permit the trainee solicitor to have paid leave to attend courses and
interviews as required by the Law Society;

   ii) pay all the fees and reasonable expenses in connection with such
   courses and interviews.

b) inform the trainee solicitor of any change:

i) in the Law Society's requirements relating to this training contract;

ii) of the training principal,

c) permit the trainee solicitor to have 20 working days paid holiday in each year of
employment in addition to public holidays;

d) complete a certificate of training at the end of this contract.

## COVENANTS OF THE TRAINEE SOLICITOR

### Duties
14. The trainee solicitor will:

a) carry out the duties given by partners or employees of [the training
establishment] faithfully and diligently and follow all reasonable instructions;

b) treat all information about [the training establishment] and its clients and their business as wholly confidential;

c) deal properly with any money or property entrusted to the trainee solicitor;

d) keep a proper record of all work done and training received;

e) comply with all requirements of the Law Society;

f) attend courses and interviews as required by the Law Society and the training principal.

### Disputes

15. a) Any dispute about this contract or the conduct of either party in relation to it may be referred to the training principal (or to another appropriate person within [the training establishment] if the dispute concerns the training principal), who must deal with it within four weeks of referral.

b) If the dispute is not resolved within four weeks the issue may be referred by either party to the Law Society or such person as it may appoint.

c) The trainee solicitor may also use [the training establishment's] grievance procedure.

**Applicable Law**
16. This contract is subject to English law.

**Notices**

17. Any notices must be in writing and given:

a) personally; or

b) by post addressed to the other party at:

i) the address set out in this contract; or

ii) any other address given by one party to the other for the purpose of
this clause.

18. Any notice to be given to [the training establishment] must be addressed to the training principal.

19. Notices will be deemed served two working days after posting.

**Termination**

20. This contract may be terminated by:
a) agreement between [the training establishment] and the trainee solicitor

b) the Law Society

i) with or without an application for that purpose by either party;

ii) following an application by [the training establishment] in the event of poor performance by the trainee solicitor.

21. This contract would not normally be terminated by:

a) the resignation or appointment of any partner of [the training establishment]; or

b) the merger of [the training establishment] with another body, firm, company or individual.

22. If the trainee solicitor:
a) has completed a Legal Practice Course, Integrated Course or an Exempting Law Degree Course

b) commenced this contract prior to the publication of the results of that course or examination; either party may end this contract within four weeks of the results being published if the trainee solicitor does not reach the required standard as set out in the letter of offer.


Signed
by:.................................................................................
............on behalf of **[the training establishment]**



Signed:
.............................................................................................

**Trainee solicitor**

# Appendix 2

## ANSWERS TO COMMERCIALITY TEST

1. Alternative Investment Market

2. A smaller company may prefer to trade on the AIM due to cost. As it is cheaper, smaller businesses will have fewer resources than a large PLC. There is also the advantage of less regulation and corporate governance, listing rules and procedures that must be adhered to strictly.

3. A bond or debenture is a debt instrument which obligates the issuer to pay to the bondholder the principal (the original amount of the loan) plus interest, essentially an I.O.U. issued by a private or governmental corporation. A company "borrows" the face value of the bond from its buyer, pays interest on that debt while it is outstanding, and then "redeems" the bond by paying back the debt

4. Selling your shares dilutes the company's shareholding, whereas a bond does not, and provides disposable cash.

5. BSkyB, the satellite television operator, bought a 17.9 per cent holding in ITV, paying out nearly £1bn. It paid 135p a share, buying out investors Fidelity and Brandes during a series of market raids.

6. You will need to consider something like this from the angle of the target company, the shareholders of the company and also the company seeking to takeover. How does the offer affect each and what would be most beneficial for those parties?

7. For example, the proposed Santander deal to take over Abbey raised an interesting point in competition law. Once it was known that Santander had laid an offer on the table, HBOS also looked as though they were shaping up to make an offer for Abbey. However, the combination of Abbey and HBOS (both UK banks) in the mortgage market would have potentially given them a greater market share than UK competition authorities normally allow, or in other words would be anti-competitive.

8. You do not need to know how every FTSE 100 share price closed on a given day (although very impressive if you did). Rather, have an understanding about which industries are doing well and which ones aren't. Also think about the reasons why this is the case. It may be easier if you look at it from the point of view of whether you would invest your own money in that area or not.

9. Emerging markets and opportunities for growth. Know which stocks and shares are doing well, also research commodities like gold or diamonds.

10. Law firms are businesses, and like all businesses they are concerned with making money. They are always on the look-out for global growth opportunities. From your reading start thinking about which parts of the world are experiencing good growth in their economies and why. Also, how can law firms take advantage of this potential growth?

11. Is a law firm a global entity? Do they have contacts and/or offices around the world? You could contact one of the new offices opened and check their precedent and steps, or answer that you may get in touch with another member of the team based in another jurisdiction that has recently opened a new office and canvass their views and their advice. This highlights that you are aware of the benefits of joining a firm with an international outlook to global business, to utilise their wealth of know-how.

12. Which institutions make up the City landscape? What kind of work do law firms do for those institutions? What is the present state of the UK and global economy, and how is this affecting law firms? There are factors affecting the profitability of law firms which will be linked to the economy.

13. a). **A thorough understanding of the law**. A good working knowledge.

b). Interpersonal skills. This will be effective in marketing to clients and retaining existing clients, as well as working with colleagues in a team.

c). Commercial acumen. Able to provide excellent advice, which appreciates the commercial context they apply their legal advice to their client.

14. The legal profession has to constantly adapt and respond to changes in business, technology, society and the political landscape. There have been some significant developments in the legal profession recently. The legal profession continues to grow at an astonishing rate, and since 1995 the number of solicitors has grown by half, with the number of women solicitors having doubled.

**Legislative changes:**

Legal Services Bill aims to put a customer focus on the way legal services are provided, to bring into force the changes recommended by the Clementi report. Among other things it would allow solicitors to form new business models, and organisations such as the RAC and Tesco possibly moving into the legal services market.

The Employment Equality (Age) Regulations 2006 makes it discriminatory to treat someone less favourably on the grounds of their age in the context of employment. This is likely to require a huge cultural shift in the business model of many UK businesses and law firms.

Company Law Reform Bill is the largest bill in history, wide-ranging reforms that will have an impact on directors, auditors and shareholders of companies.

Legal Aid: Lord Carter's controversial report on legal aid procurement, as a result of a large investigation, with recommendations to bring spiralling costs under control, primarily by making legal aid work paid for by fixed or graduated fees. The aim of the recommendations is to replace the current Legal Aid infrastructure with a smaller number of larger, "more efficient", "good-quality suppliers". This report has received major criticism of driving smaller suppliers out of business, which could lead to reduced quality of legal services to clients.

**Law firm trends.** As with any business, law firms look to grow through expansion or consolidation. There have been many recent mergers between law firms, such as Richard's Butler & Reed Smith, James Chapman & Haliwells.

**The Law Society splits** has been a significant change at the law society, with its regulatory functions divided and formed into two distinct bodies. One body handles consumer complaints and the other body is a new regulatory board that also deals with setting standards in the profession, including education and training.

**Postgraduate training.** The training pathway for solicitors (which has remained unchanged for 15 years) is being reviewed. The Training Framework review for would-be solicitors foresees the need for more flexible routes into the profession, with more emphasis on the outcomes of training and what you know, in order to make access into the profession more diverse and inclusive. We are still awaiting developments of the Training Framework review, and whether any changes will be made to the structure of the Legal Practice Course and Training Contract format.

**Diversity, access and equality will remain high on the agenda.** Although the positive note is that currently 63% of all trainees are women, while 18% are from ethnic minorities, women solicitors according to the Trainee Solicitors Group (TSG) are being paid 21% less than their male colleagues. The Law Society revealed 3% of UK partners are Asian while less than 0.5% are black, mixed or Chinese. The Equality Bill could have implications for firms with a poor track-record of gender and race equality.

**Technological developments.** With constantly advancing technology, it is an exciting time to be a lawyer and to see how technological innovation will impact the role of a lawyer. With developments in Wi-fi, broadband and the internet it will be a major challenge for law firms to embrace these developments and improve their services for their clients.